THE LIFE AND TIMES O

The Life and Times of Samuel Crompton

Whispers of the Industrial Revolution

by

David Leece PhD, MA, BA (Hons)

Oh, words are poor receipts for what time hath stole away.

Fragment from John Clare (1793-1864), Remembrances

YOUCAXTON
PUBLICATIONS

In memory of my Mother Freda Leece (nee Pimbley) whose love, support and kindness will never be forgotten.

Acknowledgements

I would like to thank the following organisations for their assistance and access to materials used in the writing of this book. Thank you to Bolton Libraries and Museums and History Centre for copyright permissions and the availability of the Crompton Papers. Also, the British Archives Online who have rendered the Crompton Papers so accessible. Thank you also to Lancashire Archives in Preston, Wigan Heritage Centre and Horwich Heritage Centre. The National Archives at Kew, also proved a valuable source of information, particularly access to eighteenth-century shipping returns, Chancery documents and online Home Office Papers. A special thanks to Youcaxton, Bob Fowke and Ella Knight for facilitating the production and distribution of this book. Thank you to all those organisations that approved the use of the illustrations listed and credited below.

Heartfelt thanks to friends and colleagues for their comments and encouragement. Professor Martin Parker of Bristol University, Professor Peter Lawrence and Dr Gordon Pearson both of Keele University. Dr Stephen Dearden and Caroline Bond. Importantly, the book could not have been written without the love and support of my wonderful family; Jan my wife and best friend, Alan and Steven my sons, Mel my daughter in law and Alex and Ollie my two grandchildren.

Contents

Illustrations

1. Commemorative Handkerchief, issued to school children by Bolton Council in 1927. Authors private collection.

2. Samuel Crompton depicted in W.A, Townsend and Company, *Famous Boys and How they Became Great Men,* New York, 1861.

3. Portrait of Samuel Crompton by Charles Allingham (1778–1850), c.1800. Courtesy of Bolton Libraries and Museums BOLMG:1902.66. HITW.

4. Firwood Fold Harold Hill (1900–1940). Courtesy of Bolton Libraries and Museums, BOLMG:2006.135.

5. Rivington Pike from the Bungalow Grounds by Alfred East (1844-1913),1909-1911. Courtesy of Bolton Libraries and Museums, BOLMG:1911.1

6. Hall i' th' Wood, Unknown Artist 1897. Courtesy of Bolton Libraries and Museums, BOLMG:1987.15

7. Portrait of Betty Crompton, Unknown Artist. Courtesy of Bolton Libraries and Museums, BOLMG:1907.1. HITW

8. Adlington Hall, Chorley, Lancashire 1846. Lithograph from Edward Twycross, *'The Mansions of England and Wales, illustrated in a series of Views of the Principal Seats in the County of Lancashire.'*

9. Sir Richard Arkwright (1732-1792), Joseph Wright of Derby (1734-1797), (copy after). Courtesy of Bolton Libraries and Museums, BOLMG:1887.32.c

10. The Spinning Mule. Courtesy of Bolton Libraries and Museums.

11. Parson Folds, 1728-1820. Unknown Artist. Courtesy of Bolton Libraries and Museums, BOLMG:1902.72. HITW

12. John Scott, First Earl of Eldon, 1815 by William Owen (1769-1825). Courtesy of the Parliamentary Art Collection, WOA 6552

13. 'Brothers in Law,' Hand coloured etching by Robert Dighton, 1793, Author's private collection.

14. Portrait of George Crompton. Photograph of a picture enclosed in a medallion, held at the Hall i' th' Wood Museum, Bolton. Courtesy of Bolton Libraries and Museums.

15. Portrait of George Rose, Member of Parliament, 1802, William Beechey (1753–1839). Courtesy of the National Portrait Gallery, ref: 367.

16. Portrait of Sir Robert Peel (First Baronet), (1750-1830), Thomas Lawrence (1769–1830) (after). Courtesy of Manchester Art Gallery, 1968, ref: 240.

17. John Blackburne of Orford Hall, (1754-1833), Unknown Artist. Courtesy of Lancashire County Museum Service, LC 58.

18. Lostock Hall, Bolton, From Captain Dewhurst's Sketch Book. Courtesy of the Local History Centre, Bolton Libraries and Museums, ref. Dewhurst Family of Halliwell, (1773-1816), *Captain Roger Dewhurst Sketch Book*, Albinson, Archive References ZZ/387 and ZZ/442/1 (Sketch book).

19. The Prince Regent, A hand coloured etching by Dennis Dighton, 1811. Author's private collection.

20. The Swan with Two Necks. Black and White Print. 1890s. Author's private collection.

21. Spencer Percival, (1762-1812), George Francis Joseph, oil on canvas, 1812. Courtesy of the National Portrait Gallery, ref: NPG 4.

22. William Cobbett, by Francesco Bartolozzi, (1728-1815), 1801. Courtesy of the Yale Centre for British Art.

23. John Bellingham, taken at his trial for the assassination of Spencer Percival, May 15th, 1812. Hand coloured etching by Dennis Dighton. Author's private collection.

24. Horse Guards, hand coloured etching by Robert Dighton Junior, 1805. Author's private collection.

25. John Crompton. Unknown Artist. Courtesy of Bolton Libraries and Museums, Hall i' th' Wood Museum, BOLMG:1975.171.

26. The assassination of Spencer Percival. Courtesy of the Royal Collection Trust / © His Majesty King Charles III 2024, RCIN 750673.

The cover illustration is Samuel Crompton Inventing the Spinning Mule, Alfred Walter Bayes, 1880, Courtesy of Bolton Library and Museums.

Prologue

As a boy I would often cycle along lonely moorland roads, laboriously struggling up winding hills only to propel myself back down again at breakneck and brakeless speeds, frequently flying over the handlebars and grazing my knees and elbows. The moors held and still hold a special fascination. With a gentle wind the heather parts in great red and buff waves, with nothing on the horizon to gain any perspective. There are times when there is no sound at all, only to be broken by the melody of a single skylark. When the rain and hail sweeps in it can feel like the top of the world and it is a wonder that people were able to build some of the now abandoned properties and the old dry-stone walls. On one occasion, caught by the inclement weather, I took shelter in a derelict cottage. Only the living room had been spared, with raised rubble where the kitchen had stood. Painted on the flaking cottage walls were mysterious figures. Bright colours wearing away with age, adults waving, sprightly smiling children and incongruous cavorting wild animals. It was impossible to date these paintings, they appeared ageless, a silent yet lively dance from the past.

It is these memories that have led me to sub-title this book *'Whispers of the Industrial Revolution'*. Fanciful it may have been, but the wind did seem to whisper, on that and other days, a confusion of voices, sadness, disappointment, determination. The book tells the story of Samuel Crompton (1753-1827), inventor of the spinning mule, set in the context of the unfolding industrial revolution. A story of invention, honest endeavour and betrayal. Crompton according to his nineteenth century biographer Gilbert French experienced his own whispers:

"The scientific discoveries of Priestley and Black reached him probably in feint **whispers** *only, but they were* **whispers** *to which his acute ear would be ardently opened."*[1]

Samuel Crompton combined this scientific knowledge with his exceptional practical expertise to construct his spinning mule an invention which had an enormous impact on the economy, society and the course of British history.

There are numerous books on the causes of rapid industrial change in Britain,[2] and in recent years many television documentaries. For the television programmes it is difficulty to catch even a passing reference to the great inventor. Indeed, there has been a noticeable tendency to leave out the cotton industry altogether; despite the clear importance given to the textile industry by historians such as Phyllis Dean[3] and Eric Hobsbawm. The latter noting that; *"to speak of the industrial revolution is to speak of cotton".*[4] There has been an inclination to focus upon the more glamorous themes, such as the influence of the Enlightenment, scientific discoveries and the economic and political liberalism of Britain.[5] One, of the aims of the book is to bring cotton and Samuel Compton back into the fore of our understanding of this tumultuous time.[6] In fact the book is a biography of his reputation as much as the story of his life. A reputation which flared or dimmed according to the dramatic events of the day, including Luddite riots and the assassination of a British Prime Minister.

Christine Macleod[7] has argued that inventors were elevated to the status of heroes as a challenge by the manufacturing class to the landed aristocracy, and a resurgence of Crompton's fame in the late nineteenth century certainly fits this model. However, there can be no doubt regarding his impact upon the economy and industrialisation.[8] The peculiar character and timidity of Samuel Crompton also explains the fluctuations in how he was viewed and treated. Through the lens of his abiding integrity, we can detect the less attractive aspects of human behavior that underpinned the industrial revolution. With Samuel Crompton we have a fixed point from which to observe a murky and calculating world. Throughout the book there are vivid examples of success based upon deceit, and privilege, rather than honest endeavour or creativity, though those virtues are also evident.

It is interesting that the one television programme to feature Samuel Crompton was an investigation into the possible haunting of Hall i' th' Wood (Hall in the Wood),[9] a complex Tudor farmhouse, part of which was home to Crompton and his family, where they spun yarn on his spinning mule. The programme suggested that the mansion is haunted by Mary, Samuel's wife, and Betty his truculent mother, who is reputed to be heard shooing away mischievous children playing about the hall. It was also claimed that Samuel Compton was *"famous in these parts."* Yet Crompton was in fact famous way beyond *"these parts"* and was visited by foreign Counts, cultivated by continental governments, and subjected to acts of espionage to discover the secretes of the mule. He was also sought after by leading industrialists such as Robert Peel[10] to be a business partner. His treatment, at times, as a humble, pestering artisan, rather than a great inventor, by a Parliament with much else on its mind, might have contributed to the promotion of the parochial view of Crompton as a merely local celebrity. Yet it is fitting that he should feature in a television documentary concerning ghosts. Crompton was a scientific man, but also deeply superstitious.

Superstition also has a place in this book. The myths and legends of Lancashire are metaphors for the fear of change that often generated virulent opposition to inventions and threats to traditional ways of living. The stories provide further insight into the attitudes and morality of the times.[11] The reader may be surprised by the occasional personal recollection. I grew up in the Lancashire town of Horwich during the 1950s, a railway town with a tradition of cotton goods manufacture, in a moorland setting. The personal stories are a vehicle to represent the legacy of the textile industry, celebrating, the sense of community and the challenges of change.

There have been several books, and short publications, celebrating the life of Samuel Crompton. In 1825, in preparation of an appeal to the British Parliament to supplement a previous reward for the invention of the mule, a young journalist, Mr. John Brown published a memorandum laying out the basis of Samuel Crompton's claim to a second remuneration. This was later published as a pamphlet,[12] though it was not widely circulated. When Samuel Crompton died on the 26 th June 1827 there appeared to be an unseemly rush to write his life story. In August of that year Thomas Cropp of the Bolton Chronicle wrote to Samuel's eldest son George expressing his desire to write a short biography and requesting family materials.[13] An even more deserving case for writing a biography was the manufacturer Mr. John Kennedy, who had been a firm friend and strong supporter of Crompton. He requested materials from the family,[14] including a family pedigree. However, Kennedy's final manuscript was a limited edition with private circulation only.[15] Again Samuel Crompton's reputation receded.[16]

The definitive text, though it contains some minor errors,[17] is the 1859 biography written by Gilbert French,[18] '*Life and Times of Samuel Crompton.*' Most subsequent books have taken French as their lead and echoed his sentiments, comments and in many cases the style and cadence of his narrative. My book is no exception in owing a great debt to French's lucid and compelling manuscript.[19] French's book can be said to be in the heroic tradition, proffering a vivid, visceral picture of Samuels obsessions, ingenuity and primarily psychological suffering. He also had the advantage of interviewing Crompton's son George.

In 1862, an obliging Manchester printer[20] set out, on a single printed sheet summaries of all the newspaper reviews of the 3rd (*"and cheap edition,"* price of one shilling) of Gilbert French's, *Life and Times of Samuel Crompton.* The reviews are interesting for what they say about the inventor, as much as comments on the book itself. For example, *The Gentleman's Magazine* intoned:

"Few men have done service of a special kind to their country than Samuel Compton did by his vast improvement in spinning machinery; and the services of few men have been worse requited during their lives, or less remembered after their deaths.......It has been Mr. French's praiseworthy object to lift out of obscurity the memory of a man who has high claims upon the gratitude of our commercial nation"[21]

The same publication claimed that by 1859 Crompton's reputation had fallen into obscurity. The 1860s and 1870s were a period when the Crompton story revived, possibly due to his appeal to Victorian rectitude and Gilbert French's campaigning. Crompton's personal struggles were perfect material for a compelling book to celebrate hard work, inventiveness and persevering against the odds. His integrity was celebrated in several Victorian publications offering moral instruction. For example, 'Famous Boys and How They Became Great Men*[22]* (1861). Also, *"The Triumphs of Invention and Discovery"*[23] (1863) and *The Living Age 1861.*[24].

Two key books were published in the twentieth century, Daniels in 1920[25] and Chapman in 1951,[26] both texts structuring their narratives around French's book. Daniels, the great scholar of the Lancashire cotton industry, was able to use newly discovered material. In 1913 a set of commercial documents, involving business between Crompton and his friend and associates John Kennedy and James McConnel were found under the floorboards of the McConnel and Kennedy factory in Ainscow, Manchester. Cameron utilised a second tranche of materials, originally in the possession of a Mrs. Irving of Blackburn, also in danger of being lost or destroyed. While both books stayed true to the biographical pathway set out by French, the newly discovered letters, manuscripts and business correspondence gave fresh insights into Crompton's thinking, business activities and life.

I have adopted a different approach than other publications by placing Samuel Crompton more firmly in the context of his times and family. My writing is informed by a wide variety of sources not available to French and later writers. The primary source was the largely unexploited Crompton Papers lodged in Bolton Libraries and Museums History Centre, replicated online by the British Data Archive. When I combined this material with the ever-growing British Newspaper Archive and the widely available out of print historical texts, not forgetting the increasingly accessible National, county and local archives, it was clear that there is a need for a new book on the life and times of Samuel Crompton.

Part I (Ruthlessness and Dreams) introduces the book and its approach, using elements of the Crompton Papers Archive to establish the context of the early stages of the industrial revolution. Part II (Superstition and Fear) looks at Samuel Crompton's childhood, along with the fears and anxieties surrounding technological change. Part III (Betrayal and Disillusion) examines conflicts over property in terms of ideas, machines, coal, and the perils of partnerships. These issues highlight the social and economic environment impinging on Crompton's fight to protect his invention and profit from its use. Part IV (Vanity and Rebellion) treats the expectation of great wealth by Samuel Crompton's family, the importance of political patronage and influential friends, and the Parliamentary campaign for a reward, amidst the poverty and social unrest of 1812. Part V (Disharmony and Persistence) deals with the aftermath of his campaign and a second attempt, in 1825, to augment the reward for his invention. Part VI (Charity and Guilt) concludes the book with a reflection on the character of Samuel Crompton and the issues raised by his life and treatment.

In this biography we will meet assassins, duelists, rioters, benevolent and scheming industrialists, abductors and guileful politicians. In some ways the book encompasses not just the saga of a reputation, but a biography of the multitude. It was impossible to research the material for these stories without meeting new and interconnected people, related through family, enterprise, shared endeavors, debt, affection etc. Each person adds to the incredible history of a society in transition. Napoleon reflecting, while detained on the island of St Helena, described his life as one that would make a good novel,[27] *"What a novel my life has been."* This book tells the story of Samuel Crompton and the spinning mule, not strictly as a novel, but certainly as an unraveling drama.

Part One

Ruthlessness and Dreams

Chapter One

A Gathering of Whispers

"History has many bypaths of, and in journeying along some of these we may pick up some pebble, hear some feint echo that perchance may lead to the discovery of some important link. In the hope that some such may be found herein has been our object."

Thomas Hampson, Horwich Its History and Legends, 1889[28]

Samuel Crompton was born on the 3 rd. December 1753 into a rural environment; a snug group of cottages known as Firwood Fold, Bolton Le Moors. Gilbert French reflected, from the vantage point of 1859, upon the nature of Bolton Le Moors in the year of Samuels birth:

"Gardens, meadows and bleaching crofts, dotted here and there with cottages stretched on the north side down to the Croal, then a pleasant stream of pure water; and, besides the comparatively considerable suburb of Little Bolton, the neighbourhood of the town was thickly studded with groups of cottages in hamlets, or folds as they are called, many of which have since been surrounded by new houses and now form part of the town itself. There were no tall chimneys in Bolton in those days, but many considerable warehouses to contain the heavy fustians and other piece goods made in the neighbourhood."[29]

Industrialisation would radically alter this landscape and the growth of factories would follow from the machines devised by inventors such as Richard Arkwright and Samuel Crompton. Arkwright's water frame facilitated the use of power to drive cotton spinning machinery, while the quality of yarn produced by Crompton's spinning mule increased the scale of production. The mule was a revolution in the spinning of cotton that added immeasurably to the industrialisation of Britain, leading to a dominance of the export market for textiles. It has been argued that the subsequent

1

increased financial returns to the British Government turned the tide of the Napoleonic wars in the country's favour. For many manufacturers this industrial change meant increased prosperity, and Samuel Crompton's later life was dominated by attempts to share in this good fortune.

Though Crompton is a neglected figure in contemporary discussions of the Industrial revolution, we can appreciate how he was celebrated in the recent past by looking back at Bolton's commemoration of his life and achievements, held 100 years after his death, in 1927. The celebrations provide a background to the story of the rescue of the many letters and documents in the Crompton Papers archive, so critical to the writing of his book.

A special souvenir booklet was published outlining a week's events lasting from June 5th to June 11th. 1927.[30] These included competitions, performances by bands, lectures, visits by dignitaries, banquets, pageants and a light opera "Merrie England" by Basil Hood, music by Edward German. On the Wednesday there was an historical and symbolic pageant by 3,500 school children to be performed at Bolton Wanderers football stadium, Burden Park.

After acting out the story of Samuel and the mule a pageant cleverly associated pictures with emotions and feelings. The opening dance was the spinning wheel and depicted *"dull monotony and weariness."* The dance of the mule and its moving parts depicted mischief, with the attempts to steal its secrets. Fear accompanied the anxieties of local people as to the consequences of the mule. Truth, Joy and progress are the celebratory feelings that follow in sequence. Finally in a grand scena, a progression of changes in clothes and fashion, paraded it is said before the *"whole world and his wife."* A final cry rendered by everyone assembled was *"All honour to the name of Samuel Crompton."* This crypto religious chant is heady material, but it is hard to think now what reverence Samuel Crompton was held in by the people of Bolton. This was a marked contrast, as we shall see, to his treatment during his life of invention when many of both Manchester and Bolton manufacturers treated his claims for financial compensation with disdain. In fact, the prelude to this pageant heralded:

"Let us hope that his memory may yet be revived, and his name worthily honoured not only in his native parish but reflected thence throughout the world which his invention has done so much to civilise, and that history may yet inscribe the neglected name of Samuel Crompton on one of the brightest pages of her annals."[31]

The souvenir programme contained thirty pages entitled *"Brief Account of the Life of Samuel Crompton"* written by Thomas Midgley curator of Bolton Museum. Midgley also produced an accompanying booklet, presenting a more detailed biography.[32] He had come into possession of the recently discovered letters and documents, relating to Crompton; with just a few weeks to read and incorporate them into his version of the inventor's life story, ready for the celebrations. It appeared to have been George the first son of Samuel and Mary (b. 1780) who preserved this collection. Then it was the widow of the grandson of George, Mrs. Irving who passed these on to Thomas Midgley, from where they were deposited at the Hall i' th' Wood Museum.[33] It is said that Mrs. Irving nearly destroyed these papers and letters, but that the fuss and celebration of the centenary of Crompton's death, then taking place throughout Lancashire, gave her pause for thought. It is this treasure trove of business and family correspondence, accounts and order books that informs the narrative of this book.

There is a handkerchief designed to commemorate the life of Samuel Compton, created as part of the celebrations in 1927, which was the winner of a competition among the students at the Bolton College of Art; a specimen of which was given to each of the schoolchildren in the town. It is a pleasing, complex pattern of the images of the silhouetted Bolton skyline, the mule and Hall i' th' Wood (The Hall in the Wood). The four corner illustrations enclose a central cartouche which displays an elephant stood on a rocky moor, supported by a red and a black lion:[34] each corner showing the tools of spinning and weaving: the bobbin and a spinning wheel. Emblazoned on the image is the town motto of *supera moras* (to overcome difficulties or delays). This book follows the spirit of this lively and colourful cloth and weaves a pattern of the rise and fall of Samuel Crompton's reputation.

A Moorland Prelude

The events and stories narrated here took place, many times, in the isolated moorland regions of Lancashire and their valleys. Earlier texts attributed a degree of wildness to both the region and its people. Indeed, Camden visiting Lancashire in 1607 expressed *"a kind of dread"* in having to approach the inhabitants.[35] Many years later in 1795 when the Kings Light Infantry, of which Beau Brummel was a captain, was ordered to locate to the unsettled North of England he was reported to have pleaded with the Prince Regent that:

"I have heard that we are ordered to Manchester. Now you must be aware of how disagreeable this would be to me. I could really not go; think, You're Royal Highness, Manchester!"[36]

The North, South divide was, as we shall see, a factor, if not the prime cause, in the struggles that Samuel Compton endured in trying to obtain recompense from Parliament for the national benefits of his invention. He was undoubtedly seen as a simple north countryman likely to be content with a small sum.[37] His simple dress and plain manner, with a painful shyness and reticence, all added to this impression of the humble mechanic who would look particularly unprepossessing in a society and political system dominated by the aristocracy, with a growing manufacturing class professing to be gentlemen.

The moorlands are a veinous network of tumbling streams which at first provided the water for the bleaching, printing and dying of cloth and later drove the new water powered factory-based inventions of the cotton spinning industry. Coal, found in rich abundance beneath the surface of the moor and its lower reaches would provide the fuel for the later use of steam engines; while the streams and tributaries, when redirected, supplied the water for the canal systems that revolutionised transport. It is a landscape populated by names of farming families long gone, and within its shifting cloak of mist horrific crimes were enacted, executions carried out and the innocent and unwary lost. Yet it was the cradle of the domestic cottage industry of spinning and weaving combined most times with small scale farming with a family perhaps keeping no more than a single cow. Families working together in an existence it is tempting to idealise. Samuel Crompton, though a progenitor of the factory system and resultant urbanisation, appeared to prefer this pastoral life for himself and his family. For a while he retreated from unwanted fame and attention to live in an isolated moorland fold named Oldham's.

Not surprisingly the moors are also the source of many mysteries and legends that lend ready metaphors for the changes wrought by the industrial revolution. One story has it that a large boulder, to be found on Turton moor, was thrown by a giant from Winter Hill, a promontory opposite, and that the giant's fingerprints can still be found impressed into the rock. There is no accompanying story as to why the giant threw the stone - through temper, fear or anxiety? In the period covered by this book the new factories must have suddenly appeared like the exertions of giants, at first as images of wonder, but later as long shadowed edifices of threat, promising very different lives. The fears and anxieties of the mill workers and inhabitants of the mill towns would express themselves in riot, at times bordering on revolution.

The environment before and after industrial change was poetically captured by Edward Baines in his *History of Lancashire*, where he describes the countryside about the settlement of Horwich, a town with the moors as a dramatic backdrop that features in the Crompton story.

"Horwich.....was sixteen miles in circumference, with its wild boars, and dairies of eagles, has long since disappeared, and their places are supplied by bleach works, cotton factories, and all the modern indications of manufacturing industry; but the woody dingles which abound in this extensive tract seem to recall the memory of those times, when the ladies and Ferrers, followed by their vassals, plunged into the thickets in the ardour of the chase, and emerged only at a distance of several miles to witness the dying struggles of the weeping deer."[38]

A noteworthy peak in this moorland terrain is Rivington Pike. The land about the Pike still shows the remains of old coal mining shafts, long since filled in, together with the drift from the disused mines. The remnants of these onetime coal pits excite the curious like Egyptian tombs, but they can no longer be accessed. On very rare occasions in inclement weather, and moorland storms, the entrances to the pits open, one time at least, revealing steps carved in the stone, descending deep into the hillside.[39] The far stretching panorama, viewed from the pinnacle of the Pike, embraces the long history of cotton manufacture in a single imagining. The romantics of the late eighteenth and early nineteenth century would have grasped the awe and infinity of the view but would have baulked at how the terrain buckled and teared as the factories and towns erupted with only the backdrop of an unwelcoming moor remaining untainted.

Look to the west from the summit of Rivington Pike and you can see the Irish sea, facing it the holiday resort of Blackpool, then further south the shimmering outline of the Welsh mountains. A more informed local glance will pick out Anderton the residence for a while of Samuel Oldknow a pioneer of cotton manufacture who introduced fine muslins to the market; and where Joseph Shaw of Bolton had attempted to make British muslins but lacked the fine yarn necessary to do that.[40] Then to the northwest, Coppull the place of one of Richard Arkwright's first factories, Birkacre, burned down by rioters in 1779. South along this visible coast is the port of Liverpool and during the seven year's war with France (1756-1763), it was possible to signal from Liverpool to Rivington Pike, to alert the population to a possible

French attack. It was feared that the infamous French Admiral Thurot was planning an invasion of England. A party of soldiers were camped on Everton hill with instructions that if Thurot appeared to signal to beacons at Ashurst, Billinge and Rivington.

It was beyond the near view from this moorland peak towards Liverpool that the cotton manufacturers, merchants and farmers increasingly turned their attention, particularly after the seven year's war, when Britain had established naval supremacy. Facing the North American and Caribbean colonies, less prone to probing and marauding French privateers, Liverpool from the mid eighteenth century grew exponentially. Not yet out competing London and Bristol it entered enthusiastically into the infamous and more risky slave trade.

The remaining two chapters, in Part I of this book, consider merchant enterprise and the arrival of inventions. Not solely concerned with the history of the industrial revolution, but rather the restless spirit and calculating behaviour of the participants. These issues are critical in understanding what motivated Samuel Crompton, and the challenges he faced within a fiercely competitive commercial environment. The early family documents in the Crompton papers offer insight into mercantile attitudes and behaviours in late eighteenth century pre-industrial society, particularly surrounding trading out of Liverpool. Were Samuel Crompton, and his family, willing and able to navigate this emerging new world and gain a reward for his contribution to the flowering of inventions and industrial growth?

Chapter Two

Of Ships and Enterprise

*The tone of the correspondence is on the whole, solicitous, civilised and Georgian, as if there were no crime to be recognised. There was undoubted guilt here; there is not even a **whisper** of shame.*

Adam Nicholson, 2011, [41] *being a comment on the slave trade.*

The Irving (Crompton) papers contain the original copies of two letters, from a Mr. James Mather, one dated 14th April 1767 and the second undated, but undoubtedly written around the same time. Together with correspondence from other sources, the letters provide a sense of the world into which Samuel Crompton was born. Through the *'favours'*[42] we hear the voices of the colonial merchants and detect the precursors of the businessmen who would drive the emerging industrial revolution. By examining the context in which the letters were written we encounter calculation and aggression. Other documentation shows the importance of business networks and political patronage, aspects of Georgian economy and society that Samuel Crompton would need to leverage to obtain any significant reward for his invention. Thus, this investigation of the early material in the Crompton archive suggests some of the personal and social requirements for material success.

Risk and Cooperation

In October 1768 a merchant ship of three hundred tons with a crew of eighteen, *"The Four Friends"*, Captain; George Wardle, constructed in Whitby in 1761,[43] sailed damaged into Portsmouth harbour.[44] Having hit rocks on its journey back from the West Indies to London it now laboured past a flotilla of the majestic warships of the Royal Navy. In port were *'The Arrogant'*, *'The Bellona'*, *'The Achilles'*, *'The Dragon'*, *'The Devonshire'*, *'The Superb'* and *'The Squirrel'*; also, two smaller ships *'The Hound Sloop'* and *'The Halifax Schooner.*[45] Portsmouth was the royal dockyard and merchant vessels would not typically dock there alongside his Majesty's ships. There must have been a sense of awe and a cast of authority, felt by master and crew, as they cautiously rounded *'the Point,'* a fortified short spit of land on the western side of the harbour.

James Mather had written to the Admiralty on the 20th of October 1768, not a letter in the Crompton Papers, but equally illuminating. He noted that the ship had a damaged hull, and that all the cargo had been unloaded at Portsmouth.[46] His request was gracious and accommodating, offering payment for any repairs made. The Admiralty replied the same day withholding permission to use the resources of the dockyard. James wrote a second letter dated 26th October 1768 requesting *"the use of a hulk"*, spotted by the master of the *Four Friends*. This could be used to heave the damaged vessel to a place it could be renovated. He noted the risk of losing his cargo if the ship could not be repaired soon. Permission to heave down and use the hulk was given on the 30th of October. Too late, perhaps, to save the cargo. This episode highlights the many risk facing merchant vessels in the eighteenth century, which included reliance for payment on creditors based overseas, piracy, war and adverse weather conditions.

While some merchant ships had the classical and intimidating names common for Royal Navy frigates, and ships of the line, such as *'The Revenge,'* there was a prevalence of whimsical, fanciful, fawning and familial names. Examples are, *'John and James'*, *'The Sally'*, *'The Bee'*, *'The Pitt'*, and the most bitterly ironic for slaving vessels, *'The Hope'*. Names such as *'The Four Friends,'* and *'The Brothers'* are suggestive of the way that ships were financed and managed. They were associations of fellow merchants, tradesmen and family members, with a *'husband'* to manage the arrangements, including the payment of freight. Life and business were risky and mutual support critical.

The Crompton Letters

The aspirations of the merchant adventurers leading them to face considerable risks can be gleaned from the undated letter (circa 1767) in the Crompton Papers. It was written on board ship, posted via Liverpool, and forwarded to James Mather's recently married wife Nancy.[47] It is clear from its content that migration to the colonies was motivated by dreams of returning with a personal fortune. The appeal of the letter is its simplicity, affection, and the whiff of fatalism should their dreams and ambitions come to nothing.

Dear Nancy, I desire thou will make thyself as easy as possible and hope that my endeavours will bring us pleasure when we are old if it please God to continue us so long. Shall always use my utmost endeavour for thy welfare as well as my own. and hope it will prosper - pray give my love to Uncle Hope and all friends there when you see them have some time to write our ship is under way and a fine and pleasant gale am thine until death. ...James Mather (circa 1767)

It is possible that the James Mather who is the author of this letter is the same person as the importuned owner of the *'Four Friend's*.[48] Researching this period is confounded by the multiplicity of family lines/clans with the same name, reproducing identical patterns of Christian names, cascading down succeeding generations. There are James Mather's in profusion with families in Scotland, Northumberland, London and the various Parishes of Lancashire: Winwick, Radcliffe, Little Hulton, Rivington etc. A James Mather of London established an eighteenth-century shipping empire and was a member of *'the first fleet'* transporting convicts to Australia and purchased Captain Cooks Endeavour[49]. A James Mather famously became the Mayor of New Orleans and was taken to the Court of Chancery by James Mather merchant of London.[50] James Mather of Newcastle pursued the abolitionist cause.[51] From the seventeenth century onwards, the Mathers find their way from Lancashire to Virginia in North America.[52] Thus, the name Mather is emblematic of seventeenth and eighteenth century enterprise and colonial settlement.

The second letter in the Crompton Papers from James Mather is dated April 14th, 1767,[53] and franked Liverpool. Dr Johnson's confidante and biographer Hesther Thrale wrote glowingly of Liverpool, after a visit there in 1788:

"....the streets embellished with showy shops all, day and lighted up like Oxford Road all night: A harbour full of ships: a cheerful opulent commodious city."[54].

Mrs. Thrale might have limited her perambulations to the more fashionable parts of town which broadcast the prosperity of Liverpool. The guts and pace of frontier like development of eighteenth-century commercial activity and new urban centers are best exhibited by an alternative view. Even by 1796, when prosperity led to general municipal improvements James Wallace[55] was able to state that only a few years before the streets had been dirty, mean and *"much too narrow for the health and the convenience of the inhabitants."* It was from this raw yet prosperous Liverpool that James Mather and William Pimbley chartered their ship, *catching* the Mersey tide to venture to the West Indies.

The second letter puts devotion and aspiration to one side, outlining the business to be completed before James and his partner John could board the ship. The letter is addressed to *"Cousin William Pimbley" who was* the father of Crompton's wife Mary Pimbley. French claimed that James Mather and William, exported oatmeal to the West Indies.[56] The government subsidised the export of corn, based on the mercantilist belief that a countries prosperity depended upon exports and the accumulation of gold. James and William would have received a subsidy for their cargo. However, this item of correspondence was more concerned with cloth, highlighting how the early textile trade was bound together with agriculture and other mercantile activities.[57] The letter states:

"Shall send the cloth which is eighteen yards by the Never man to be left at the Griffen".

"I have only just saved my distance in coming to Liverpool time enough to settle matters before we go which are done in the following manner. "

In what follows we see the last-minute preparations for the voyage, the favours called in, the financial transactions completed and the concerns with bills and the all important insurance:

". ...was obliged to draw an order on Mr. Richard Milne for £27-2-0 and desired Mr. Fullerton Ge (Gentleman) to join him in part payment thereof....I called upon Mr. Tyer but could only get a parcel of old book orders for Liverpool which was my trouble for my pains."

"Take care of in regard to the insurance."

The most likely ship in which the partners sailed was 'The General Blakeney,' owned by Mr. Jonathon Brookes,[58] which left from Liverpool for Jamaica two days later, on the 16th of April 1767.[59] The letter notes that:

"Mr Brookes is insisted that the freights of all the goods should be paid before we sail and likewise Johns paperage and mine or else we should not go in the ship".

The *General Blakeney* arrived at Kingston Jamaica on the 15th of June 1767,[60] having sailed from Cork on the 26th of April, a journey of some 11 weeks.[61] The Colonial Office shipping records show that the cargo was beef, butter (probably loaded at Cork as these were prime Irish exports) and 4 casks of Barley.[62] Barley and oats were key agricultural products in the

Warrington area and Merseyside and would be a likely export for William and James, particularly as William was a husbandman as well as a merchant. Barley could be used as substitute crop for oats in brewing, thus quenching the thirst of colonist. The cargo on the return voyage were the imported luxuries of sugar, mahogany, rum punch, juices, and wine.

With respect to the success or failure of the commercial adventure on the *General Blakeney* and any rewards reaped by James Mather and William Pimbley, French states:

"....little is known of the profits from this enterprise other than there was a monkey that was a firm favourite of the family".[63]

Perhaps, on occasion, the monkey gained its freedom, wreaking havoc and provoking giggles from the children as it bounded chattering from rustic table to makeshift chair. It may have symbolised a fancy for the exotic, a child's request for a pet derived from a travelogue, a symbol of trade and extended horizons, or a tick mark for the successful completion of a hazardous voyage, perhaps all these things.

Of course, a disturbing background to these merchant adventures was the slave trade. A list of the Company of Merchants trading to Africa and belonging to Liverpool,[64] dated 24th June 1752, shows 112 enterprises, among which there are four members of the prominent Lancastrian family the Blundell's. There is even a John Crompton, though we cannot be sure that he is any relation of Samuel's. Even the urbane and humane textile factory owner Samuel Gregg is incriminated through the inheritance of slaving interest in Dominica, West Indies and on the island of St Vincent.[65] However, his wife Hannah Gregg (nee Lightbody) was an active and committed abolitionist. The Brookes brothers Joseph and Jonathon further signified their own and Liverpool's participation in slavery by the building of the Liverpool town hall. Designed by John Wood, there is an idiosyncratic frieze, portraying a slave's head. It was the plan of the slaving ship *'The Brookes'* that figured in the abolitionist campaign of William Wilberforce.[66] The drawing illustrated the cramped and inhuman conditions under which slaves were transported.

There is no evidence that William Pimbley and James Mather dealt with slaves. William Wilberforce made much of the fact that slave trading was not necessary to further prosperity. However, by 1759 Manchester's export trade was over £300,000, having grown by £100,000 from £14,000 a year in 1739;[67] over one third of this value resulted from cloth exported to Africa in exchange for slaves.[68] In the 50 years prior to 1807 it is estimated that a third to one half of shipping tonnage in Liverpool consisted of African slave and associated trades.[69]

Privateering, Business Goes to War

The *'General Blakeney'* was a ship[70] with a privateering pedigree, that emerged from the seven years' war cleansed for trade. It was a one hundred and forty ton vessel with a crew of fifteen. It was a 'French ship captured by the British ship the *'Neptune,'* subsequently used as a privateer with a larger crew of thirty five men, including a lieutenant, carpenter, and advisably, a surgeon. Several major engagements were reported including the capture of a large Dutch East Indiaman.[71] The owner Jonathan Brookes had eagerly participated in the 'privateering boom' during the seven years' war, having two other ships granted letters of marque by the Admiralty Board; the *Tiger*[72] and the *Ellen*.[73] The *Tiger* was the larger vessel with its crew of forty and its eighteen carriage and twelve swivel guns.

During the Seven Years War (1756-1763) the merchants of Liverpool and Lancashire took to legalised piracy with ease and profit. Possessing letters of marque,[74] the whole of the Wirral coast appeared to be involved in the production of ships for attacking French, Spanish and Dutch merchant vessels. Privateering became a major industry. It produced its own heroes such as Fortunas Wright of Liverpool. Louis XV of France had two special ships constructed for the sole purpose of capturing Wright and offered a prize double the value of his ship, a pension of 3,000 lires per annum and the Order of St Louis.[75] Wright disappeared killed in action or dying in captivity, but there were continued rumors of his return to battle.

The confrontations between armed merchant ships could be as long and as bloody as any royal navy engagement. There was a code of honour, with prisoners expected to be treated humanely and with dignity, by both sides.[76] When in January 1759 the *'Bird Cartel'* ship arrived in Gosport carrying seventy six officers and men from St Malo, most of them wounded and taken from the hospital at Dinant, they commended the French surgeons for their humane treatment.[77]

The merchants rewarded their returning victorious captains. Lloyds of London offered prizes to the battling traders. Fortunes were made and lost. One such award was to Captain Lockhart; a cup and salver being sent to Lloyds for the inspection and approval of the merchants of the city. For those who preferred an abstract rather than visceral representation of bloody conflicts the twenty six inch diameter salver was embossed with the seven French privateers that Lockhart had captured, in addition to a picture of his own ship and arms. The inscription read:

"The Gift of the two public companies, the underwriters and Merchants of the City of London to Captain John Lockhart, Commander of the Tarter for his signal service in supporting the Trade by distressing the French privateers in the year 1757".[78]

A particular feature of this form of 'enterprise' was the capture, use and recapture of ships, a violent form of recycling. Renamed by their captors, the vessels were used to engage with the merchant ships of their nation of origin. On the 23rd of December 1757 the inauspiciously named Captain Death, commander of the ship *'The Terrible,'* captured the *'Grand Alexander'* from St Domingo, a French ship sailing to Nantz.[79] This was a formidable prize, being a four hundred ton vessel with twenty two guns and a crew of one hundred men. There was, as one newspaper report understated, *"a smart fight of two hours and a half"*. In fact, this bloody encounter resulted in the loss of Captain Death's brother, and sixteen of his crew. However, lurking in the picturesque walled Northern French port of St Malo, menacing lair of the French privateers, was the *'Vengeance,'* a larger ship than the *'Grand Alexander'* with thirty six guns and three hundred and sixty men.

The *'Vengeance'* pursued *'The Terrible' and its prize*. Weakened by the fight, *'The Terrible'* was soon sighted and another fierce battle ensued; described as *"the most bloody and desperate engagement ever known"*. The losses were horrendous, with four hundred fatalities, including Captain Death and his officers. *'The Terrible'* had had its fangs drawn. In a deplorable, wrecked state, with just twenty six of the crew surviving, sixteen of which had lost limbs, with ten badly wounded, it was funereally escorted, by Captain Bourdas, into the eagerly waiting port of St Malo. There it was refitted and returned to battle, renamed and scrubbed clean of the blood of its hapless British sailors.

By 1767 Britain was enjoying and exploiting the confidence resulting from its mastery of the seas. Not that the economy and society were untroubled. There were high grain prices and social unrest. In 1768 merchant seamen, bemoaning the atrocious conditions and excess discipline under which they laboured, marched in protest through London.[80] Nevertheless, colonial expansion progressed. The prospect of great wealth encouraged enormous commercial and corporeal risk. The privateering, demonstrating the raw resolve of these merchants, exhibits the primal human forces that forged the industrial revolution. Perhaps the aggressive stance of privateering merchantmen served them well in the expansion of commercial activity during the peace. Capture and recapture, plunder and profits were the commercial motif of this period.

The enlightenment had encouraged skepticism and rational thought, with a celebration of scientific progress. Thus, there were those who opposed slavery and privateering, though sympathy for them varied geographically. The abolitionist Thomas Clarkson was in fear of his life when surveying slave trading in Liverpool but would have been more comfortable in areas of Lancashire and Yorkshire, such as Leeds, where the abolitionist cause was enthusiastically supported.[81] This was also true of privateering, which was not viewed with universal approval even by the people of Liverpool.

"Towards the conclusion of one of my sermons preached at Liverpool, I was led by the proximity of the subject to condemn, in terms of the utmost asperity, and somewhat hyper tragical, the horrid practice of aggravating the calamities of war by the rapine and injustice of private hostility."[82]

Thus preached the Reverend Gilbert Wakefield who observed the acrimony of his parishioners towards him, but with self-congratulatory delight pointed out:

"....but learned some years afterwards, that the nerves of one lady were so agitated by the thunder of my lecture, as to allow herself and husband no rest till he had sold his share in a privateer." [83]

Class, Patronage and Connection

The Mather letters, in the Crompton papers, are personal promotions of education and social standing. The flourishes and swirls of writing with random variation in the use and style of grandiose capital letters herald class and aspiration. Subtle personal positioning was necessary in a society where class distinctions could be a matter of fine gradation, not always, though often, a social chasm.[84] A weaver who owned a cow was a cut above someone who simply wove. A chapman or middleman dealing in corn or textiles was of a higher class than a hawker proclaiming his wares in the muddy streets of towns and villages. A yeoman was higher than a tenant farmer and certainly of a higher station than agricultural workers dispossessed by the increasing numbers of enclosures of the land.[85] The grandfather of Henry Fox, Stephen Fox, was a humble cottager who through his services to Charles II became the richest commoner in the country. Individuals were not averse to self-attribution with the terms yeoman and gentleman often loosely applied. When James Mather married Nancy Kirkham in 1766 his marriage bond proudly proclaimed him a gentleman, son of Ralph Mather of Warrington, a weaver.[86]

Imagine James Mather adorned in the clothes of a gentleman of the merchant class, wearing long waistcoats, called flap waistcoats, with pockets in the great swinging flaps, with ornamental buttons known as basket buttons. Then in a further show of prosperity short breeches and gold or silver buckles on their shoes. The clothes all of one colour, the wrists ornamented by ruffles. For the headwear a cocked hat with a pointed front and a raised back. Silk stockings and a walking stick with an opulent prominent head of gold, silver, ebony or amber.[87] So cutting a fine figure and making the point that who was judged a gentleman was in part a matter of dress, displaying profitable business dealings and ample funds for investment.[88] This attire was highly prized by Mr. John Sparling High Sheriff of Lancashire in 1785, and mayor of Liverpool in *1790*.[89] Commensurate with his status and the aggressive money making of Liverpool, Sparling had a privateer named in his honour '*The Sparling*'.[90]

In the Crompton Papers there is an intriguing receipt dated 27th March 1760,[91] for payment made by a Mr. Thomas Townsend,[92] one of the tellers of his majesty' exchequer, for the enormous, precise sum of sixteen thousand, three hundred, and eighty two pounds, thirteen shillings and eleven pence. Corruption sneering behind the mask of precision? This was part payment to Henry Fox of an even more incredible amount of eight hundred thousand pounds for the service of his majesty' guards, garrisons and land services, referring to the date 26th June 1727. Henry Fox, father of Charles James Fox and at one time Paymaster General of his Majesties Forces, was renowned for enriching himself at the expense of the public purse.

It is not clear how or why the Townsend receipt found its way into the Crompton papers, but it provides evidence of the fabulous sums of money involved in the movement of provisions and the importance of position, favour, patronage, and sometimes corruption. There is a link between the recipient Henry Fox, Manchester and the textile industry through Samuel Touchett (1705-1773). Touchett can be described as a *dependent of Henry Fox,* providing a striking example of the importance of patronage. The son of a Warrington pin maker, he was a Manchester manufacturer of check ware. He made his fortune exporting '*Guinee Cloths*' to Africa, the West Indies and North America, in addition to his direct trading in slaves.[93] He influenced government policy, particularly as the advisor to Charles Townsend (1725-1767), Chancellor of the Exchequer. Indeed, he ill-advised Townsend to increase taxes in the American colonies, a major cause of the American war of independence. He often presented petitions on behalf of Manchester manufacturers. Moreover, he supported Lewis Paul, an early inventor of spinning machinery, thought to be the first to conceive of using rollers for spinning, though Lewis Paul's efforts were largely unsuccessful.

Samuel Crompton's manner and clothes suggested a common artisan with modest needs. He would never aspire to be a gentleman, in the evocative manner portrayed above. However, fashion and connection would prove important to his sons and place pressure on their father to provide the wealth to underpin their aspirations. Patronage could be an uncertain commitment; opportunistic or based upon genuine admiration and support. Samuel's later efforts to seek a reward from Parliament would sorely test the mettle of his connections.

§

The Crompton correspondence indicates the importance of family and business networks for the finance and support of commercial activity.[94] A further requirement for success, and dealing with risk, may have been the possession of a calculating, if not ruthless, personality. Other authors[95] have noted the aggressive money making mentality of British commercial society in the eighteenth and as early as the sixteenth century.[96] This view should be modified as more deeply religious and principled people, carrying the political and discriminatory burdens of nonconformity, thrived in manufacture and trade.[97]

To understand the importance of Samuel Crompton's invention and the factors that could make a difference between poverty and great wealth it is helpful to trace the development of the cotton industry and the experiences of other inventors. For example, Richard Arkwright. shows just how calculating and ruthless you might have to be to succeed. There could be no greater contrast to the humble, introverted Samuel Crompton.

Chapter Three

Preface to a Revolution

The poplars are fell'd farewell to the shade
*And the **whispering** sound of the cool colonnade:*
The winds play no longer and sing in the leaves,
Nor Ouse on his bosom their image receives.

William Cowper, The Poplar Field (1784)

Hobsbawm considered the likely view of a hypothetical foreign visitor to Britain in 1750:

"Yet if we placed ourselves in the Britain of 1750 without the wisdom of hindsight, would we have predicted the imminent Industrial Revolution? Almost certainly not. We should like the foreign visitors, have been struck by the essentially 'Bourgeois' commercial nature of the country. We should have admired its economic dynamism and progress, perhaps its aggressive expansionism, and we might have been impressed with the remarkable results of its multifarious and hardly controlled private entrepreneurs."[98]

By 1767 however, there was more than a hint that seismic economic and social transformation was under way. There was certainly a glimpse of the prospects of greater wealth. The 1760s saw the emergence of some of the key foundations of the Industrial revolution. The flow of capital from land to industry, urbanisation increasingly evident in places such as Liverpool and Manchester. There was the growth of commercial and consumer culture; evidenced by the rotting cargo of the 'Four Friends' and the rum and mahogany in the hold of the 'General Blakeney'. The colonies, including the land gains of the seven year's war, provided new markets for manufactured goods, particularly cotton wares. Agriculture had already undertaken gradual changes in the previous century with the beginning of enclosures of the land,

17

crop rotation and selective breeding. It was to witness a remarkable rise in productivity post 1750; an increase that accommodated rapid population growth.[99]

The organisation of the Lancashire textile industry was also changing. The old system of trade consisted of merchants buying cloth and transporting it on pack horses directly to the traders in the towns; in the process extending them credit. Pack horses wended their way to Bristol, Liverpool and London, transporting the cloth to be shipped overseas. Postlethwayt, writing of the industry in 1766, noted this as the chief way of distributing goods and estimated the annual value of cottons to be £600,000, a figure thought credible by Baines.[100] Any goods not sold would be stored at various inns. This form of distribution, by so called chapmen (*"Manchester Men"*), was being gradually replaced by pattern books containing samples of the wares, and order books with orders fulfilled via the new means of transport. There were improved roads, and more navigable stretches of the Lancashire rivers. Water transport was enhanced by canals, such as that constructed by James Brindley in 1761, for the Duke of Bridgewater, connecting his coal pits at Worsley with the Manchester markets. Even more critical for Liverpool, in 1762 an Act of Parliament was passed for the building of a canal from Manchester to Runcorn where it would join the river Mersey to Liverpool and conjoin Liverpool and Manchester.

The changes in the organisation of the textile industry presaged the coming industrialisation and the relationships between capitalist employers and the textile workers. The traditional system involved self-employed, small, producers of fustians and other wares. These 'manufacturers' purchased raw materials, produced the goods and sold them directly to customers. Though not completely this system was being surpassed by a more capitalistic form of enterprise, with merchants supplying materials on credit and purchasing finished cloth back for sale; the so called "putting out' system. Daniels states that there was no rapid economic and social transformation in moving to factories, as workers under this system were effectively employees of capitalist enterprises.[101]

Until the 1790s the domestic market for cotton appears to have grown more rapidly than exports[102] offering a stable environment for domestic production, while promising a potential surge in overseas sales if finer yarns could be produced. However, in the twenty or thirty years prior to 1795 foreign markets were important enough for the agents or partners of many Manchester manufacturers to reside abroad.[103] Thus the motivation and the infrastructure of overseas trade, exhibited in the Mather letters, was in place to take full advantage of any benefits of technological change in textile production.

In 1764, James Hargreaves introduced his spinning jenny, reputedly named after his wife. A Blackburn carpenter and spinner by trades he conceived of the idea that the productive capacity of spinners could be enhanced by spinning thread on multiple spindles. Hargreaves is said to have knocked over his wife's single spindled spinning wheel and observed that as it hit the hard flagged cottage floor, the spindle continued to spin, despite no operative spinning it.[104] A dreamy, ethereal glimpse of mechanical motion to come. The idea was formed, turn one spindle and automatically spin more. Hargreaves also realised that spindles could be positioned vertically, as well as in the traditional horizontal position. Though his invention was not patented until 1770 it was being adopted, modified and used by domestic producers throughout the intervening years.[105]

It is with Hargreaves's jenny that we observe the first reactions to technological change in this era. The extensive opposition to the machine is a prime indicator of the perceived threats to the precarious existence of agricultural cum cottage based textile workers. Opposition to new technologies recurred with a vengeance as the industrial revolution progressed. The spinners, perceiving the jenny to be undermining their livelihoods, attacked and ransacked Hargreaves's home. Intimidated and anxious he fled to Nottingham where he set up a small-scale spinning concern, in partnership with Thomas James, Arabella Sadler and Thomas Marlow.[106] The business was not successful, and Thomas Marlow left the partnership in August 1776 with Hargreaves and Arabella Sadler assigned to pay off the debts. In 1777 Hargreaves died, uncelebrated, in poverty, in a Nottingham workhouse. A portent for inventors to come.

The productivity of weaving had been markedly enhanced by the invention of John Kay's flying shuttle in 1764, and this further exacerbated the imbalance between the output of the spinners and the greater demand for thread by the weavers. Baines reflected, poetically:

"The one-thread wheel, though turning from morning till night in thousands of cottages, could not keep pace either with the weaver's shuttles, or with the demand of the merchant."[107]

Thus, there was a pressing need for increased productivity in spinning adding a further impetus to the emergence of new machines.

The Era of Invention

When the Mersey tide was favourable and the *General Blakeney* sailed from Liverpool, on the 16th April 1767, on its voyage via Cork to Kingston Jamaica, a Mr. Richard Arkwright (1732-1792) peruke (wig) maker in Bradshawgate, Bolton, was raising the finance for his proposed new cotton spinning machine. The water frame was a device that transformed the production of the cloth that the merchants, such as William Pimbley and James Mather, were handling; eventually creating an eruption of three story factories across Lancashire and the North. Arkwright's Water Frame utilised the fast flowing streams of Lancashire to power his new machine and spin the thread. The warp and the weft are the vertically and the horizontally woven threads. It was the course warp that, even in the damp Lancashire air, snapped so easily. As a result, weavers made fustians, using linen for the warp. The solution was provided by Richard Arkwright and his new machine. He was a man who would seize a concept, and turn it into practice, while the originator of the idea was still reflecting on it in his bathtub. A man who knew how to corner a market, a charmer who literally teased the hair from young women at fairgrounds to make his wigs.

In March 1767 Arkwright met with John Kay, a clockmaker of Warrington. John Kay had worked for a Mr. Thomas Highs of Leigh in Lancashire and developed a system of spinning by using rollers that was first conceived of, but never implemented to any practical effect, by Lewis Paul and John Wyatt of Birmingham. This was the origin of the disputes and accusations over who invented what, with Arkwright being accused of stealing the ideas of Kay and Highs. There existed an ultra-competitive environment, generating further invention, the continuous improvement and modification of machines and ever present industrial espionage. Just as the General Blakeney was captured and reused in the seven year's war, the great innovations of the Lancashire textile industry were captured and modified in the pursuit of riches. It was an environment that provided the hard edge to commercial life that was so unsettling for an honest, introverted man such as Samuel Crompton.

The cotton industry was a thriving concern throughout the seventeenth and early to mid-eighteenth centuries, even before the new inventions established themselves. There was limited government regulation, compared say to the French textile trade. There was also a skilled workforce and established links with overseas markets. Thus, the scene was set for a further wave of ingenious mechanics and inventors to design and manufacture new and improved 'engines.' Arkwright's water frame solved the snapping of the yarn but did not produce cotton goods fine enough to compete with the muslins and cambrics imported from overseas, such as those from India. So, there was commercial pressure to improve the quality of cotton goods. Moreover, the process of invention was not as simple as one man made one new machine, which then revolutionised a process and a trade. To some extent the markets in which the new technologies would prosper were also created alongside the invention.[108] However, as Baines put it:

"We have now arrived at the era of invention; and a series of inventions is to be opened, which for ingenuity and importance has never been equaled in any other manufacture." [109]

Samuel Crompton was 10 years of age in 1767, displaying the shy introverted behaviour that would be a salient aspect of his adult personality. The ruthlessness of the privateers and the nascent industrial espionage constituted unknown worlds and behaviours to him as he was hidden away in the half light of an old hall, Hall i' th' Wood, weaving his daily quota of cloth. He would not know about the mercantile adventures of James Mather and William Pimbley in the scorching, fevered West Indies. He may have been aware of the reactions to the spinning jenny, certainly by 1768 when a group of spinners broke into Hargreaves's house and destroyed his machines. Superstition and certainly fear may have played a part in the reaction of the population to the challenges to traditional ways of life.

John Roby in his book *'The Traditions of Lancashire'*[110] argued that the stories that communities preserve and relate illuminate their feelings and beliefs. The *'Tale of the Spectred Horseman,'* which follows, is a story that highlights the tensions between rationality and superstition, an unsteady balance that corresponds with the contradictions in Samuel Crompton's character and foreshadows the conflicts to come.

Part Two

1753-1779

Superstition and Fear

Chapter Four

Prelude to Fear

There she weaves by night and day
A magic web with colours gay.
*She has heard a **whisper** say,*
A curse is on her if she stay
To look down to Camelot.
She knows not what the curse may be,
And so she weaveth steadily,
And little other care hath she,
The Lady of Shalott.

Alfred Lord Tennyson, "The Lady of Shalott," 1832

The story of Samuel Crompton may be one of practicality and invention, business and industry, but it is also a narrative involving a good deal of superstition. We may relish ghost stories, creaking doors, random knocking and phantasmagorical shadows. They entertain and are keener for a dose of exaggeration. When people embrace superstition there can be cause for concern if it is attended by misanthropy and political persecution. The ghostly legend of Rivington Pike.[111] publicised by John Roby[112] in 1872, reveals the anxieties of 18th century communities in the North of England. It reflects the power of religious beliefs and the mingling of superstition, with the threat of change that populates the next few chapters.

The legend involves three 'sportsmen,' Pilkington's,[113] Norton and Mortimer who with their servants, dogs and *'paraphernalia'*, go hunting on the moor for grouse and game. The tale commences at the close of the day, on the glorious 12th August, following a stay at a *"little wayside tavern at the foot of the descent."*[114] On the distant horizon, at the far side of the valley, a dark and menacing storm was brewing. Keen to observe the storm the party trudged higher up the steepening slope of Rivington Pike. As the weather worsened the 'sportsmen' sought shelter in the cramped stone tower at the Pike's summit, which acted as a hunting lodge.

Undulating sheets of water swept across the moorland, accompanied by relentless thunder and lightning. The rain searched out the crevices in the roof and windows of the tower. The dogs fearful of the battering gale barked and howled. Inexplicably there was a clattering of horse's hooves on the cobbled surface outside. The door swung open and there on a baying horse sat a menacing figure, the brim of his tricornered hat obscuring his face. Retreating as fast as he had arrived, the horseman charged down the fell into the eye of the forbidding storm.

To everyone's surprise the apparition was chased, on foot, by Norton, who cried out that the phantom was his long lost Uncle. Martin, a servant, convinced the party that it was sensible not to follow Norton and to stay in the tower, until the storm abated. He had experienced the chilling antics of this horseman before. Twelve years previously, on the eve of St Bartholomew, Martin's father had gone hunting with his favourite dogs, Crab and Pincher. However, the dogs had returned alone scratching at the cottage door. Frantically searching the moor, for his father, he was unable to find him. Was he injured and lying in a bog trap? Returning to the house he retired to bed. He was jolted awake by the clanging of the outside gate. His father had returned, looking wretched and a lesser man. Sighing, he collapsed into his rocking chair, moaning I've seen the '*owd un.*'

He had climbed the Pike and met with a small man on a large black horse. With the dogs trailing, tails down and out of sorts, the horseman led them to a high point of the moor, *The Two Lads*, a cairn commemorating the death of two young boys who had perished in a freezing moorland storm. They were reputed to be the sons of a Saxon king. A place of wildness and grief. The horseman commanded that the stones marking the spot be moved. Martin's father, reluctant to disrespect the memory of the boys, refused. The incensed horseman caused the stones to rise and remove themselves.

A deep hole opened in the earth and a long arm beckoned the servants father to enter. *"Take what he offers you"* shouted the horseman, but he again refused. The specter screamed in demonic frustration, that *"he will miss his time."* A stranger appeared on the crest of the moor. The horseman, anticipating a more cooperative victim, moved on. Martin's father was kicked away. He muttered an old charm and lost consciousness. When he woke the stones were back on the cairn and the moonlit night was calm. A few days later the village gossips reported that a traveller had disappeared while riding on the moor. Martin's father was a changed man, more readily consulting a neglected bible. He never again wandered the moors alone.

The hunting party listened to the story with trepidation, trying to disentangle the *'marvelous'* from the facts and offer a rational explanation. In the hope of finding Norton, they returned to the inn. Alas! he had not returned, so they raced to *The Two Lads*. The rain persisted and the banks of the river Douglas had been breached. During their treck Pilkington was alarmed by a rush of air. Mortimer fancied that he heard a voice warning them *"Go not"*. Approaching the stones, they heard the piercing cries of Norton. Suffering from delirium he was carried back to the inn. For several weeks he relived a terrifying nightmare.

Norton's uncle had disappeared on the moor, some twelve years previously. He had been the unsuspecting stranger abducted instead of Martin's father. Norton told his story of how on reaching the *Two Lads* the horseman had exhorted him to wait until he returned at midnight, when all his questions would be answered. On his return the demon had a hideous appearance *"Thou art mine"* he had cried. He grasped Norton's arm who struggled to escape the unearthly grip. Eventually he escaped, crediting his good fortune to divine intervention.

The story of the Spectred Horseman and the *"owd un"* is undated but given that John Andrews built the Pike Tower as a hunting lodge in 1723, the tale is likely to have originated in the eighteenth century. It may be a composite of earlier stories of morality and menace. It portrays the fears that surrounded the upper reaches of the moor, serving as a warning to those who might stray unattended, or ill prepared, into this beautiful but unforgiving environment. There is a clash between rational thought and superstition. A lesson for keeping faith and reading your bible. Superstition was rife. The wealthy landowners and nascent industrialists, the Blundell's' had their hair cut short every midsummer eve, as a precaution against attacks by werewolves.[115]

The *Romantics* of the late eighteenth and early nineteenth centuries professed a love of nature that contrasts markedly with the legend of Rivington Pike. The man of feeling Babbitt suggested *"finds the savage deserted nook full of beauties that seem horrible to mere worldlings."*[116] The characters in our story are *worldlings* rather than Romantics. The Romantics were stimulated by diverting from well-trodden pathways and venturing into the unknown. The solitary exploration of nature was the essence of personal freedom. The Spectred Horseman has elements of wonder but presents the wilderness as an adversary, rather than a kindred spirit.

The Two Lads were a warning of the perils of natural forces while the demolition and rebuilding of the cairn depicted the threat to order. Samuel Crompton's religious inclinations would present him as a compromise between the romantic and the *worldling*. However, the worldlings were advancing. The machines and edifices of the emerging industrial age provided the focus for wonder and threat. Industrial and technological change advanced like the menace of a rapidly encroaching moorland storm.

Chapter Five

Hall i'th' Wood
(The Hall in the Wood)

*And conscious reason **whispered** to despise His early youth misspent in maddest whim; but as he gazed on truth his aching eyes grew dim.*

Child Harold, Lord Byron, 1812-1818

I recollect a game that the young boys of my town, in the 1950s, used to play on or around Guy Fawkes night. Discarded bobbins from the local cotton mills could be scavenged from the nearby rubbish tip. There was nothing more satisfying than placing a couple of 'tuppeny canons' - particularly loud explosive fireworks - inside these makeshift hollow missiles, blasting them as high as a lamp post. We were not even sure what the bobbins were used for, and though some members of our families worked in the mills, spinning, weaving, carding etc. were arcane mysteries. Unlike children of the industrial revolution, we knew little of the deafening powerful looms within the factories, the scale of which represented the culmination of the impact of the mechanical device first constructed by Samuel Crompton. The terraced streets in which we played, descending steeply away from land that would have once been the lower reaches of the moor and touching the steam whistling railway works, were named after the pioneers of the textile industry. For example, Cartwright Street was adjacent to Arkwright Street. We did know that the mills must be deafening places; relatives signing to each other and lip reading in the weaving sheds would, once outside the factory, use emphatic mimes and silent enunciation to hide their tastier snippets of gossip from the children.

The cacophony and tumult of the textile factories belied the quite country life that was the environment of the early cotton industry. Samuel Crompton experienced a very different childhood than my contemporaries, being fully versed and engaged in the craft and labour of spinning and weaving. Samuel was subjected to a harsh working and domestic regime, enforced by his petulant Mother Betty Compton (nee Holt) of Turton. He was locked away in a sparsely furnished darkened room with a quota of cloth to spin, using Hargreaves spinning jenny. Regardless of the fragility of the yarn he would not be released until his target had been reached. Betty was not averse to slapping him and could be harsh and snappy. His father George would have done little to ameliorate any discipline, deferring most matters and decisions to his wife. Dying in at the age of 35 years in 1758, even his will abandoned all pressure to make decisions and bequeathed everything to Betty to dispose of as she pleased.[117] Betty Crompton would have been more than capable of such financial management.

§

The Crompton genealogy was extensively spelled out by Gilbert French, the lineage including a poet and a significant number of farmers. French noted that the Crompton pedigree also included renowned authors, and had strong links with the clergy; including the Rev John Okey of Bolton, the Rev Oliver Heywood and the Rev Mr. Goodwin.[118] The poet was a Mr. Hugh Crompton, who immodestly styled himself: *"Son of Bacchus and Godson of Apollo"* and among his works was to be found the surreal rendering: *"Poems, Being a Fardle of Fancies, or a Medley of Musick stewed in Four Ounces of Oil of Epigrams."*[119] Thus on this observation alone the more practical and modest Samuel Crompton would have little genetic indebtedness to his forebears. Rather, we need to look to his more immediate family and social situation to better understand the formation of his character. However, the inestimable Mr. Hugh Crompton does, in the final stanza of his poem on *"Grief"*, offer advice which, throughout his troubled life, Samuel Crompton would be severely challenged to adhere to :

"If accident should chance to fall, it falls from heaven above; then let no poverty or thrall Your soaring spirits move: Nothing but sin can require; then grieve for sin, else grief expire."[120]

For several generations the Crompton family had owned and farmed land at Firwood Fold. Samuel's grandfather George Crompton (1651-1755) could be described as a yeoman farmer. Firwood was a typical Lancashire fold, a collection of diminutive cottages, smaller than a hamlet, but large enough to facilitate a viable working community. There the Crompton's would have tended a few cattle and practiced farming on a small scale. Unfortunately, the families wealth and status, which was tied up in land, was to be compromised and they were forced to sell their holdings to the Starkie's of Stretham, a noteworthy family originating from the Great Budworth area in Cheshire, the origin of Mary Crompton's ancestors the Pimbley's.[121] The sale of Firwood Fold reflected the tendency for agriculture to become concentrated in larger units, as landowners enclosed their lands and increased the scale of their operations. Many yeoman farmers lost their wealth and status, becoming renters and relying upon spinning and weaving for employment. The great nineteenth century historian of the industrial revolution Arnold Toynbee[122] lamented the eventual disappearance of the independent yeoman class (the small freeholders) during the eighteenth century, which he described as *"a silent revolution."*[123] Land was the prime source of wealth and merchants and manufacturers who craved political power and social status became large scale landowners, driving out the smaller independent yeoman farmers.

The Crompton's' remained at Firwood Fold as renters, but they were eventually obliged to move to a smallholding at Lower Wood in Tong. Thomas Midgley attributed this move to the difficulties of combining farming with cotton manufacture, with consequent adverse effects on the ability to farm,[124] George Crompton also had significant debts. It is a tribute to the character of Betty Crompton that in 1758, on her husband's death, she managed to raise the standing of the family by securing a lease from the Starkie's on an old manor house, Hall i' th' Wood. This was an Elizabethan yeoman farmers house, black and white timber framed, its location can be pictured as a romantic idyll, situated on a hillside, refreshed by a clear bubbling stream and the whole immersed in an ancient woodland. The internal structure of Hall i'th' Wood was complex, and one can imagine how the young Samuel might have scampered from room to room, avoiding the attention of his controlling mother and questioning adults. Midgley goes so far as to state:

"The remote situation of the Hall and the number of spare rooms in it had a considerable influence on the character and temperament of the child and afterwards were of supreme value to Crompton whilst he was secretly

experimenting with the spinning machine which is ever connected with his name."[125] .

There is a small, cloistered part of the upper story of the Hall that is known as *'the thinking room,'* a space associated with Samuel's preoccupation with the spinning mule. On the few occasions he was not working it may also have served as a refuge from the intrusive and intimidating world of adults. Samuel later challenged his isolation by making his own violin and practicing music.[126] If today one was to imagine ghostly sounds associated with the old Hall it might be the retreating thud of Samuel's clogs[127] on the creaking timber floors and stairways, together with the background murmuring of commercial and family chatter in the rooms below. And from Betty a mother's impatient shout to her young son, to return to his work on the jenny. Betty Crompton was undoubtedly self-assured and further demonstrated her resolve and organising abilities by becoming overseer of the poor for Turton and Haugh; an onerous, unpaid role involving the raising of a rate of assessment to meet the 'needs' of the poor. This was a vacancy typically filled from the ranks of yeomen, husbandmen and craftsmen. Though an organised man Samuel would inherit none of his mother's natural assertiveness. As for his father, he undoubtedly facilitated his son's practical development. George Crompton had started to build an organ for the local church which he did not finish. The family attributed his early demise to fatigue from this commission. It was Samuel Crompton who completed the construction of the instrument.

Samuel was a shy, diffident youth but also a determined, single minded, industrious artisan who was influenced by contemporary science and industry. His ability in mathematics and his neat writing style are attributed to his private education under the tutor William Barlow of Little Bolton, while further advances in his education were gained at evening school, which at the age of 16 offered him some reprieve from the jenny. Given this background and his musical ability, then he was different from many other artisans who contributed their inventions to the industrial revolution, such as James Hargreaves and Richard Arkwright, both of whom were less formally educated. His parents and family could not be described as 'entrepreneurial' with little propensity to invest and speculate in the manner of many yeoman farmers. The Crompton's' adhered to a traditional lifestyle, facing sufficient risk from changes in the price of food and cotton goods, together with the general assaults on health and life typical of the times, without embracing the risk of business.

There was one family member who may have had a significant impact on Samuel's personal development. Eccentricity can be a bulwark for the survival of family memories; and one singular character was Samuel's uncle, Alexander Crompton. Piercing the calm of a misty moorland Sunday morning, around 10.0clock, the bells of St Peters Church would peal across the wooded vale of *Hall i' th' Wood* summoning the Cromptons' and the other spinners, weavers and small holders to morning service. Alexander was confined to his room by a walking disability, therefore excluded from weekly worship and social gathering. On hearing the beckoning church bells Alexander would, perhaps unsteadily, change into his best Sunday clothes. Unlike Methodist churches where dressing in any kind of finery met with censure, the congregations of Anglican churches favoured dressing *"decently"* on a Sunday; clean simple white or black clothes being the measure of decorum.[128] Moreover, the invention of the spinning jenny by Hargreaves had allowed the production of more affordable garments that could serve this purpose.

Alexander was fully prepared for this weekly ritual and had a sermon to hand. Perhaps hastily scribbled by himself, or provided by an obliging vicar, he would read the script aloud. The sermon had become an integral part of Anglican Services in the eighteenth century and good speakers could attract a congregation from several parishes;[129] though the attractions of self-delivery are difficult to divine. He also sang the hymns, gruffly or sonorously. He was determined to act out his religious duty; albeit pared down to a lonely core of ritual and obligation. The performance accomplished, he would place his Sunday best clothes back in the country cupboard, until the evening service, which could be as early as 3.pm, when the whole process would be repeated. Or so goes the story of Alexander Crompton!

The description of Alexander's singular piety and homemade Sunday Service may be a family exaggeration.[130] However, he was disabled and so as French noted *" there was but one step between his bed and his loom."*[131] According to Cameron the disability meant that if Samuel's uncle could not see the world, the world would have to come to Uncle Alexander.[132] Thus, young Samuel Crompton was introduced to a network of bleachers, dyers, spinners, weavers and merchants who milled around the small room in which his uncle was confined. Cameron speculates: *"in his uncle's room where he so often was, there was but one topic, spinning and weaving and all that concerned their improvement."*[133] He suggests a parallel between the physical isolation of Alexander Crompton, and the introspection of his nephew.

The image of this bustling commercial gathering may not be accurate as dealings with the textile community lying outside Uncle Alexander's bedroom could have easily been undertaken by the highly competent Betty Crompton. However, we retain this colourful and frenetic image to note the variety of individuals that had to be dealt with by the small-scale spinners and weavers. Certainly, there is one significant influence that the single-minded Uncle Alexander would have on his nephew, and that was religious piety and devotion. It was here that the reach of Samuel's more notable reverend ancestors might be found. To quote French:

"One cannot help respecting the character of this simple but sincerely pious recluse, who thus cut off from the world, worshipped his God and at the same time did honour to himself. Doubtless his nephew remembered and respected this example through life." [134]

French also noted the revolution in science, technology and industry that was taking place at the time. There was the genius of the great Duke of Bridgewater and his engineer James Brindley. French speculated that if Samuel did have a day's holiday it would have been spent surveying the wonders of the canal system at Worsley (built, 1761). Not an altogether unlikely happening as the labyrinth of underground canals were a great source of contemporary fascination and attracted a multitude of visitors. One commentator noted in 1765 that *"At first view you would think the work was intended to astonish."* [135] As early as 1776 there was a full timetable of boat trips along the canal from Warrington to Manchester; a place in the grand cabin travelling from Norton cost 3s and 6d with children on the lap free. [136]

He would also have heard of the *"fire engine" which was year after year passing like himself from youth to giant manhood under the tending of James Watt.* [137] One newspaper editor noted in 1772 that he had received J. Bells, *Remarks on Some Improvements in the Fire Engine*, being *"too obscure in various parts to be understood."* [138] A correspondent writing in 1775 announced a fire engine *"of a new construction"* that made twenty strokes a minute, with no beam and reduced in size to less than one third the usual height, using less fuel. [139] Clearly Watt's engine was growing in complexity. No doubt the excitement of invention and change captured the imagination of the young Samuel Crompton.

By 1774 Samuel was contemplating the building of a prototype of his spinning mule, and reflecting on how to create a finer, but strong yarn. Perhaps, from the vantage point of the mullioned windows in *'the thinking room,'* he exercised his imagination, peering across the then densely wooded landscape and verdant pastures, contemplating how to draw upon his natural inventiveness to ease the frustrations of his trade. Samuel the dreamer, the violin player, the extraordinarily diffident and industrious young man began constructing his spinning machine. A machine introduced into an increasingly fractured traditional world with views of technological change alternate between wonder and fear. In developing his spinning mule Samuel would have to traverse this turbulence and protect himself and his invention.

When Richard Arkwright built his cotton spinning factory on a moorland site at Birkacre, Coppull, near Chorley in 1779 it harnessed the force of waterpower, but it did not tame the torrid emotional responses of the populace. Emotions were readily excited in the eighteenth century and never more so than when traditional ways of living and livelihoods were threatened.

Chapter Six

Ghosts, Riots and Disorder

*'Oh, do not use violence! He is one man, and you are many'; but her words died away, for there was no tone in her voice; it was but a hoarse **whisper**"*

Elizabeth Gaskell, North and South, 1854

Coppull lies on a hill 300 feet above sea level, with a river perceived to run from the ocean towards the Pennine moors. It is as though this stretch of water, that could power the wheels of Arkwright's revolutionary new machine the water frame, was physically feeding industry in the way that the financial capital from seafaring trade flowed steadily into new investment and cotton manufacture. The name Coppull means a hill rising to a peak.[140] A key location in the development of the cotton industry it faces the east across the *"owd uns"* lair; the complex of sweeping moorlands, Rivington Moor, Horwich Moor, Deane Moor. Scattered over this terrain and its valleys were the cottages and folds inhabited by the outworkers of the domestic system of textile production. Given its rarity, the spinning house built by Richard Arkwright, Jedediah Strutt, Samuel Need, Thomas Walshman and John Cross at Birkacre,[141] Coppull, in 1779, was a mesmerising feature of the local landscape.

Today Birkacre is a pleasant country park embracing the bubbling river Yarrow, providing summer recreation for picnicking families, with excitable children wading and bathing by its banks. In the summer of 1779 moving faster than the river, were rumours and troubling news. In August there were reports that the French had captured the *'sugar island'* of St Vincent in the West Indies. In September there were accounts of the capture of Grenada, an important cotton producing island. These conflicts had arisen from the American Revolutionary War (1775-1783) which had a devastating impact upon trade. By June 21ˢᵗ 1779[142] the war had widened as Spain joined France against Great Britain. Social unrest was inevitable.

In July 1776 Lord North, First Lord of the Treasury, attributed riots in Liverpool to a decline in trade; one newspaper report claiming that the rioters had been appeased by *"taking them into the royal navy."*[143] Also in July the *"poor people"* employed in *"clothing manufactory"* in Bradford, Trowbridge, Westbury and Frome, had planned an armed assault on a spinning jenny at Shepton Mellet.[144] Rioters were selective in their targets,[145] only destroying spinning jenny's with more than twenty four spindles;[146] a fine calculation suggesting that the merits of the jenny were appreciated, but that too great an hike in productivity was a threat. The clothiers paid for protection by dragoons, and armed volunteers, which was sufficient to stop many planned attacks.

Assaults took the form of a guerrilla war involving *"flying parties."* This degree of organisation predated the Luddite machine breaking disturbances of 1811-1813. The flying parties had destroyed a mill at Bolton by the Bridge and had 'visited' Bury and Radcliffe. Mr. Taylor of Ardwick was *"collecting men"* to protect his mill at Altringham, while Messrs. Dales of Stockport borrowed cannon from Sir George Warren to defend their premises.[147] Given this agitation the spinning house at Birkacre was unlikely to avoid attention. Distress and anger were compounded by the rumour that an owner of one of the larger cotton spinning enterprises was to lower his prices for spinning. Unfortunately for Richard Arkwright and his partners, the new mechanised mill at Birkacre was a provocation to a much agitated populace. Initially viewed as a monument to progress that rapidly changed to a perception that it was an engine of misery and poverty.

On Saturday 2nd October, 1779[148] a few hundred angry people[149] ventured onto the moor to attack the Birkacre spinning house. The only approach to the factory was a narrow stone gully, severely disadvantaging the assailants. Given this hazard it was easy enough for the owner, with the assistance of a few neighbours, to ward off the attack. Unfortunately, the defence of the mill was ferocious, possibly disproportionate, and involved the shooting dead of two of the attackers. Another person was reported to have drowned in the Birkacre stream, while several people incurred serious injuries. As with modern disturbances there were contradictory reports regarding the number of casualties. One newspaper[150] claimed that an assailant was killed on the spot, 50 wounded, with 4 or 5 dying later; while the Annual Register claimed two rioters killed and 8 wounded. Whatever the casualties they ignited an unquenchable passion for revenge. It is worth remembering that what were subsequently described as a mob, or *'brutes'* involved many otherwise respectable tradespeople.[151]

On the Monday which followed the initial fracas, the aggrieved locals decided to arm themselves with what they could and return to Birkacre. Pewter pots and other pieces of metal work were melted down to create bullets and weapons. Guns, scythes, and anything else that came to hand, were used to arm a crowd speculated to be 4,000 to 5,000 people, though Josiah Wedgwood claimed 8,000. With banners waving, drums beating, hearts pounding, they marched on Birkacre, vowing its destruction. Sympathy for the rioters and their cause had extended beyond the neighbourhood. They were joined by miners from the Duke of Bridgewater's estates at Worsley. Independently minded, forming a vigorous subculture in eighteenth century England, the colliers would have been a formidable ally.[152] Once again they approached the spinning house through the narrow stone gulley.

Waiting for the assailants was Sir Richard Clayton (1745-1828) of Adlington Hall, Baronet and Magistrate. The militia, under his command, were the 'Invalids', being soldiers retired from the regular army and in receipt of a pension. The Baronet showed great courage by attempting to dissuade the rioters from any action. It was also clear to Sir Richard that any resistance would lead to substantial loss of life. It is also possible that General Saville, commander of the York militia had forewarned Sir Richard to exercise caution. Saville had arrived in the area noon the day before,[153] but clearly felt it safer to stand down. It was common practice to use militia from outside an area, thus minimizing the defenders sympathy with rioters. So outnumbered and having failed to persuade the attackers to return home, the Baronet and his ageing part time soldiers prudently stood aside and allowed the crowd to destroy the factory.[154] It was said that the flames from the burning spinning house lit up the surrounding moorland, even at midnight of that day.

The agitation surrounding the riot, and the disturbances in general, were observed by Josiah Wedgwood, whose four sons were attending a boarding school in Bolton run by the Rev Philip Holland. One son was sick, and Wedgwood had come to take him home.[155] He alluded to the rioters wider destructive ambitions.

"On Tuesday morning we heard their drum at about two miles distant from Bolton, a little before we left the place and their professed design was to take Bolton, Manchester and Stockport in their way to Cromford and to destroy all their engines, not only in these places but throughout all England."[156]

The rioters who destroyed the Birkacre factory, were subsequently apprehended and put on trial at the General Quarter Sessions of the Peace for the County of Lancaster held at Preston, chaired by Alexander Butler Esquire, Sheriff of Lancaster. Sir Richard Clayton of Adlington Hall also sat in this court. The testimonies give some indication of the size of Arkwright's factory and the extent of the destruction. One Mary Leicester was accused of destroying 20 spinning frames, 20 spinning engines, and in perfect symmetry wrecking 20 each of carding engines, roving engines, twisting engines, twisting mills, cotton wheels and cotton reels. This busy systematic lady was sentenced to twelve months imprisonment in the castle prison, Lancaster. Surprisingly, the arrests which followed did not lead to any executions, and the harshest sentence was meted out to Giles Fletcher, a miner and the presumed leader of the attack, in the form of two years imprisonment. The court gave thanks to General Saville[157] and Sir George Fawcett and other officers of the militia for their actions in controlling the riots, albeit too late to save Birkacre.

Having examined the circumstances of the riots the magistrates pronounced five resolutions. The court adopted a balanced view of the motives and actions of the machine breakers, though mill owners might clearly have been antagonistic. Arkwright applied to the government for compensation for the loss of his factory and its machines but was refused. While recognising that the rioters feared a reduction in earnings, they felt the need to proclaim the beneficial nature of those inventions and engines which had led to the building of the spinning house. In sharp contrasts to the proprietorial claims of Richard Arkwright, whose patents gave him an effective monopoly of highly mechanised spinning, the commission saw this progress as the property of the world. Indeed, if an invention was not applied in this country, it would soon enough be adopted by others. The progress of invention was considered relentless. The court claimed, *"It is impossible to restrain the force of ingenuity when employed in the improvement of manufactures."*[158]

Many local magistrates adopted a sympathetic view of the riots. The justices of Wigan, in the aftermath of the events at Birkacre and elsewhere, called for the banning of what they described as the *"patent machines"* which used waterpower. However, as a further indicator of divided opinion there was an exhortation to 300 respectable households in Blackburn to join the militia and oppose the *'insurgents,'* with the magistrates' granting permission for them to arm, a clarion call that newspaper reports[159] stated was enthusiastically heeded. So, regardless of social class the new machines were not universally perceived as threats to an ordered and customary ways of life. Randal states:

"From the first, therefore, the battle over machinery saw different value systems in opposition, with respective forces of custom and innovation vying not only over the physical introduction of new technologies but also for the moral high ground of public support."[160]

Birkacre was not the first spinning house to be powered by water, that honour went to Arkwright's other establishment at Cromford in Derbyshire.[161]In 1770 Arkwright had commissioned Samuel Stretton, a Nottingham builder, to convert an existing property into a mill, though due to the experimental nature of the enterprise the factory was not fully working until 1772. Arkwright may have been taken by surprise by the destruction of Birkacre, but his capacity for organisation meant that he was prepared for any onslaught on his talisman premises at Cromford. A dozen or more mills were destroyed in the disturbances, but Cromford remained intact. He had an 'army' of 1500 men bearing small arms, menacingly equipped with spears attached to long poles.[162] The potentially bloodiest confrontation of the troubles was avoided, as the rioters did not get within 50 miles of Cromford.

Arkwright's defence of his mill invited some observations on the nature of the rioters and the defenders. Often the attackers were seen as *"unhappy and deluded people"* misled by *"the artful persuasions of a few wicked and designing wretches."*[163] The Cromford defenders were not only *"the gentlemen of the neighborhood"* but also 5000 to 6,000 men and miners resolved to protect the factory *"by which many hundreds of their wives and children get a decent and comfortable livelihood."*[164] So the riots were no simple expression of class conflict between employers and workers, the latter as with the miners often took different sides.

Amidst the noise and fire of these disturbances, Samuel Crompton continued to work on his spinning mule at Hall i'th' Wood. He had laboured on this project since 1774, suffering the frustrations of a lack of tools and little experience in using them. In his nocturnal activity he rendered his own clanging and banging noises, leading to the widespread belief that the ancient hall was haunted. Worryingly he could hear the commotion of rioting and destruction resounding from the attack on a carding shed in the Folds, a nearby property.

Gilbert French was informed by Mr. James Crossley and Mr. Samuel Crompton (Crompton's grandson) who had both visited the hall, that they had discovered a trap door above the room in which Samuel had worked on the mule. [165] There was a square cut into the ceiling with the clay in the room above replaced to cover the hole. The current resident Mr. Bromiley, a tenant farmer, had been in the hall long enough to talk to Samuel Crompton on one of his many visits, and had asked him about the aperture. He had explained that on hearing the shouts and jeering of the rioters he had dismantled his invention, and with the aid of a rope and skip hoisted it's various 'parts into the attic. On peace being re-established, he would retrieve the components and laboriously reconstruct his machine. French speculated that Crompton believing in the potential and symbolic significance of his invention, anticipated even greater acrimony, should it 's existence be discovered. [166]

French considered that the rioters demonstrated their *"own ignorant prejudices against machinery"* and added that this was made much worse by many of the middle and upper classes who also expressed a dread *"at the changes in manufacturing and trade that they saw approaching."*[167] However, just as privateering could be viewed as piracy or legitimate private military action there were different perspectives on social disorder. The interpretation of who was an insurrectionary or a defender of rights could be fragile and changeable. There were other tensions that led to disaffection. For example, organising the workforce into a factory system meant that the outworkers lost some of their independence, though they were often organised along industrial lines. [168] The evidence also suggests that it was not mechanical innovation per se that led to riots and discontent, but general economic conditions and the consequences of war [169]though there was still some ferocious opposition to machines. Also, inventors could appear selfish, pursuing their own material interests in defiance of customary ways of working and living. [170] It is tempting to interpret the actions of Richard Arkwright in this way. However, Samuel Crompton appears to have had mixed motives, though economic advantage for his family was undoubtedly one.

Arkwright never returned to Lancashire after the Birkacre incident, while John Kay of Warrington inventor of the flying shuttle (1733) fled to Nottingham and eventually France, where he died in poverty in 1780. [171] The inclination was for manufacturers and inventors blighted by discontent, not to rely upon any local enforcers to ensure their safety and property, but to move to more accepting environments. [172] For example, Birkacre had been allowed to be burned to the ground. Robert Peel (Parsley Peel, 1723-1795) grandfather of the eventual Prime Minister Robert Peel was a spinner and calico printer who had his machinery thrown into the river in Oldham. He retreated to Burton in Staffordshire and built a cotton spinning concern on the banks of the river Trent. This tendency to retreat from disturbances momentarily held back the development of the textile industry in troubled areas of the country. [173]

Samuel Crompton never abandoned his native town and continued to work in isolation and secrecy. In his own words:

".........which machine to complete to my satisfaction cost me years of study and personal labour and at the expense of every shilling I had in the world unaided directly or indirectly by anyone."[174]

So, emerging from the din of violence and destruction and the mists of the ambiguity of invention there is Samuel Crompton and his spinning mule. The tension between the private rights of inventors and notions of the public good were ever present. The Preston court saw mechanical invention as the property of the world, but for Samuel Crompton this would prove to be a treacherous path to follow.

1. The Crompton centenary commemorative handkerchief, 1927

2. A depiction of Samuel Crompton being spied upon

3. Samuel Crompton

4. Firwood Fold, Samuel Crompton's birthplace

5. *Rivington Pike*

6. *Hall i' th' Wood*

7. Samuel's mother Betty Crompton

8. Adlington Hall

Part Three

1780-1805
Betrayal and Disillusion

Chapter Seven

The Reign of the Conjurers

*The **whisper'd** murmurs of the gathering storm; Shuts her sweet eye-lids to approaching night; And hails with freshen'd charms the rising light.*

Erasmus Darwin, from 'The Loves of the Plants, Mimosa and Tremella', 1791

The Arrival of the 'Mule'

By 1779 Samuel Crompton had built his Hall i'th' Wood machine and was soon producing the yarns that would intrigue and mystify local spinners, weavers and merchants. He rewarded himself, from the proceeds of his sales of the finely spun thread, with the purchase of a splendid silver watch, for 5 guineas, from Mr. Hodson of Bolton. He visited the watchmaker regularly to check the progress of its construction. This small piece of precision engineering would have been a personal accoutrement that represented the height of male fashion, manly status, and a representation of the combination of the sciences and the arts. The complexity of the watch is both an apt symbol for the knowledge and engineering precision evident at the time and indicative of an actual source of the craft and engineering skills that facilitated the progress and application of wider mechanical invention. For example, John Kay inventor of the Flying Shuttle was a clock maker.

The inventors, and the mechanics who perfected the engines, were known as the 'conjurers'. There was a prevalence of talented amateur engineers, including clock and watch makers, to aid the continuous development of the new engines. There was also ample business acumen to harness the power of the machines, or in some cases to develop the markets that made them profitable applications. It has been argued that Richard Arkwright was successful because he not only applied a new machine but integrated the process of production into a water powered factory system.[175] Arkwright's capacity to organise production and market his ideas and goods contrasts with the more technically focused Samuel Crompton. Osborne describes inventors such as Hargreaves, Arkwright and Crompton as *«artisan plus»* all tending to have a craft and commercial background.[176] Foster notes that innovators were from families who were commercially minded and proud of their business, passing enterprises on from son to son, or in the absence of a son to nephews.[177]

The motives for Samuel Crompton's perseverance in developing the mule have not been debated by his biographers, but they have been differently expressed. French suggested that Samuel Crompton's chief intent was to ease his own burden and the lot of the domestic spinner, with no inkling of the impending factory system and its miseries. Osborne asserts that the motive for working on the mule, as with all the inventors, was pure financial gain.[178] I adopt an eclectic view. Crompton's motives were undoubtedly mixed and may have included obsessing over the challenge of solving several technical problems on which his calculating and practical mind would thrive.

The spinning mule *"combined the drafting rollers of Arkwright's water frame and the spinning action of Hargreaves jenny."*[179] The water frame facilitated the use of a source of power to drive the machine, initially horsepower, but later at Cromford Mill in Derbyshire water. Arkwright's machine had significantly reduced the problem of the snapping warp that so frustrated Samuel. However, it could not produce the fine threads to compete with the imported cotton goods from the Far East. [180]It was Crompton's mule that solved that problem.

The mule came into wider use after 1785 and corresponded with an expansion in the volume, value and variety of cotton goods produced and exported.[181] This justified the use of the new machinery and further encouraged the growth of the factory system. Samuel Crompton was not averse to proclaiming the significance of his invention.

"At that time 1780 the cotton trade was in its infancy compared to what it is now and I dare affirm that its rapid increase was owing under Divine Providence to this invention whose powers are the most unlimited and perfect of any machine yet known, if I had destroyed it rather than give it up I do not hesitate to say, this country would have lost the only piece of mechanism that has produced and increased one of the first manufactures in Europe..."[182]

The mule did two things simultaneously, very well. It stretched the cotton by drawing it away from multiple spindles around which the cotton was wrapped, also twisting the thread to give it strength. Imagine the raw cotton (the roving) being stretched and flattened at the same time by several rollers, then a spindle putting in the twist while using a moving carriage to draw the cotton out even further. So, flatten, stretch, twist and stretch again while reeling this on to the twisting spindles. The cycle was then repeated, and the mule produced its magic. In essence it was the stretching of the yarn, by the moveable carriage, that solved the problem of the uneven threads. The principle was clear to observe, but this was a remarkable technical achievement at the time.[183]

Comparing Arkwright's water frame and Crompton's mule presents some telling contrasts. The former was fashioned in metal and had fluted metal rollers and toothed gears. However, the mule was initially made of wood with its few metal parts provided by the local blacksmith and the machine operated by a system of rollers, pulleys and bands. Clock making had its technical reflection in the precision and beauty of the moving parts of the water frame while the mule reflected Crompton's sense of craft and his preference for working in wood. Even the financing of these machines reflects the different personalities of the two inventors. Richard Arkwright was a master deal maker with access to sources of credit and fellow investors.[184] Samuel purchased his materials and tools with money raised by playing the violin in the Bolton Theatre, for one shilling and sixpence a time. Music and invention combined. Perhaps he visualised the rapid movements of his spindles and the mule carriage as the bow of his violin expressed harmony, co-ordination and vigour. The image of the racing carriage loudly banging from its start to its finish, drawing out the threads - a harbinger of the future hellish, thumping, unmusical din of the mills - is a potent one.

Playing the violin symbolises a distinctive creative edge to Samuel's practical ability which when combined with his patience and focus fueled his inventiveness. He performed in the orchestra alongside his blind friend Billy Lonsdale (1733-1833), a composer and organist in the Parish Church. Samuel Crompton had many musical associates, including Edward Harwood a celebrity musician and composer, to whom he is reputed to have taught musical theory and practice.[185] Billy Lonsdale was less salubrious and was later removed from his post, by Canon James Slade, for being drunk on duty.

Lonsdale was a popular local character. He was kept out of poverty by public subscriptions and charitable donations. Subscriptions and donations, sometimes the provision of an annuity for a pension, were a way of supporting individuals whose merit had not been adequately recognised by the government or the marketplace. It was a form of reward that Samuel would seek for recognition of the importance of his spinning machine. Meanwhile Arkwright was demonstrating the value and difficulties of having a patent and enforcing it in a commercial environment primed for the theft of ideas.

Whose Machine Was It Anyway?

Some historians have seen technological change during this period as nothing more than could be achieved by a *"reasonably well educated and practical man."*[186] But this argument ignores nascent industrial espionage and the determination of some overseas governments, particularly the French, to appropriate the new technology. In some cases, British entrepreneurs were enticed to establish complete factories in France. The secrets of Arkwright's water frame were carried off to America by Thomas Slater (1768-1835;) *"Slater the traitor,"* later celebrated as the father of the American industrial revolution. Samuel Crompton was pestered and spied upon to distraction, all suggestive of sufficient novelty and ingenuity, not to mention potential profitability, to credit inventors such as Crompton with a degree of uniqueness and possibly genius. There was also a superstitious tendency to imbue him with magical powers. In his own words *"the production of a nail could create wonder."*[187]

Foster argues that the main impediments to the development of inventions were social and cultural. [188] However, the technical problems should not be understated. It took a considerable amount of experimentation for Samuel Crompton to develop his machine to the stage that it worked, slowed down of course by riots and disorder. While the technical expertise required to develop the new engines might be a matter of debate, the impact is not so contentious. Osborne states that the inventions *"ushered in an entirely new kind of productive economy, and again that all of the inventions of this period had "effects that were threefold."*[189]

A key feature in the development of new machinery was the collective skills used to improve the working of the engines. Networks of business associates, families and friends, and the secondhand market, supplied the fertile ground in which the mechanical devices were spread and modified. When the friend, advisor and benefactor of Samuel Compton, John Kennedy, addressed the Manchester Philosophical and Literary Society on the 20th of February 1830, his brief life of Samuel Crompton outlined the modifications of the spinning mule.[190] Henry Stones of Horwich recommended metal as opposed to wooden rollers, Baker of Bury applied vertical cylinders or drums in the carriage which allowed the carriage to be extended significantly. There was also a diagonal shaft devised by Baker that dropped out of gear when the rollers were to stop and so on and so on. Kennedy summarised the process:

"For, if in the course of their working the machine, there was any little thing out of gear, each workman endeavored to fill up the deficiency with some expedient suggested by his former trade; the smith suggested a piece of iron, the shoemaker a welt of leather, &c. all which had a good effect in improving the machine."[191]

Innovation proceeded apace with the application of power. Kennedy noted the use of steam, and the replacement of human effort by the energies of the machine.[192] The collective modifications reflected a scientific cast of mind that meant the mule found its optimum state in a very short period.

Secondhand mules and other cotton spinning machines soon enjoyed a lively and extensive market which facilitated their further spread and development. Typical was an advertisement in the Manchester Mercury, dated 8th December 1789, where anyone wishing to purchase a prospective Christmas present could avail themselves:

"..... at Mr. Ralph Foggs, Bank Street, Manchester, four second hand spinning mules, two of 84 and two of 96 spindles"[193]

Anyone believing the mule to have been a medieval construct, with little from the enlightenment to inform its construction, should consider questions that troubled Crompton. For example, the need while the spinning was taking place *"to accurately control the translatory motion of the rapidly rotating spindles, relative to the precisely driven drafting rollers."*[194] The mule was a *"complex and ingenious device."*[195] A reductionist view suffers from 'hindsight bias', that is a tendency to think that an original idea or application, having been revealed was obvious. It is critical to judge the revolutionary nature of an invention and its complexity in the context of the prevailing resources and tools. With these arguments in mind Samuel Crompton's invention was a heroic achievement with enormous social and economic consequences. Moreover, the fascination with its complexity was apparent in the blatant attempts, as with Arkwright's water frame, to steal its design.

The casual conversation with a tipsy workman in the local Inn, the inquisitive elegantly dressed tourist mesmerised by the intricacies of James Watts steam engine, or carefully sketching the latest technological wonder. The clandestine illegal exporter of valuable cotton spinning machines, operating in the night and shipping, probably via Ireland or Rotterdam, to France or America. The late eighteenth century was an age of industrial espionage. Beware the seemingly innocent bystander, the secrets of invention were not safe. Machines such as Arkwright's water frame or Crompton's mule were too complex to simply carry the image in the mind. Compared to the spinning jenny, for example, they had an intricacy that required detailed calibration. Sweden, Denmark, Holland but particularly France was eager to catch up with the 50 years march acquired by the British textile industry.

If you could not steal the secrets of the mule and the water frame directly then those well trusted mechanisms of bribery, and monetary incentives would do. Skilled workmen were enticed abroad and whole factories constructed in France to exploit the new techniques of production. An infamous example was John Holkar, an English refugee from Bonny Prince Charlies failed uprising in 1745. He was cited as a lieutenant in the Manchester Regiment and a rebel.[196] Arrested in Carlisle, he was subsequently held in Newgate prison. He escaped from Newgate, with a companion, by climbing through a breach in the wall. Holker, being *a very square bulky man"* got stuck.[197] His fellow escapee widened the hole. Holker wriggled free and scampered off into infamy.

After five weeks hidden away in London, by a woman who ran a green stall,[198] Holker escaped to France. Enjoying French royal patronage, he attempted to establish a competitive textile manufacturing sector. In 1754 he built a textile factory in Rouen, and smuggled machinery to France through Rotterdam. The French paid him to return to England to spy on textile manufacturing in Manchester, and the Lancashire towns. He arduously sought a royal pardon, but it was never granted. Eventually he fully morphed into a Frenchman by being promoted to the French aristocracy. He died 28th April 1786, cited as Knight of the Order of St Louis and 'Inspector General of the Woollen and Cotton Manufactories of France,[199] and having served honorably in the Irish Brigade.[200]

For France and other competitor countries, even successful espionage was never going to impart that frantic thrust to industrialisation that was being experienced in Britain. The British had a less interfering government, a developing transport system, and methods of industrial organisation and small-scale factory management that had imperceptibly emerged over the previous decades. As noted, the emergent complexity of the machines also acted as a bulwark against simply copying them. The French attempted to sidestep the intricacy of the new machinery by looking for the essence of things, a feature of Enlightenment thinking. However, when George

Garnet introduced Arkwright's machine into France in 1787, he left out the important *"crank and cog "* mechanism - a feature which John Kay was thought to have introduced. The consequence was that the counterfeit machine did not produce the fine yarns of the original. In April 1785 an Irish Newspaper, in a debate on duties placed on Irish goods, complained that Irish copies of Arkwright's spinning machine were inadequate: [201]

"Models indeed have been brought over, and imitations have been executed from such, but on so confined a plan as scarcely to be productive of one fifth of the real advantages that are enjoyed by any one manufacturer in the West of England, who has gone to the trouble and expense of the same."

The cost was just too great, and so the Irish manufacturers must be satisfied with:

"a less complicated and consequently a less beneficial construction."

The extent to which the invention of the water frame could be credited to Arkwright was a matter of dispute. He was openly cynical regarding the importance of who first had an idea. His notion was that if a practical man should first spot and exploit the opportunities provided by an embryonic invention or prototype then that was to his credit and to the benefit of the industry. Intellectual property rights had little purchase on the personal and ethical posture of Richard Arkwright, though he was a man of considerable creativity, for example, he invented a waterproof coloured dye for the wigs that he sold.

Given this ultra-competitive and opportunistic. environment it was essential that inventors protected their rights and garnered the potential financial gains from their innovations. How well you could do this could depend upon your vigilance and character, but also your ability to apply the patent system to your advantage. When it came to combining ambition, business acumen, creativity and inventiveness these were exquisitely represented by Arkwright. Arguably, to understand Crompton and the course of his life and fortunes we need to appreciate the behaviour of his mirror image Richard Arkwright. A patent for the spinning mule would be one option for Samuel Crompton. Arkwright's experience, and the ideas that he was protecting, were critical to informing Samuel's choices.

The Inestimable Mr. Arkwright

The challenge to Arkwright's patents provides another example of the attitudes to inventors and invention and the unremitting search for profit that characterised the British commercial environment. The patent system was a tangle of ambiguous judgements, layers of committees and uncertain purpose. As with the magistrates contrasting views on riots and disorder, judges differed in their opinions on the merits of protecting the rights of the inventor and sharing the benefits of invention with the wider commercial world.

The patent system did not defend intellectual property rights. Emerging from the Elizabethan obsession with granting monopolies, letters patent were focused upon generating returns for the government and granting favours. It was through the court cases that inventors had to protect their rights, imperfect protection gained at considerable personal expense. Yet the ambiguity was fertile ground for the conjurers to flourish. The patent system, though expensive in time and money, did provide some protection, but it had enough loopholes to facilitate the noted incremental change that was so important in bringing the machines to perfection, and facilitating their use on a wider commercial scale. Though the specification for any invention did not need to be that precise, there was a requirement that a competent engineer be able to reconstruct the machine from any plans.

The challenges to Arkwright's patents and the ensuing court cases requires a degree of untangling, primarily because they involved two inventions. One was a carding machine the purpose of which was to remove the cotton (the roving) of its impurities. The second was the famous water frame spinning machine. The issues are further conflated because the two machines operated on similar principles, both involving the use of rollers.

The spinning machine was Arkwright's first patent, taken out in 1769. The carding machine was patented six years later in 1775. The similarity between these two machines meant that Arkwright could try to extend the patent of the spinning machine by extending the life of the patent for the carding machine, and vice versa. So, though the focus is often on the water frame the patent for the carding machine and the court cases involving that engine were also critical.

In 1781 Richard Arkwright challenged nine manufacturers - though only one case involving a Colonel Mordaunt was taken to a trial - over the infringement of his carding machine patent. This provoked the ire of the wider Manchester cotton manufacturing community. As a result, they called a meeting of *"The Committee Representing the Cotton, Linen, Silk and Small ware Manufacturers of Manchester and District"* which replaced the committee of 1774 which had been named *"Committee for Protection of Trade in Manchester.*"[202] The manufacturers presented the defense in the Mordaunt trial and the judicial reformer the 1st Earl of Mansfield, Lord Chief Justice of The Kings Bench, found against Arkwright based on the vagueness of the specification. [203] Arkwright had argued that his machine could be constructed from the patent and that any remaining ambiguity was there to combat theft by overseas competitors.

Having lost the 1781court case Arkwright moved quicker than a flying shuttle and reverted to challenging the abuse of his rights over the spinning machine. He sought an act of Parliament to extend the life of this patent. He also argued for a joint patent to cover both inventions, which would have extended protection for the spinning machine by six and a half years. We can imagine Arkwright's intense lobbying of Parliament and people of influence. A process that 29 years later in 1812, Samuel Crompton would replicate. The success of such lobbying was always hostage to economic conditions, wars and Parliament's other overseas and domestic concerns, in this case the ongoing American Revolutionary War (1775-1783). The Manchester committee submitted a counter petition and Parliament did not agree to Arkwright's request to combine the two patents.

In February 1785 with just a few months of life left for the spinning machine patent Richard Arkwright demonstrated his resolve and appealed to the Court of Common Pleas. He took legal action against several manufactures using his spinning machine without license. No doubt assisted by James Watt's evidence regarding the ability to construct the machine from the patent, he won this legal dispute. Encouraged, Arkwright returned to the carding machine patent and made a further attempt to get it extended.

The Manchester manufacturers were not about to let him re-establish control and in June 1785, challenged him in the Court of the Kings Bench. The judicial proceedings were concerned with who first invented the carding and spinning machines, a key aspect being the first use of rollers in the stretching of the yarn. The prime witness against Arkwright was John Kay, who argued that the spinning machine was first developed by Thomas Highs of Leigh. Kay and Highs were partners, and it was on the visit to Warrington in 1767 that Arkwright had taken away two models of the machine. However, Kay and Arkwright had parted bitter enemies, casting doubt upon Kay's testimony.

Any reader confused by the rapid movement between court cases can be forgiven for focusing on this last dispute which involved both machines. Arkwright faced formidable opposition including Robert Peel (1750-1830).

Sir Robert Peel (later the first Baronet) was a powerful manufacturer and political figure who featured in Samuel Crompton's claims for a reward for the spinning mule. In a final declamation judge Mansfield found against Arkwright, and the patents were revoked. Emphasising the finality of this decision was the judgement that he could not have recourse to any other court - for example the Court of Chancery - which would have judged his case on fundamental fairness. Though his patents were revoked Richard Arkwright was a very wealthy man. It is estimated that at the time of his death on August 3rd. 1792, he was worth half a million pounds, two hundred million pounds in today's spending power.

Inventors continued to contest the use of improved versions of their machines. For example, James Watt legally challenged the use of a possibly superior Hornblower engine developed by Richard Trevithick, Arthur Woolf and William Bull. An example of how progress might have been hindered by a successful court case.

Inventors not only had to be alert to the threat of espionage, but also to conflicts within business partnerships and/or the breach of informal understandings between fellow manufacturers. For example, in 1795 Crompton legally challenged Adkin of Ainsworth Hall. The dispute concerned Crompton's suggested modifications to the spinning jenny. This is also interesting because it illustrates that the jenny was still in use and that adoption of new inventions was far from instantaneous. Crompton's later 1811 survey of the use of the water frame, mule and spinning jenny revealed its continuing use.[204]

Adkin advertised his proposal as an *"improvement in common spinning"*. Crompton claimed that having advised him on how to modify the jenny to increase its productivity, Adkin launched a subscription inviting interested parties to pay £100 in exchange for the 'secret'. Crompton was also irritated by the suggestion, in the advertisement that he had approved of the plan. [205]He objected to the scheme on the grounds that Adkin:

"...had any right to sell no more than we have a right to advertise another man's house or estate for sale and buyers should not know it."[206]

By 1780 Samuel Crompton's spinning mule, though not yet fully developed, was a demonstrable technical success. He now had to decide how best to release its secrets into the pestering, duplicitous world. The pressure of espionage, as we have seen, was relentless. Patents were of uncertain merit, expensive and could be challenged. However, the spinning mule could not be hidden away in Hall i' th' Wood forever.

Chapter Eight

Of Heartbreak, Love and Betrayal

Spirit of her I love,
Whispering *to me*
Stories of sweet visions as I rove,
Here stop, and crop with me
Sweet flowers that in the still hour grew-
We take them home, nor shake off the bright dew.[207]

John Clare (1793-1864), Mary

Mary Crompton

To fully understand Samuel Crompton, we ought to know more about his wife Mary. Here there are the perennial problems in researching the lives of eighteenth-century women, anonymity and a lack of records. Despite the representation of female virtue in the sentimental literature of writers such as Richardson, and later the heroines and 'society rebels' in the works of Jane Austin, there is a paucity of information to inform female biography.[207] Though Mary provided immense support to her beleaguered and sensitive husband, we struggle to piece together a complete picture of her life. Of a 'blue stocking' such as Mary Wollstonecraft, or a member of the demi monde (the fashionably impure), such as Harriet Wilson, we know a good deal, but for a virtuous woman of the lower or middling sort we know very little. Even the simple headstone in the grounds of Bolton Parish Church, that marked her death in 1796, was removed and the stout and weighty monument to her husband placed firmly on top.

There is no surviving personal correspondence between Samuel and Mary, though a shopping list in the Crompton papers is written in her hand and is an indication of her domestic economy.[208] Touchingly, there is a page in Samuel's Accounts for 1796 relating to her death and her personal possessions that concern, *"my dear wife's clothes,"* among which are the evocative items of black stockings, leather gloves, a black and French grey skirt and a silk and satin bonnet with feathers.[209] The dominance of black and white presents a vision of a simple neat style, a plainly dressed north country woman.

Mary Crompton (nee Pimbley) was possibly much younger than Samuel when they married in 1780. [210] This would have provoked little disapproval. Given his debilitating levels of shyness he may have found a humble younger woman less intimidating. It seems that Crompton was impressed with Mary for two reasons, one that she was slender and attractive, secondly, that she was adept in the use of a spinning wheel. There is a description of Mary arising from French's conversations with George Crompton in 1859; that she was *"a very handsome dark haired woman of middle size, and erect carriage though of somewhat delicate constitution."*[211] Subsequent biographers have emphasised this physical attractiveness. Writing in 1951 Cameron reflected that *"Mary had good looks and a figure trim enough to invite warmer feelings even in one so shy and diffident as this solitary man";*[212] However, technical dexterity should not be underestimated as a motive for marriage. To the skills and refinements of domesticity, for a woman of Mary's class, must be added productivity. Even more compelling was her ability to protect Samuel from intrusion.

There is a story that she would shoo away the children, to prevent them disturbing their father as he sat reflecting, balancing his cup of tea on his knees. She was considered to be a very perceptive person, which may further explain Samuel's attraction to her. She had the ability to reassure him and offer protection. To quote her son George she possessed:

"....something like a second sight by which she could tell a rogue in an instant and warn her family to have nothing to do with him."[213]

She soon had many opportunities for keeping *"rogues"* with prying eyes away from her home and preserving Samuel's secrets. This would include a visit from the formidable, most certainly inquisitive, Richard Arkwright.

Prying Eyes!

During the 1960s Dobson and Barlow Ltd was an extensive factory complex in Breightmet Bolton, a walled citadel dominating its local landscape.[214] Established in 1790 the company was an early manufacturer of the spinning mule, by 1799 extending the capacity of the machine from 8 to 408 spindles.

[215]When I worked in the factory, as a commercial apprentice, it was a thriving manufacturing plant. A cathedral of light illuminating the dark winter evenings as the workers streamed through the wrought iron factory gates, often in the fog and mist, to catch their buses home. I was unaware of the link between Dobson and Barlow and Samuel Crompton and the powerful legacy of the Hall i' th' Wood machine. I processed costing sheets for the detailed parts of the machines; never glimpsing, in the tedium of the clerical work, the whole gleaming, magnificent outcome that was the modern mule. It would have been an impossible task, had I been a spy, to divine the secrets of the beautifully engineered machines. They were technological colossuses, produced for export to those countries such as India which would eventually compete away what remained of the Lancashire textile industry.

Even in the eighteenth century the mule was becoming ever more complex, but the Crompton family were not immune from the pressures of espionage. After their marriage in 1780 Samuel took his bride back to the rural idyll of Hall i' 'th' Wood. They were careful to live in an adjoining apartment, separate from his overbearing mother Betty Crompton. It was in this beautiful setting that the couple worked together using the mule, spinning the fine yarns that excited so much interest in the Lancashire markets. No one could understand how they were able to achieve such high quality thread. They could sell as much as they could make. Consequently, the farcical attempts to steal their secrets gained momentum. People called on false pretenses. Others gawped through windows. One person hid in the attic, having placed a hole in the ceiling through which to observe them. To escape these unwanted attentions Samuel and Mary worked behind a screen. John Kennedy reported a conversation between himself and Mr. Lee and Samuel where Crompton stated:

"....that a man had a very insecure tenure of a property which another could carry away with his eyes."[216]

There is a graphic in the book *"Famous Boys and How they Became Great Men."*[217] Samuel, not a good likeness, is sitting at his desk, presumably at Hall i' th' Wood in the thinking room. He is unknowingly besieged by inquisitive individuals, one peering through a keyhole and the other observing through the hole in the loft. Notably absent is Mary who also suffered these indignities. Such intruders could be repulsed but the more subtle and devious forms of spying could not. There was a young lady named Betty Woods, who was a dear friend of Mary Crompton, but also a daughter in Law of Richard Arkwright. Betty visited Mary when she was ill and invited Arkwright to accompany her. Samuel was not present during the visit and the mule was concealed behind a locked door. There is no record of Crompton's thoughts about this incident, but he was subsequently ill disposed towards Arkwright, making a cryptic reference, in a letter outlining the history of the mule, to being harassed by people from sixty miles, being the distance between Arkwright's residence at Cromford and Hall i'th' Wood.[218]

For Samuel Crompton the hunger of the world for the secrets of his machine became increasingly onerous and threatening. He would have to relieve the pressure and placate the appetite for profit, creating privacy for himself and his wife. Moreover, he wished to supplement the financial gains from his produce with a reward for his invention. He now had to make his most difficult decision. Should he patent his machine? Or he could raise a public subscription and release his secrets to the cotton manufacturers on the promise of a just reward. Recognising his own vulnerability around this choice he consulted a trusted friend, John Pilkington. Pilkington was a cotton merchant/manufacturer, and he advised him to release the secrets of the mule and to raise a public subscription. Samuel Crompton agreed. Pilkington was certainly well meaning in this advice and there was no suggestion that he encouraged this disclosure for his own private commercial interest.

Given the stress and anxiety that Samuel was experiencing, the advice to launch a subscription and garner some immediate recompense might be what he wished to hear,[219] Arkwright's patents had not yet been revoked, so that he may have faced determined opposition from that quarter. Given the nature of the patent system, he would have had to be constantly alert to breaches and be willing to prosecute pirates of his invention. He may have been reluctant to experience the same travails as Arkwright. French suggested a personal reason for choosing a subscription. That the choice arose from the *"kind and trusting hearts"* of Crompton and Pilkington.[220] Though it is worth noting that John Pilkington was a member of *"The Committee Representing the Cotton, Linen, Silk and Small ware Manufacturers of Manchester and District"* that opposed the use of patents.[221]

With hindsight Pilkington did not give Samuel good advice. Crompton presented a model of his spinning mule to the Manchester Exchange. Custom and practice dictated that any model displayed on the floor of the Exchange should receive the sum of £200 by subscription. Save for a few, the hardheaded, calculating cotton manufacturers of Lancashire where not willing to pay for something that was no longer a secret. Samuel's erstwhile biographer John Brown cited an example of the treatment meted out to Crompton as he knocked on the heavy wooden office doors of the then small mills, humbly reminding the manufacturers of their promise. According to Brown; A Mr. Alexander Kay of Blackburn :*"called him an imposter and asking him how he dared to come on such an errand."* This rebuke despite being shown his signature on the agreement to pay.[222]

Samuel Crompton despaired of human nature:

"Many subscribers would not pay the sums they had set opposite their names. When I applied for them, I got nothing but abusive language to drive me from them; which was easily done; for I never till then could think it possible that any man could pretend one thing and act the direct opposite. I then found it was possible, having had proof positive."[223]

The list of 84 manufacturers who paid the subscription, still survives and includes prominent names such as the company of Peel, Yates and Co. The most frequent contribution was £1. 1 shilling (a guinea), with some, perhaps less wealthy, giving 10 shillings and sixpence each,[224]One person gave 5 shillings and 6 pennies. However, several of the subscribers for the lower amount of 10 shillings and sixpence subsequently became prominent businessmen, such as the bleachers Peter Ainsworth and Thomas Ridgeway. What no longer exists is a list of those manufacturers who reneged on their agreement. In the end Samuel gained little from this subscription with some dispute as to the amount, Mr. Kennedy saying £50 and Mr. Pilkington £106, a generally agreed estimate being £60.[225] These sums were invidious trifles compared to the enormous personal fortune amassed by Richard Arkwright.

The subscription money allowed Crompton to construct a new spinning machine with just four extra spindles, being an increase from 48 spindles to 52. The poor response to the subscription was Samuel Crompton's first major disillusionment with his fellows in the trade. Thus, the scene was set for a later campaign for justice, particularly as the use of the mule, in its continuously modified form, would soon be spreading exponentially throughout England, Scotland and Wales. In the years that followed the manufacturers and merchants of Bolton would be accused of having treated Samuel Crompton with cruelty and disdain.

Disillusioned, Samuel and Mary left Hall i' th' Wood and sought refuge in a pastoral life, at Oldhams, a remote moorland fold. Arguably, life at Oldhams was how Samuel conceived it should be. He was less pestered by unwelcome visitors or burdened with any responsibility other than to his family. It was here, in 1781, that their youngest son George was born. Events leading up to the birth of George give further insight into Samuel Crompton's superstitious nature. Mary was experiencing a difficult labour, so he walked the 14 miles from Bolton to Winwick to bring back his mother-in-Law, Alice Pimbley, to assist in the birth. Trudging along the bumpy road back to Bolton, in the light of the full moon, an hare darted out of cover, sitting upright it stared at him intently, as if to convey a silent message. Marking the time on his watch he later suggested that the animal had materialised at the exact moment of his child's birth, encouraging him on his journey home. This is an example of both his superstitious nature, and his propensity to walk long distances, an ability that he would need to draw upon in his future campaign in London.

The family were content to lead a traditional life at Oldhams.[226] George Crompton recollected how as a young boy he was placed upright in a bowl of milk where after the cotton had been combed (carded), he trod it in preparation for spinning by his mother and grandmother.[227] But if Samuel thought that there would be no further pestering in this rural idyll, he was to be sadly disappointed. There was not the scale of mischief of the intruders at Hall i'th' Wood, and the enquirers were often more salubrious. For example, the Cromptons' were visited by Robert Peel (1st Baronet), highly successful cotton manufacturer and father of the future Prime Minister Robert Peel (2cd Baronet).

Peel Senior made two visits to Oldhams. On the first occasion he exercised his option to inspect the mule, as per the agreed subscription where he had paid one guinea. He was accompanied by two of his workmen whose task was to inspect and memorise the key features of the spinning machine. Peel caused offence by offering a small, in fact quite paltry sum of one sixpence per man, for the privilege of the inspection. Samuel Crompton may have been timid and ruminative, but he was also proud with a strong sense of personal integrity, and he was injured by this reaction to his generosity, in allowing them to inspect the machine, likening it perhaps to paying off a hired hand.

On the second visit by Robert Peel Samuel was not present and it was the childish innocence of George Crompton that nearly revealed the mules secret hiding place, behind a door leading to the upper story of the cottage protected by a secret fastening. George's memory was undoubtedly sharpened by the recollection that Mr. Peel gave him half a guinea, the contribution of many manufacturers to the Crompton subscription. Mary, having gone to the dairy to fetch Mr. Peel a drink of milk, young George was questioned as to where his father carried out his labours, which would include developing the machine. His mother returned just in time to stop George revealing the hiding place. She gave him a glance that read halt; a look that only mothers can give, in unfamiliar company, where a direct scolding would not be fitting.

Robert Peel remained an admirer of Samuel Crompton and offered him a partnership whereby he would have the freedom to continue with his *"conjuring."* Despite what would have been an enviable coupling of business acumen and inventive genius he refused the offer. He was to decline many other approaches including requests to work abroad. When he did move from Oldham's, around the year 1791,[228] it was to begin his spinning business in King Street, Bolton. One explanation for the move was that he had been asked to be Overseer of the Poor for Sharples a role his more assertive mother had performed admirably in Tong and Hough. For Samuel Crompton this would not have been a comfortable responsibility.

Samuel did not escape the problems of keeping his work and innovations secret. The young men he employed as apprentices/assistants, who would have intricate knowledge of the working of the mule, were enticed away by other manufacturers. Such was his frustration that on one occasion even this gentle man exploded with rage. Constructing a development of the carding machine, he smashed it to pieces with a hammer, furious at the duplicity of those with whom he had shared his time and knowledge.

Makeshift spinning factories were spreading throughout Lancashire and his King Street premises were a prime example. Cottage homes were the sites of industry and commerce intertwined. While seeking business success and employment for his sons his hope that there could yet be some reward for the mule had not faded. Meanwhile, escaping his disappointment and constant betrayal he found comfort in a non-conformist religion, the Swedborgian church.

Chapter Nine

The White Doe of Rylstone

*Again, the Mother **whispered** low,*
Now you have seen the famous Doe;
From Rylstone she hath found her way
Over the hills this sabbath day
Her work, whate'er it be, is done,
And she will depart when we are gone;
Thus, doth she keep, from year to year,
Her sabbath morning, foul or fair."

Wordsworth, canto first. The White Doe of Rylstone: Or the Fate of the Norton's. (Completed 1808, published 1815).

Just five years after its invention, the use of the spinning mule had spread throughout the country. They were largely situated in converted lofts and repaired barns, even cowsheds.[229] However, small groups of cottages, or Folds, could accommodate mules, provide a rental income and be a source of capital for those selling or leasing the land on which they were built. Capital that could be invested in the growing textile industries of Lancashire and Yorkshire. One such settlement was constructed on a small moorland agricultural estate named Nevy Fold, situated in Horwich, on the high ground to the Northwest of Bolton.

Nevy Fold rests on a tufted, soggy incline sweeping down from Horwich Moor, serenaded by the piercing cackle from nearby rookeries, the echoes emphasising the great empty spaces of the upper moorland. The land was intractable to farm but provided the perfect setting for the arts of spinning, weaving and bleaching. Here, in 1784, Mary Crompton's brother, Joseph Pimbley, and his father in law James Blakeley Junior, built four adjoining cottages.[230] They had purchased the original lease from Mr. John Heaton and his wife Anne. The name Heaton was to become associated with success in the cotton industry, but tragically not for John Heaton.

Anne was the original proprietor of the land at Nevy Fold, and John possessed a farm in the nearby village of Blackrod. John Heaton, married Anne in 1794, consequently owning both estates. He subsequently sold the leaseholds of the two farms to finance the building of a textile factory on the site of an old corn mill at Rylstone, near Skipton in Yorkshire. The topography was reminiscent of the moorland areas of Lancashire,[231] having textile production and coal mining. However, the industrial and civil unrest that had plagued the Lancashire textile industry was less of a problem in Yorkshire, where the new inventions in cotton spinning where more readily accepted. Yet the history of Rylstone was a turbulent one.

The White Doe

William Wordsworth's epic narrative poem *'The White Doe of Rylstone'*[232] concerns the rebellion of the Northern Earls in 1569. The poem describes a 'White Doe' regularly roaming over Bolton Moor (the Yorkshire Bolton) and laying down upon an unmarked grave. This was the resting place of Emily Norton, the embroiderer of her father's banner, as he rose in rebellion against Queen Elisabeth I. Norton was slain in battle, and Emily's brother Richard, who had tried without success to dissuade his father from insurrection, was captured and died. To complete the tragedy their grand ancestral home at Rylstone was laid to waste. The vanquished Hall had stood, as the poem expressed it:

"......southward far, with moors between; Hill-tops, and floods, and forests green"

Emily fled, only to return and befriend the 'White Doe' who followed her devotedly until, destitute she died of a broken heart. Such was the bond between Emily and the Doe that it continued to repose on her grave. The history, and the legend were inauspicious for John Heaton's adventurous new enterprise. The factory was situated just a short distance from the crumbling remains of Rylstone Hall.[233]

John Heaton invested the whole of his capital in the new mill.[234] However, a minor rebellion occurred in the form of a dispute over his access to the factory, via a track. It was necessary to use this byway because the mill was several hundred yards distance from a good road. The neighbors' objected to the carts, transporting raw materials and taking away the finished cotton goods. The dispute was costly and inconvenient, though through the good offices of a local barrister the argument was resolved by arbitration. Despite extensive expenditure on capital equipment, the prospects for the mill did not improve. There was a sharp decline in trade and a run on local banks, so that liquidity was short.

In 1797 John Heaton was declared bankrupt. Though Anne Heaton sold the lease of Nevy Fold to pay some of the debts this was not enough to avoid financial catastrophe. John decided to avoid possible incarceration in Lancaster or Skipton Castle, by escaping to Argentina. Around the year 1812, he died there of yellow fever. Nancy, despite selling off machinery and stocks to rescue the family fortune, was plunged into poverty. In the manner of the retreat from burning Rylstone she fled from the wreck of the business to Manchester. The Heaton family decided to act and found her wandering the streets of the town. Her three brothers in law recognised their family duties, took pity upon her, and accepted the care of her eight children, ranging from a few months to 14 years of age.

The liquidation of land and agricultural capital for investment in a single manufacturing enterprise had led to impoverishment and an ignominious death. However, this specialised form of investment was a gamble that was to pay dividends for some. A more successful enterprise was that of another John Heaton who had a typical small five story mill in Picton street, Doffcocker, Bolton. The annual accounts of the machine makers Dobson and Barlow (Dobson and Rothwell at that time) for 1797/1798 show the sale of a mule with 252 spindles, 1 1/4 distance,[235] price £69 to John Heaton of Doffcocker.[236] In fact the accounts show sales of 19 mules, indicating a thriving market in the machines, even in this difficult year, and despite the extensive use of secondhand machinery. The Picton street mill[237] was converted back to living accommodation in the late 1800s.

The Swedenborg Church

The White Doe of Rylstone is a poem of passive heroism and quietude, a natural contemplative religion. It offers a metaphor for the story of John Heaton and his failed factory. It presents a portrait of risk and the pathos of failure. Samuel Crompton continued to be troubled by the failed subscription of 1780, the stresses of commercial life and the recurring betrayals. He would have been aware, through his brother-in-law Joseph Pimbley, of Heaton's failure at Rylstone. However, his troubled mind would be focused less upon the failure of others, but more upon their success as they availed themselves of the productivity of the mule, enrichment in which he was not sharing. However, the calm sense of resignation in the legend of the White Doe hints at a palliative for Samuel Crompton's disquiet. He sought contentment in the reassuring embrace of a non-conformist religious movement, the Swedenborg Church.

In 1796 Samuel Crompton needed all the comfort that he could get when his beloved wife Mary died, followed in 1797 by the death of his mother Betty. Two of his youngest children also departed, leaving six children for him to care for. There is a school of thought regarding reactions to the death of family members in the eighteenth century. The family unit, it is argued, was more important than the individuals comprising it, hence the rapidity with which men remarried on the death of a wife.[238] This says nothing of personal grief and implies a harder heart than was the case. Religion may have provided some comfort, premature bereavement was a frequent occurrence, and the cohesion of the family was paramount, but grief there was. Even the austere, much disliked Lord Chief Justice Eldon was in the depths of despair on the death of his beloved wife Elizabeth (d. 1831). [239]There is further evidence of Samuel Crompton's supernatural disposition as he told how, when he returned from her funeral, the spirit of Mary greeted him at the door of their house in King Street.

Though remarriage was a common practice, and for some classes of society advisable, Samuel never took a second wife. Goldsmith's fictional Vicar of Wakefield, objected to second marriages for a priest of the Church of England, on ethical grounds.[240] He placed a framed epitaph, addressed to his wife, on their chimney piece *"extolling her prudence, economy and obedience till death"*, there to remind her of her duty and his fidelity but also *"inspiring her to fame"* and *"constantly putting her in mind of her end."* In Crompton's case, though Mary's virtues were equally well appreciated, remarriage was less likely due to a lack of inclination and debilitating inhibition. There is no doubt that he would have benefited from a female companion, as he found his family responsibilities, especially his errant and alcoholic daughter Betty, a continuing strain. The natural shyness and diffidence, that Mary was able to sensitively manage, may have continued to act as an impediment to forming any new romantic, or even pragmatic attachment. Instead, he sought companionship and spiritual comfort with the Swedenborg church a group that accommodated his temperament.

Based on the teachings of Emanuel Swedenborg (1688-1722), the 'church' enshrined the idea of the spirit co-existing with the physical body, developing as it was nurtured by love. Everybody, regardless of religious denomination, was eligible for entry into the Kingdom of Heaven. Thus, it rejected the Calvinist notion of the elect, and though espousing a work ethic this was not based on material aggrandisement, but rather the daily, almost ritual, performance of simple tasks. While a minority religion it had proved popular among many intellectuals and artists including William Blake. Though its teachings and practice, could be associated with Jacobinism and radical political views, its creed was moderated to reflect the spiritual needs of an increasingly materialistic culture.[241] Emanuel Swedenborg was a religious leader and mystic, but also a mineralogist with an established scientific background, having written several books on mineralogy. He also owned coal mines in Denmark and was appointed by Charles XII of Sweden as assessor extraordinary at the *Bergscollegium* (Board of Mines).[242] This combination of science, profit and religion were a comfortable fit for Samuel.

Samuel Crompton retained a good relationship with some members of the Anglican faith including Parson Folds, Lecturer,[243] at Bolton Parish Church, who had married Samuel and Mary. Samuel's son James married a relative of the Parson.[244] Clergy could be commercially inclined, supplementing their meagre stipends with property investments, business partnerships and agricultural land. Parson Folds had extensive investments in land and property, owning several smallholdings and cottages.[245] Leases and other documents confirm several commercial transactions. For example, the sale and leasing of property in 1786 to a Mr. John Greenhalgh, weaver, for the purposes of building;[246] involving the payment of £55 7s 6d with an annual rent of 8 shillings. His diary includes an account of his rental income for the year 1786 (May 12th) amounting to £71, fifteen shillings and two pence.[247] So, the commercial 'fit' with a religious group could be important.

Suspicions of the true extent of the involvement of the clergy in commerce are aroused by the apparent reserve associated with these extracurricular activities. Parson Folds was asked by a farmer, on who he often called to take a glass of sherry, as to the value of his income. The Parson asked the farmer *"Can'st ta keep o' secret"*, to which he answered *"Aye"*, the Parson responding *"Un so can I."*[248] In fact James Folds was considered a comical and likeable character, with a servant named *"Sorry"*. The Parson was responsible for starting the annual football match, blindly throwing the ball over his orchard wall to land, as if from heaven, amidst the opposing teams, poised in anticipation of a ferocious physical battle. His apples were particularly sought after by the local boys who sneaked into his orchard. Though generally a kindly man he was disposed to give any boy that he caught a sound beating.

A more likely source of clerical aggravation for Samuel Crompton was the Reverend Richard Whitehead, vicar of Bolton Parish Church, Parson Fold's superior. Whitehead was a haughty character with whom the Parson had an uneasy relationship. Certainly, he had many disputes with the Vicar's arrogant, opinionated son Richard. In one diary entry Parson Fold's writes of seeking refuge from the son:

"On a quarrel not the vicar his son. Gave me such a specimen of his arrogance and pride has determined me to retire to my chapel"[249]

The Swedenborgian religion offered Samuel Crompton more amicable personal relationships than the Anglican Church. The Swedenborgian's were a small group among whom he had more control over his life, with less prying, and the personal support typical of an extended family.[250] He was content within what French described as *"this unpretending and philanthropic body."*[251] This association might have distanced him from other manufacturers towards whom he felt continuing resentment. Not that business connections were absent; a fellow Swedenborgian Richard Wylde had a longstanding business partnership with Samuel and his sons.[252] Midgley notes that many of the workmen and small manufacturers to whom he suppled rovings were also Swedborgians.[253]

French considered Samuel's engagement with the Swedenborgian church to have been the outcome of *"a natural inclination towards the supernatural"* and a reaction to the *"cold teachings"* of the established church.[254] The reported visions of Emanuel Swedenborg and the ritual free faith relying upon divining the spirituality implicit in biblical texts exposed Swedenborg's followers to accusations of occultism. Carl Jung in exploring his theory of synchronicity[255] was impressed by Emanuel Swedenborg's premonition of a fire in Stockholm on the 17 th July 1759, while he was having dinner in Gothenburg, some 400 km away. [256]

If this unorthodox church provided Samuel Compton with a religious 'family' he did not neglect the care of his own children. He was a considerate father, though his daughter Betty (b. 1784) severely tested his paternal tolerance. The death of his wife Mary in 1796 removed a source of stability from the family. Four years later, in 1800, the sixteen year old Betty was coaxed into an unsuitable marriage. This reflected heightened local expectations that riches were just around the corner for the Crompton's. Betty's marriage was the result of the scheming of the housekeeper whom Samuel had employed on his wife's death. The bridegroom was a hard drinking relative of the housekeeper. He soon died, but life with this degenerate had led Betty to drink to excess, a habit she found difficult to conquer. Soon after becoming a widow, she married a Mr. John Dawson who proved to be equally unsuitable, and the bouts of heavy drinking continued. Later correspondence contains entreaties from Betty to her father, and at times her brothers, for financial assistance.[257]

The Swedenborgian's provided an environment in which Samuel Crompton could express his creativity. He played the organ, an instrument that he had made himself. He composed several songs for the young ladies of the choir, the titles of the hymns reflecting the more feminine nature of this religion and Samuel's fondness for his fellow worshippers. Three female singers, apparently his favourites, had songs named after them; *Mary's Joy*, *Martha's Comfort* and *Ellen's Delight;* though strangely two pieces are named after localities *Bury Street* - the place of the New Jerusalem Church - and *King Street,* reflecting his fondness for both locations.[258] The songs were sung at choir practice in his home in King Street where he also held a family service. [259] Worship within the home was common with non-conformism. Suggestive of his ease in this environment, in marked contrast with his public persona, he would read the scriptures aloud, with no apparent self-consciousness. So, Samuel's religious activities provided him with some comfort, coalescing with his home life. However, his residence in King Street was also a factory. Could Samuel Crompton avoid the fate of John Heaton? Would the Lancashire cotton manufacturers relent and reward him for his invention?

Chapter Ten

An Englishman's House is His Factory

*For many are the **whispers** I have heard*
From beauty's lips - loves soul in many an eye
Hath pieced my heart with such intense regard
I looked for joy and pain was the reward

John Clare (1793-1864), From Child Harold

The morphing and conversion of property was the leitmotif of social and economic change in Lancashire during the Industrial Revolution. From the old halls of the gentry converted to tenements for aspiring tenant farmers, or families of spinners and weavers, to the transformation of cottages into makeshift factories. A needs' driven philosophy as the factory system found its footing; to use the existing infrastructure, *'mend and make do!'* During the 1780s Manchester, and its surrounding area, experienced a property boom.[260] Urbanisation took place around previously isolated communities. New cottages were needed even for the outworkers of the textile industry, in particular weavers, who despite the emerging factory system still largely practiced their craft as a domestic activity.[261]

John Heaton was an example of the desire to burst out from the parlours and attics of cottages to embrace purpose-built factories, harnessing the power of the new inventions. During the 1790s, steam engines were principally used to pump water back into the mills[262] to turn the wooden paddled wheels,[263] so, there was still a dependence upon waterpower. Thus, the typical Georgian factory would still be situated by water.[264] The larger establishments were long and narrow four-story stone-walled, slate-roofed buildings, illuminated through numerous small glass windows. Arkwright's factory at Cromford, by the river Derwent, and the Gregg's factory at Styal, exploiting the gushing River Bolin, are aesthetically pleasing locations to the modern eye, but they also attracted contemporary praise. Not Blake's dark satanic mills.[265] In his epic poem *The Botanical Garden,* Erasmus Darwin eulogised Arkwright's mill noting the action of the river Derwent on the water wheel:

"His ponderous oars to slender spindles turns, And pours o'er massy wheels his foamy urns.".[266]

Samuel Crompton was not successful enough to own an enterprise of the magnitude of Styal or Cromford. Small scale manufacturers often diversified their activities to minimise risk. For example, Peter Rothwell was a timber merchant and farmer as well as a manufacturer of Crompton's mules. Crompton's brother-in-law Joseph Pimbley had an astounding range of business activities which included, saddler, farmer, innkeeper, coal mine agent, wood merchant, limestone dealer and manufacturer and undoubtedly spinning and weaving, all sustained by a large family of 17 children. Samuel Crompton did have some investment in property, drawing rent from Spring Gardens in Manchester,[267] but by specialising he was vulnerable to the vagaries of the market. He could have shared some of this risk with a partner, or partners, but generally chose not to do so.

The King Street Business

When Samuel moved to King Street, he joined together three adjacent houses.[268] The buildings were near to other manufacturers and markets; but in a picturesque setting with gardens, an unpolluted river and cultivated fields. In the conjoined attics of the three properties, he installed and operated two spinning mules. His family grew by two more sons, John (b.1791) and James (b. 1793). The two eldest children, George and Samuel Crompton Junior, nine years and eight years of age respectively, worked the mules, while the whole family lived in the frugal surroundings of the bottom room of the middle house. Spinning and weaving were family activities and members of the extended family were also a part of commercial networks. Samuel's account books for 1790 shows the debits and credits attributed to George Pimbley, a brother-in-law, with charges for rovings' plus credits for slipping and spinning, amounting to 4 pounds, 9 shillings and 11 pennies.[269]

From 1794 to 1797 the Crompton family did not use the mules for spinning, but instead produced high quality roving's, supplying the various small 'factories' scattered about the town. His business books offer an intriguing glimpse of the eruption of small enterprises along the banks of the river Croal. Not until 1798 did he begin spinning, using yarns that he received in payment for his rovings. 'Occasionally, he returned to weaving, using the cloth for barter rather than receiving cash. Handkerchiefs, mops, wine and a watch are examples of the items he traded. [270]

Despite others prospering from the mule, the Crompton business was not a source of great profit. However, there was still a body of manufacturers sensitive to his plight, and appreciative of the contribution of his 'engine' to their prosperity. So, in 1802 a group of the leading merchants of Manchester established another subscription.[271] Given the twenty years since the disastrous subscription of 1780 the mule had amply demonstrated its utility, meriting some generosity. Led by his two great supporters Mr John Kennedy and Mr George Lee the subscription foundered yet again. The trickle of money, between May 1803 and December 1807, resulted in £444 out of pledges of £872;[272] an outcome offering some recognition, but no significant financial recompense.[273]

Though a list of the subscribers to the 1802 appeal has not survived, one contributor has been identified. Mr. Richard Arkwright Junior. Richard Arkwright's son recognised the victory of a *"bitter rival"* and Crompton's success in making finer yarns than those produced by the water frame. [274] Arkwright Junior contributed the considerable sum of 30 guineas. The manufacturers of Bolton were, once more, found wanting with not a single subscription. It should be acknowledged that an obstacle to generosity was Napoleon, whose victories combined with a bad harvest, led to the plummeting of trade in the textile industry.

The £444 allowed Samuel to open another factory, the rented upper story of an existing establishment, with two power driven mules, one of 360 spindles[275] and the other 220. With typical generosity he also donated £100 to the construction of a Swedborgian chapel in Bury Street. He was attracted to the factory by a steam engine on the ground floor in proximity to the river. This allowed him to utilise Kelly's self-acting mule, the power being conveyed to the upper stories of the building via a shaft. In 1792 William Kelly, a clock maker of New Lanark, had registered a patent for a self-acting mule. He was an ingenious engineer who also designed a heating system for the New Lanark Mills of Richard Dale and acted as an efficient site manager. His patent only automated part of the spinning process by driving the spindles at high speed during the drawing and twisting at the head of the machine. Children still had to intervene at some point to handle a guide which set the spindles in motion.[276] The site, which was neglected and damp, hampered the operation of the machinery so Crompton took responsibility for the engine, deducting the expense of its maintenance from his rent. He distributed his yarn to a network of weavers, then used the woven cloth to produce muslins.

While working in King Street and Back King Street he continued to experience the problem of educating his employees to master the intricacies of his mule, only to have them coaxed away by competing manufactories. The skill his deserting employees took with them must have embraced the way Samuel operated the machines, though knowledge of any small modifications to the machinery were a further inducement to poach his workers. On one occasion one of his own sons was enticed away by higher wages; albeit only for a few weeks.[277] The market economy was no longer a respecter of family ties, though we can only speculate regarding other family frustrations that may have led his son to desert him.

If we are to understand the lack of fit of Samuels character with the rabid commercial environment of the industrial revolution, and ultimately his obsession with seeking a reward from Parliament, we need to ask why he refused so many offers of partnership, even from friends and trusted manufacturers? He never invested in coal mining but clearly the rapid growth of that industry was a key feature of the industrial revolution. The next chapter involves coal, but more tellingly portrays the perils of partnership and interaction with the legal system as other aspects of the social and economic environment that Samuel and his sons would find problematic to contend with.

Chapter Eleven

The Curious Case of Ichabod Eccles

*There was a **whispering** in my hearth,*
A sigh of the coal,
Grown wistful of a former earth.
It might recall.

Miners, Wilfred Owen, 1918

Sir Richard Clayton

Imagine the scene on a chill, clear night, in a small moorland settlement under the north stars guilty wink. A swarthy individual, lacking either the will or expertise of a housebreaker, takes advantage of a trusting young man who leaves his creaky wooden door unlocked. The horse tethered to a post down the roughhewn street neighs in the confusion of this diversion from its usual pathways. The stairs are no less noisy as Joseph Pimbley treads, as cautiously as he can, from step to groaning step. Ichabod[278] Eccles half turns restlessly in his tussled bed, barely conscious and rendering a repelling grunt. Joseph pulls at the drawers of an oak chest, a little hesitantly, because though never a drunken person he is an innkeeper, and a hastily swallowed drink has fuelled his courage. At last, he finds what he is looking for, a set of accounts and proof of his claim to a larger share of a coal mine on the lands of Sir Richard Clayton. Or do they contain the damming evidence that he is entitled to less than he claims?

Samuel Crompton's brother-in-law Joseph Pimbley was the innkeeper of the White Bear Inn in Adlington, close to the village of Rivington, adjacent to a major coal field. His landlord, Sir Richard Clayton, Baronet, of Adlington Hall was the minor aristocrat who had led the 'invalids' against the Birkacre rioters, sitting in judgement at the subsequent Quarter Sessions. He was admitted to the Inner Temple in 1762 and called to the Bar in 1771. The Clayton family owned the properties of Adlington and Worthington. He was created a Baronet in 1774, served as Constable of Lancaster Castle and was Recorder of Wigan for the period 1815-1828. He was made a fellow of the Royal Society in 1802. In 1825 he was appointed British Consul to the state of Nantes.[279] Sir Richard provides a clear example of the power of patronage and the involvement of the aristocracy in industrial development.

The home of the Claytons was Adlington Hall;[280] Elizabethan, but with a new hall built around 1771.[281] This fine Georgian red brick building had a broad inviting approach, welcoming parades of emblazoned coaches, speeding phaetons, and distinguished guests. The hall dominated the local landscape, a symbol of wealth and privilege The building and its surroundings were praised as the loveliest pieces of architecture and countryside in the country.[282] The main residence was described as having a southerly aspect and *"appears to the eye at a distance as if: "Bosm'd deep in tufted trees."* [283] Antique prints evoke an Arcadian scene of peaceful vales and grazing cattle, while nineteenth century maps indicate the pockmarks of disused coal mines that gradually erupted about the estate.[284] There is a sales piece of 1858 indicating the buildings size; with a drawing room, morning room and eight best bedrooms and servants rooms on the second floor. It was described as a property *"suitable for a gentleman."*[285] An earlier reference to the residence, in the 1790s, noted that the hall exhibited a fine painting of the severed head of Charles Ist.[286]

The autobiographic sketches of the essayist and notorious opium addict Thomas De Quincey (1785-1859) reported a visit to Manchester of Lady Clayton. Remarking upon Sir Richard Clayton's literary achievements:[287]

"Amongst the families that were thus attentive to her, in throwing open for her use various advantages of baths, libraries, picture-galleries, etc., were the wife and daughters of Mr. White [a famous Manchester Surgeon] himself. Now, one of these daughters was herself the wife of a baronet, Sir Richard Clayton, who had honourably distinguished himself in literature by translating and improving the work of Tenhove the Dutchman (or Belgian?) upon the house of the De' Medici, a work which Mr. Roscoe considered "the most engaging work that has, perhaps, ever appeared on a subject of literary history."

Sir Richard was a 'sportsman' and a singular example of this is a *"Treatise on Greyhounds, By a Sportsman."* A flamboyant manuscript with precocious smatterings of Greek, Latin, French and Italian text; all considering the history, breeding, quality and attributes of the current stocks of this magnificent dog. A delicious irony, as with industrialisation the greyhound became a robust emblem of working class sport and leisure. He notes:

"A Welsh proverb intimates a gentleman may be known by his hawk, his horse, and his greyhound; and Mr. Pennant J has observed, by a law of Canute, a greyhound was not to be kept by any person inferior to a gentleman."[288]

In 1780 the Baronet was an erstwhile Whig politician hoping to emulate his father, who had been a member of parliament for Wigan (1747 to 1754) . Unfortunately, he had acrimonious disagreements with the 'conservative' Whig the Duke of Portland. Despite writing two ingratiating letters to the Duke, assuring him of a correspondence between his principles and his own, he failed to get any patronage and support. If indeed he did share Portland's values they would include a reluctant approach to catholic emancipation, opposition to parliamentary reform and an austere view of radical opposition and dissent.

It is likely that Sir Richard was more liberal than Portland. Having abandoned any pretence of being in sympathy with Portland the Baronet was roundly beaten in the Wigan borough election of 21st August 1780. The unanimous choice was Henry Simpson Bridgeman,[289] son of Sir Henry Bridgeman Bart.[290] Sir Richard blamed his defeat on the undue influence of an unnamed peer of the realm (probably Portland), and the importing of burgesses from other boroughs.

"Yet there are the men loud in the cry of patriotism in one corner of the Kingdom whilst they are poisoning the very vitals of the constitution in another."[291]

So ignominiously defeated Sir Richard, classical scholar, sportsman and gentleman focused, as he had promised, in his open letter published in the Manchester Mercury (September 1780), on the interests of the burgesses of Wigan, and the borough. This would, of course, facilitate the management of his own business activities. For example, in May 1783, a coal pit for sale on his lands, bridging Blackrod and Adlington. [292] It was then another 15 years in 1798 that a further coal mine was established, and Samuel Crompton's brother-in-Law Joseph Pimbley became involved, and experienced the perils of partnership.

The Perils of Partnership

Joseph Pimbley had several business dealings with Sir Richard Clayton and his agents. One significant meeting took place, in the year 1800, on the premises of a coal mine in Blackrod of which Joseph was part owner. Bluntly, the Baronet informed him that the pit would be closed. The mine had been *"sunk,"* in 1798, on the properties occupied by Mr. John Law and Mr. Richard Makinson, both of whom received an unknown amount of compensation for the loss of the lands current use, most probably pasture. We can picture the mine from the description of its contents given by one of the other partners, Ellis Ratcliffe. He cites *"wheels, pumps, an engine pit, outbuildings, a small house and a smithy"*. Sir Richard had insisted on the erection, at the pit head, of an engine to pump water out of the mine. This would be the machine, with its great see sawing beam, invented by Thomas Newcomen in 1712, described by Samuel Smiles as, *"wheezing, sighing, creaking and bumping."*[293] This evocative evidence of how the landscape was changing with industrialisation.

The mine would have employed 20 miners or less, including women and children. It was probably a bell pit where the vertical shaft widened at its base in the shape of a bell, offering, albeit suspect, support to the roof. Joseph Pimbley was the agent for the colliery, the pit manager responsible for the employment of the miners, purchase of materials, sale of the coal and the general operation and maintenance of the mine.

Sir Richard would have had no direct concern with coal mining. Like many aristocratic landowners the discovery of coal on his land was fortuitous. He secured his interest by having a lucrative contractual relationship with the partners. The Baronet agreed to a revenue sharing scheme where he received one shilling for each batch of 26 baskets of coal taken from the mine, and sales per annum had to be sufficient to pay him £200 per year. Many coal mining ventures were short lived as the coal pits were depleted or became uneconomical.

Joseph reacted with incredulity to Sir Richard's insistence that the pit be closed. He certainly objected to the subsequent financial distribution from the sale of the coal mines assets. As the dispute became protracted Sir Richard stood ever more aloof and Joseph became increasingly frustrated. He believed that the other partners were avoiding him or treating him with contempt. Ultimately the lack of consensus led to the dispute being taken to the Court of Chancery. This was a court associated with great expense and delay, so the decision reflected the rancorous relationship between the partners.

The Lord Chancellor of England, who presided over Chancery, was Lord Chief Justice Eldon (1751-1838), Keeper of the Great Seal (1801-1806). If the celebrated Whig politician Charles Fox, according to Edmund Burke, *"was born to be loved,"*[294] then it is tempting to conclude that Lord Chief Justice Eldon was born to evoke contrary sentiments. This may be unfair as on a personal level he was judged able and good humoured, showing his humanity by profound grief in the loss of family or friends, together with exemplary faithfulness and devotion to his wife. However, in matters of the law he was severe and reactionary. When on the occasion of the execution of a croft breaker, James Holland in 1786, the Reverend Edward Whitehead of Bolton raged against the corruption and vices of the times, he anticipated the rationale for the public execution of petty criminals of Lord Chancellor Eldon. A man is hanged, the reverend proclaims, *"not for stealing a horse, but that horses might not be stolen."*[295]

Eldon's severity generated a great deal of antagonism. According to an anonymous early nineteenth century biographical note he was *"viscous and mean."*[296] Percy Shelley responded with despair and indignation, to Lord Chief Justice Eldon's denial of his rights to care for his two children by his first wife Harriet, who had committed suicide. Shelley in his 'The Mask of Anarchy,' written in 1819, at the time of the 'Peterloo Massacre,' portrayed Eldon thus:

"Next came Fraud and he had on, Like Eldon an ermined gown; His big tears, for he wept well, Turned to millstones as they fell"[297]

A later piece in the Biographical Keepsake thought to be by Mary Shelley yearned:

"Many of England's most deserving people have suffered by his intolerable delays and doubts ...we can never forget a thousand proofs of his mean and cruel intolerance....whenever it shall please the disposer of all events to remove him from the world, the nation will respire with still greater freedom."[298]

To be fair to the Lord Chief Justice his detractors had probably not fared well in the court cases on which he deliberated. Chancery was involved in thorny and emotive disputes, often relating to family disagreements and contentious entitlements to land and property. For example, circa 1823, Samuel's eldest son George Crompton was a plaintiff in a dispute over the distribution of property and the payment of rents to his infant daughter Sarah Crompton (nee Lancaster), arising from the death of her grandfather Thomas Lancaster, in contention with George's brother-in-law John Lancaster. [299]The rents related to Wensley Fold which was the site of the first purpose built cotton spinning mill to be built in Blackburn.[300]

Real name John Scott, Eldon had a romantic past. The son of a Newcastle coal merchant, at the age of 21, with the customary ladder and the assistance of a good friend, he eloped with Elisabeth Surtees the daughter of an influential local family of coal merchants. It was some time before he was redeemed in the sight of his parents and in laws. Overshadowed by his cleverer elder brother the assiduous John studied obsessively, developing prodigious feats of memory that would serve him well in the law. His habit of taking home the bills and answers of the Chancery court cases to ponder every minute detail, along with his refusal to reform the court, caused an extreme backlog of cases.

In considering Eldon we see the pressures for change and the resistance to them. He deliberates on the great issues of the day, hovering above the seething conflict and rancour engendered by rapid industrial and social change. A land dispute here, inheritance there, a contention over the share in a mine, a challenge to ancient rights, the rights of lessee's and copyholders,[301] and even challenges between merchants at home and overseas. When Joseph Pimbley made his appeal to the court in 1804, he may not have been aware of Eldon's reputation, it was not yet established, or he was so convinced of the justice of his case that he abandoned caution and risked great expense. Subsequent court cases, and Joseph's relationship with the Wigan attorney Henry Gaskell, suggest a fondness for litigation and legal challenges.[302] But how would the overworked, unyielding Eldon respond to this dispute?

The details of any dispute bound for Chancery were presented to the court through written documents.[303] The plaintiff asked questions of the defendants who supplied answers, with the possibility of a further sequence of questions and answers. These fascinating parchments, yellowed with age, in fading pencil, were written by the clerks of the court. They are of varied length and intelligibility, powdered with the accumulated dirt of ages. Tightly rolled, they often refuse to flatten and yield their secrets to the investigator. Though legal documents with stock phrases and grandiloquent expressions, there is peeping out from the statements and rejoinders a hint, sometimes strong at other times weak, of the characters and voices of the defendants and their accusers. There is a sense of indignation, surprise, strident accusation and even a smattering of paranoia. We obtain from the parchments a feeling of the disquietude of the actors in these conflicts, over which the Lord chief justice presided.

The Joseph Pimbley case is an example of the potentially fractious nature of partnerships in eighteenth and early nineteenth century Britain.

In 1798, Richard Smalley, Ellis Ratcliffe and John Catlow tread upon Sir Richard Clayton's land, and as the Court of Chancery put it *"to sink a pit"*. Ellis Ratcliffe was the 'required' gentleman of money, from Haslingdon near Blackburn. The principal, most canny, investor, he gradually withdrew from the increasingly troubled business. It was quarrels around the sale of a slice of his ownership to Joseph which was a key feature of the legal dispute. Cantankerous Ratcliffe fulminated the most, generating an enormously wordy testament of his actions and suspicions. He displayed a remarkable grasp of detail that would have impressed Eldon. He had previous experience of litigation, albeit minor, when in 1796 with John Roscoe, stone cutter of Haslingdon, he made a claim in the Borough of Clitheroe court, against a Mr. James Hindle for the nonpayment of five pounds seven shillings for coal.[304]

John Catlow, a farmer, was another partner. Catlow was timorous, less intransigent than Ratcliffe, more the procrastinator. The case also involved a female investor, Anne Smalley. Invariably women investors were widows, who had property. Anne felt isolated and possibly intimidated by the male partners and their claims. She was emphatically informed by Ellis Ratcliffe that the mine was *"a loosing concern,"* and that there was no money available for distribution. To protect her interest, she hired a young attorney from Darwen, Ichabod Eccles. It was John Catlow who accused Joseph Pimbley of entering the premises of Ichabod Eccles while he was sleeping and stealing a set of accounts. However, the disputes and maneuvering all begin with the death of Anne's husband, clergyman of the established church the Reverend Richard Smalley.

The Reverend Smalley conjures up an image like the accident prone Dr Syntax,[305] the poetic creation of William Combe, amusingly sketched by Thomas Rowlandson, to whom: *"A sudden thought across him came and told the way to wealth and fame."*[306] Smalley was a good caricature for a contemporary satirical print. His father Robert had presided, for many years, with compassion and affection, over the parish church in the village of Lower Darwen. Unfortunately, his sons haughty and arrogant manner led his congregation to desert him, preferring the ministrations of the nearby non-conformist chapel.

Richard Smalley was no Parson Folds. His investments were not successful. In 1799 he died intestate, leaving his widow impoverished, keen to learn if there were any monies due from the recent sale of the coal mine in which her husband had been an investor. Richard Smalley had an history of failed enterprises. In 1792 on the death of his father Robert, in partnership with his brother Robert junior, he was directed to offset their debts against his father's estates, lands and tenements.[307] One of the trustees with oversight of this process was John Catlow, suggesting that Joseph Pimbley was encroaching on a well-established Blackburn business network. There were bankrupt partnerships in 1794, 1795, 1797 and 1798.[308] These involved banking, manufacturing and general trade. He does not declare himself reverend, because to claim the protection of a bankruptcy order you were required to be in trade.

In 1800 the partners met at the pit head to resolve their differences. To the disgust of Ellis Ratcliffe, Joseph Pimbley had invited his attorney, Mr. Henry Gaskell of Wigan. Henry Gaskell was a highly successful local attorney whose name is scattered like corn among deeds, mortgages and commercial agreements throughout the district. In contemporary culture attorneys were viewed with derision and even contempt. Hence Dr Johnson's quip that *'he did not care to speak ill of any man behind his back, but he believed the gentleman was an attorney.'*[309] The caricaturists Robert Dighton (1756-1814) often portrayed attorneys as parasitical beings draining the financial vitals from their clients.

As a poor singer, actor, artist, portrait painter and print seller Dighton was well acquainted with lawyers. He is said to have been rolled into his benefit night at the Haymarket Theatre by sympathetic Draymen, concealing him in an empty beer barrel, to avoid the bailiffs pursuing him for debts.[310] Ellis Ratcliffe's disapproval is understandable in this context, and recourse to an attorney posed a challenge to informal, traditional forms of dispute resolution. Moreover, as Dighton's etching of the ragged John Doe and Richard Doe, entitled Brothers in Law implies, the cost of legal disputation could be mutually ruinous.[311]

A Tangled Web

The disputes between the actors in this querulous scenario concerned several issues. These included whether Sir Richard Clayton sold a lease to the partners, the need to sell the mine, the receipt and distribution of money from its sale, and the size of each person's initial shares, all involving a set of accounts that had gone missing. It was this type of wrangling over property and money in which the Court of Chancery excelled. However, it would have been socially approved for the dispute to go to arbitration;[312]

though often the decisions arising from arbitration had to be subsequently enforced by the courts.[313] The diplomatic Sir Richard, though not entirely disinterested, would have been an obvious choice of arbitrator. Frustratingly for Joseph the Baronet refused and it proved difficult to find anyone else to oblige. Sir Richard maintained a cautious distance and was more concerned with retrieving his capital and exercising petty clams to equipment, than determining a just and fair disposition of funds.

On one occasion discussions between the partners were delayed, awaiting the return of the Baronet from fashionable Bath, a return journey he may have been tempted to delay. A meeting was arranged at the hall, but Joseph was ill and could not attend. There were several failed attempts to arrange a meeting in Blackburn. Then, when they finally do get together, Joseph marched out in disgust. He was convinced that the other partners were consorting behind his back and that an unnamed individual was actively conspiring against him. [314]

The dispute was rendered venomous by accusations of theft. Work tools and equipment were highly valued and passed between generations. Joseph was accused of taking a wheelbarrow and rope to the value of £15. Then in a final rebuke Joseph Pimbley is accused of having managed the mine badly, paying too much in costs and receiving too little for the coal.

The general sense of the complaint to Chancery is one of a conspiracy, and by implication fraud. Joseph concluded that they *"often act as if there was no agreement and at times admitting that they wished he had never been admitted as a partner to the concern"*. Moreover, they refused to allow him to inspect the approved partnership books of account. He stated that he was happy to go to arbitration, to which they first agreed, but that they used various excuses not to do this. There is a real sense in which he is not considered an equal of the others and does not appear to have been given all the information necessary to establish his claims. What is difficult to untangle is the role of subterfuge, error and imprecision, or the clash of subtle differences in social rank.

The outcome of the litigation was presented in the report by Master John Simeon, dated January 1806. The memorandum noted that on the 7th of December 1805 Josephs case was dismissed by Eldon and that he was requested to pay expenses of £28, 4 shillings and 10 pennies to cover Ellis Ratcliffe's legal Bill, this to be reduced to £18, 10 shillings and 10 pennies if the costs were paid early. It is not surprising, given the complexity of the transactions and the inadequacy of the records, that the case was lost.

This Chancery case introduces leading characters in the playing out of the industrial revolution, at the local and national level. Sir Richard Clayton, minor aristocrat with ownership of mineral rights, Lord Chief Justice Eldon representing conservative opposition to reforms, a veritable barometer of the pressures of industrial and social changes. Joseph the enterprising yeoman, with others of the 'middling sort' who provided the finance for new ventures, the 'men of money.' Also, the farmers and trades men, the impoverished widow and the attorney. Collectively, these characters delineate the calculating commercial environment and its key actors that Samuel Crompton had to engage with. A partnership would be one way forward for Samuel and his family. But given the above example, of which he would have been aware, was that an attractive proposition?

The Desirable Partner

If Joseph Pimbley did clandestinely sneak into the bedroom of Ichabod Eccles, it was because the usual mechanisms of mutual trust, community oversight and arbitration had failed. It was a grasping for formal proof in a contentious murky debate of accusation and counter accusation. The stakes could be high, as indicated by the fate of Anne Heaton and the poverty of Anne Smalley. Business failure could lead to impoverishment, destitution and prison. Samuel Crompton had found that the promises, symbolised by the bold assertive signatures of cotton manufacturers could not be relied upon. Partnerships were fragile and business networks could be transient as they became stretched to incorporate new associates. In the future the litigious Joseph Pimbley would advise Crompton's sons, who were often in dispute with their partners in manufacturing and trade.

Despite the problems it was common to enter a partnership with a fellow manufacturer who could inject capital. This allowed plant to be better utilised and added new areas of expertise. For example, Robert Peel combined with Yates and Halliwell (circa, 1794).[315] Samuel Crompton was pursued as a potential partner by William MacAlpine, an ebullient and forever pressing general merchant based in London, who he had known since at least 1785.[316] MacAlpine acted as a commissioning agent, selling the wares of Crompton and other northern manufacturers to the London market. He also exported goods through Hamburg. Germany was the major European customer for cottons and the Hamburg fairs were the entrepôt for other areas of Europe. MacAlpine and his associates wished to add their capital to Samuel's technical expertise. He exuded an infectious Georgian optimism, this despite his own experience of bankruptcy in 1788.[317] He was a close friend of the family, writing:

"....no object I have so much at heart as to form a solid and permanent establishment with you being confident that with your knowledge in spinning and manufacturing and my experience and powers affecting sales. Something of decisive advantage may yet be done between us...."[318]

In 1805, MacAlpine offered the tantalising prospect of a partnership in a cotton mill at Cromwell Park, Perth, Scotland.[319] The particulars for a later sale of this property, in 1808, stated that it was a five story building:

"....wrought by a wheel of about 15 feet in diameter, and about 13 feet broad, and a fall of about 20 feet commanding 4032 water twist spindles on two floors............"[320]

The factory had adjacent cottages and managers houses situated *"amidst the most picturesque scenery."* It had the *"unrivalled"* pure water of the river Almond. There is a hint of the romanticism attached to early descriptions of changes in the industrial scene, resonating with the paintings of industrial landscapes by Joseph Wright of Derby. Unfortunately, Crompton seems to have let this opportunity slip away. MacAlpine was forever chastising him for the slow response to his letters and business propositions.[321]

"I have been daily expecting your answer but am much surprised I have not yet been favoured with it."

The distance from Lancashire to Perth (and possibly some isolation from London) may have discouraged Samuel and his family from investigating MacAlpine's business proposition any further. They never acted upon an invitation to visit the mill.[322] However, it was undisclosed changes in the circumstances of the proprietor, Mr. Hunter, that caused the deal to collapse and relieved Samuel of the burden of taking any decision.[323] Duncan Hunter had retired from the House of Sterling Hunter, with *"a fortune from business."*

A second proposition involved a smaller cotton mill much nearer to home, just seven miles east of Nottingham. MacAlpine described it as having four floors, 90 feet long and 27 feet wide, with a strong river running into the front of the mill. Moreover, there was an adjacent house as large as the mill, just perfect for bleaching, plus 8 or 9 cottages.[324] Critically the factory was just 125 miles from London with plenty of coals on the spot. The factory had 1000 spindles based on *"water twist,"*[325] but MacAlpine thought the factory perfect for the use of spinning mules. He wondered if one of Samuel's sons would like to work the establishment, which could be rented for £350 to £400 per year. He noted the use of little boys and girls on looms, weaving beautiful calicoes and cambrics being sent to a factory previously belonging to Mr. Oldknow of Stockport. These cotton mills are vivid examples of the impact of Arkwright's water frame on the emergence of factory production.

Despite its attractions the second business opportunity was also missed. Samuel may not have been timely, though in most of his affairs he was far from dilatory. More likely he had a reluctance to engage. He had already rejected the enthusiastic approaches of Robert Peel. An exception was his comparatively long standing partnership, at 6 years., with Richard Wylde, a fellow Swedborgian, and his son William Crompton. [326]This ended, circa 1813, with a calamity. Delph Mill, which they were supplying with cotton, was flooded. William withdrew from the business and the assets were sold to cover the losses.

MacAlpine often focused upon Samuel's sons. George for example, might establish himself in London, or at least the sons might act as agents in the north commissioning cloth for London and overseas sale. Observing a member of his wife's family's involvement in fractious litigation may have convinced Samuel of the wisdom of working alone, or only with members of his immediate family. However, family disputes would soon be threatening the stability of even these arrangements.

Business networks were critical for the manufacturers of the early industrial revolution, supplying credit, expertise and legal support. The Manchester manufacturing networks were particularly well organised, demonstrated by the opposition to Arkwright's patents. Engagement with the power and privilege of aristocratic landowners, such as Sir Richard Clayton, was vital as they 'sat' upon mineral resources. The more successful businessmen married into their families, providing a route to power and ostentation. The aristocracy could also be significant actors in economic networks, encouraging manufacture. To influence Parliament aristocratic patronage was still important. When Samuel Crompton decided to seek a government reward, he would need to canvas support from both his manufacturing associates and vested aristocratic interests.

Elements of business networks could coalesce into partnerships, with all the attendant problems. The Chancery case presented an evocative picture of the potentially torrid nature of disputes over capital, equipment and ownership. A clash of personalities, or at other times the death of a partner could cause a renegotiation of the ownership, rights and obligations of a business. Partnerships were one way of combining skills and seeking wealth.

Less robust was the spending of anticipated wealth, based on a sense of entitlement and inevitable reward. When this is a shared misconception, easing dalliances with the powerful and influential, but with none of the material common interest to be found in the alliances of farmers, colliers and gentlemen of money, then the sense of wellbeing is a chimera. Though still working at their trade, this was the nebulous course of *'enrichment'* pursued by Samuel Crompton's sons.

Part Four

1806-1812

Vanity and Rebellion

Chapter Twelve

Wealth Anticipated

Too long alas my inexperienced youth
Misled by flattering fortunes specious tale
Has left the rural reign of peace and truth
*The bubbling brook; cool cave, and **whispering** vale.*
Elegy written in the garden of a friend,
Mason, 1758

Of Wild Oats and Credit

In 1807, Samuel Crompton's sons, according to Gilbert French, had reached manhood.[327] Credit was available to them at every turn; the victualers, the coffee shop and most particularly the tailors. No Dandy's, or Macaroon's, but fine well dressed young gentlemen enjoying social life and spending their fathers anticipated fortune. Moreover, with a continental war in progress to avoid dressing as a soldier would be remiss. To look fine, do one's duty and attract the ladies was an irresistible combination. Consequently, George and William enlisted in the local volunteers, later joining the militia. French noted how they would *"sow their wild oats"* and consort with *"flattering and dangerous companions."*[328] Fortunes had been made from the use of the mule, surely their turn would come?

In the Crompton papers there are examples of the credit given to the eldest son George. A bill dated March 27,[th] 1804, for £4 and 7 shillings from Mr. Stubbs, for scarlet and blue cloth with silk and twist.[329] A later bill from Henry Wilson Draper of Exchange Street Manchester *("funerals completely furnished")* covering white stockings, pantaloons the making of a scarlet coat, a further plain coat and blue nankeen trousers to the total of £4. 10 shillings.[330] In a letter 7th May 1810[331] Lieutenant George Crompton was ordered to the orderly room by Colonel Ralph Fletcher to march, no doubt proudly in Scarlet and Blue, through the streets of Bolton. In the words of the elegy by *Horatius* (pseudonym) writing in the Lancaster Gazette of 1st December 1810 on the loss of a subaltern's epaulette:

"How oft with Martial strut and martial air. Or at the ballroom or the thronged parade, I've sported thee before the admiring fair, and all thy glittering honours bright displayed."[332]

No doubt the elder sons found most of their diversions in nearby burgeoning Manchester. They might have attended the *Theatre Royal* to enjoy an intriguing composite of entertainments; on one occasion beginning with the comic opera *"Love in a Village"* (the part of young Meadows played by Mr. Hill). This to be followed by the new ballet dance suggestively named *"Love and Danger,"* the whole long evening to conclude with a song sung by '*Little Pickle*' *"the spoiled child,"* perhaps reflecting a contemporary concern.[333] Changing times and social stresses were also indicated by a performance at the Theatre Royal entitled *"Wives as they were and maids as they are."*[334] Or they may have ventured slightly further afield to the equally prosperous Liverpool; perhaps responding to Madame Catalani's call to the nobility, gentry and public to come and hear her sing in the Music Hall.[335] All of the performances *"illuminated by wax"*.

The Crompton sons were well educated and may have attended the debates in the Manchester Assembly Rooms, just down Exchange Street from Walthor Wilson, George's tailor. [336] Here they would participate in disputes that reflected contemporary concerns. One such: *Is the old adage true? that the world grows wickeder every day; or on the contrary are they not in a moral and intellectual point of view improving.*[337] Then tellingly embedded in the invitation the prescriptive *"RELIGION and POLITICS must be excluded from any share in the debate"*. Given the prevalence of social unrest and non-conformist agitation this may have been an understandable restriction, though leading perhaps to a rather sterile discussion, focused on the agendas of the moral improving societies, such as the Society for the Reformation of Manners. Yet the sons may have reveled in the debate: *"Which of the following characters is the most inimical to the good of society, a knavish attorney, an illiterate quack, or a dissipated divine?"*[338] Troubling notions for uncertain times, reaching out from the eighteenth century, animatedly discussed amidst the warmth of *"well kept fires"*.

The Cromptons' enjoyed many fine dinners at the houses of the increasingly prosperous manufacturers, such as Peter and John Hewitt (gentlemen), tenants of the grand Peel Hall, Little Hulton, a productive site for coal mining. The Hewitt's had been in business with Joseph Pimbley at a colliery and lime manufacturing enterprise in Adlington, the partnership being dissolved in 1807.[339] In a letter to his father dated 28th April 1812 George Crompton noted how the Hewitt's were fearful that Luddite rioters would burn down their home.[340]

Family connections extended to London, usually Lancashire emigres who found the capital more compatible with their cultural or business interests, such as William MacAlpine. Or Edward Harwood,[341] a celebrated composer, born in Blackburn. Samuel reputedly taught him to play the organ. There was the supportive George Lee of Milk Street, who owned a cotton warehouse in the capital. Then a particular friend of George Crompton, Joseph Nightingale, who taught him shorthand while they were incarcerated in the Fleet prison in 1813, for insolvency. Nightingale was a Methodist and prolific author who had distressing personal experiences of imprisonment, being involved in cases of defamation, bankruptcy and theft.

Though the sons were furiously socialising, they continued to attend to their father's business. They presented goods to the Manchester market and assisted in running the enterprise in King Street.[342] Not all five children were content to exploit their local celebrity. An unrecorded family dispute led the fourth son John (1791-1864) to run away to sea. Perhaps he was overshadowed by the pretensions of his older brothers, unable to emulate their finery and posturing. He did not remain in the navy for long, and a discharge document exists from his commanding officer Samuel Colquitt, noting that he served on the Frigate *Princess*, from 11th July 1808 until the 13th of August 1808, just one month, and that he acted as a supernumerary.[343]

As a landsman John Crompton had half the worth of an experienced mariner: and as a supernumerary would have worked in the cramped conditions below decks. His discharge was facilitated by a *'willing substitute'*, Thomas Cuddy, a book binder, from Dublin. John's discharge could have been a smooth application of the rules or eased by Samuel Crompton's Liverpool connections. It was not unusual for the Commander of a receiving ship to be given a request for the release of even those forced into service.[344] The appearance of Samuel Colquitt in the Crompton family story provides a fascinating insight into the importance of patronage in early nineteenth century society. Samuel's sons were not entirely foolish in socialising and seeking out connections. As the story of Samuel Colquitt shows, if you had powerful friends, you might literally get away with murder.

Of Patronage and Power

The *Princess* was a guard ship of 26 guns and had sailed from Plymouth to Liverpool on the 10th of August 1803.[345] It was a receiving vessel for volunteers for the Royal Navy and impressed men. The early days of the ship were marked by a near disaster, when in December 1803, strong tides and ferocious winds swept the frigate on shore between Woodside and Seacombe. Calling for assistance, by firing three of her cannons, she excited the local militias (*fencibles*) into action to defend the port against a presumed enemy attack; *"zealous to protect the lives and properties of their townsmen."*[346] The neurosis of war meant that the privateers no longer announced their return to port by firing their cannon in the estuary. To further emphasise the ongoing conflict, the same day saw the arrival of the buccaneering Captain Cochrane in the *Arab* with provisions for the *Princess* and another guard ship the *Castor*.[347]

There is an evocative description of the *Princess,* written in the memoirs of an early nineteenth century seafaring resident of Liverpool.

"We had a venerable guard ship in the river, the Princess, which we believe, had originally been a Dutch man-of-war, and if built to swim was never intended to sail. There she used to lie at her moorings, opposite the Old George's dock pier, lazily swinging backwards and forwards with the ebbing and flowing of the tide and looking as if she had been built for that very purpose and no other. Her very shadow seemed to grow into that part of the river in which she lay. But beside her, we had generally some old-fashioned vessel of war which had come round from Portsmouth or Plymouth to receive volunteers or impressed men."[348]

Discipline on receiving ships was singularly harsh, especially given that they were often used as holding stations for impressed sailors. The press was deeply unpopular in Liverpool as it denuded the merchant vessels of the best mariners and broke up families. One list of impressed men handed over to the *Princess* in 1807 recorded 200 names.[349] In principle landsmen, those with no seafaring experience, such as John Crompton were exempt from the press. However, when John in his fit of pique ran away to the dank embrace of the receiving ship then he placed himself at the mercy of its severe and controversial commanding officer, Samuel Colquitt.

Samuel, Martin Colquitt was born into a well established Liverpool family. His father John held the prestigious public office of distributor of stamps. His grandfather Scrope/Scroop Colquitt was a major ship builder and military figure. However, by the time John arrived in Liverpool in 1807 Colquitt was a man of notoriety. He is an example of the potency of social status, and the class of people with whom John's brothers were fraternising.

In 1802 Colquitt was promoted from lieutenant to commander. In 1804. he transported Nelson's dispatches to the Admiralty, on their arrival from Gibraltar. [350]In 1803 he had dined on the *Princess* with Prince William of Gloucester, *Commander of the North*. The Prince had been conducted to the Princess in a 12 oar barge, with his aides De Camp which included Colonel Bolton of Liverpool.[351] The ship fired her guns and raised the royal standard. As the band struck up, twenty thousand people witnessed this *"novel and pleasing sight."* Newspaper reports cited the presence of distinguished members of Liverpool Society. Mr. Roscoe President of the Antheum coffee room, and Nicholas Ashton a deputy lieutenant of Liverpool.

Following a brief trip to Manchester, Prince William returned to Liverpool to reside at 'St Domingo *'the seat of Mr. William Sparling'* which he had requisitioned as his headquarters. St Domingo was another echo of the seven year's war, and involvement in slavery. The property was originally held by Mr. George Campbell, West India merchant and sugar refiner. One of his privateers captured a rich French Prize off St Domingo, so he named his estate in honour of the event. The property was purchased by Mr. John Sparling, father of William Sparling, in 1773 for £3,476.[352] The house was *a* palatial looking structure that would have appealed to Prince William as a residence and HQ. William Sparling, and Samuel Colquitt were friends and no doubt linked through their family businesses. The royal and other connections were going to prove critical to their mutual survival.

In 1804 William Sparling Esq, late lieutenant in the tenth regiment of dragoons, commanded by his Royal Highness the Prince of Wales, and Captain Samuel Martin Colquitt of the *Princess* were accused of murder by the coroner's court at Liverpool. Dueling was illegal and deaths arising because of such ritualised fighting were acts of homicide. Sparling had shot and killed a ship builder named Edward Greyson and Colquitt had acted as his second. William Sparling had promised to marry Greyson's niece a Miss Renshaw, but allegedly, through the persuasion of his mother, who thought the match unsuitable, reneged on the arrangement. Mr. John Blackburne, Lord High Sheriff of Lancashire who would be a key character in Samuel's 1812 campaign for a parliamentary award had written to a Mr. Park, noting that he was aware of the gossip surrounding Sparling's treatment of Miss Renshaw and *"that it was the general report at Liverpool and its neighbourhood."*[353]

Greyson responded to the outpourings of his broken hearted niece with an onslaught on the dishonorable conduct of Sparling. One public lambasting occurred in the celebrated Antheum coffee rooms. Sparling through the mediation of Colquitt challenged Greyson to a duel. A reluctant Greyson was pressurised, albeit in a 'gentlemanly' manner by letter, and by visits from Colquitt, to cease delaying and attend the 'contest' at the appointed time and place. With Sparling's military background the fight was never going be an equal one. Greyson was shot in the hip. He lingered for a week *"in great agony"* before dying.[354]

After the coroner's verdict William Sparling and Samuel Colquitt absconded, hiding it was thought, in the hold of some sympathetic frigate in the Mersey estuary. However, they were persuaded by powerful friends to give themselves up and face a trial by their peers. Late March, or early April 1804, they presented themselves for trial at the Assizes, Lancaster Castle.[355] The President of the court was Sir Alan Chamber; Sergeant Mr. Cockell, Mr. Scarlett and Mr. Clark acted for the crown and Mr. Park, Mr. Wood, Mr. Topping, Mr. Raincock and Mr. Healde represented the defendants. The pair faced a formidable prosecution led by James Scarlett (1769-1849, First Baron Abinger). Scarlett was thought to be a scholarly man, though not an eloquent speaker.[356] While at Cambridge he refused to join the '*True Blue Club*,' a dining club no doubt involving some mischief and high jinks, but presumably no great measure of scholarly exertion. Scarlet preferred instead to *"read hard"*. However, he was reputedly tall, handsome and gentlemanly with an ability to distil the essence of a complex case and generally coax a jury to arrive at his preferred conclusion.

The defendants challenged eleven members of the jury, leaving a group of influential more sympathetic citizens. After the cross examination of witnesses to the crime there was a parading of illustrious character witnesses, including leading military officers and dignitaries. Who could not be moved by the testimony of Mr. Northcoate, who on questioning from Mr. Wood, was asked if Colquitt was liked by his sailors, and replied:

".......he reigns as much in the hearts of the sailors as our beloved sovereign reigns in the hearts of his faithful subjects."[357].

Colquitt's fate rested on whether Sparling was found guilty of willful murder. Sparling had a veritable who's who of aristocratic character witnesses, all attesting to the gentleness of his character and amiable disposition. Lord Viscount Carleton, ex Lord Chief Justice of Ireland stated that:

"It appears to me that he is a very quiet, civil, well-conducted gentleman, perfectly free from any disposition to give offence, or to quarrel"[358].

A total of seventeen character witnesses attested to Sparling's 'saintly disposition'; including five Lords, one major general a major, and four good reverends. Back home at St Domingo Sparling's royal house guest, Commander of the North, may have cast a protective dark shadow over proceedings. Dr Henry Parker, who attended Greyson during his dying hours, and was well acquainted with Sparling and Colquitt even testified that Greyson with his last precious words had asked that the defendants not be prosecuted.

« *...whatever my opinion may be as to Mr. Sparling's conduct, I freely forgive him the injury he has done me in giving me this wound, and I beg my friends may not prosecute him."*[359].

In fact, Parker had known Colquitt since birth and had *"brought him into the world."*[360] On the few occasions a witness testimony contradicted the benign view of Sparling, or Colquitt, it was generally held up to ridicule. William Ashley a post chaise driver of Liverpool had transported the wounded Greyson from the scene of the duel and reported hearing Colquitt say,

"egad it had done me good"[361].

The derisory response of the defending counsel was to ask:

" Now sir I ask you, and look the jury in the face, do you mean to swear sir that that brave naval officer at the bar used the expression you have mentioned, or that Captain Colquitt is a man who would use such an expression............ believe it who can!"[362].

It was perhaps no surprise even after an intense trial, though only lasting twelve hours, that Sparling and Colquitt were acquitted. A pamphlet giving the details of the trial noted in its preface that death because of dueling was, according to the law, unambiguously murder, but that no court had found a gentleman guilty who was defending his honour.[363] It was unlikely that the court would find against Sparling and Colquitt despite the presiding judges plea to be brave and consider the matter of the law. A naval commander in time of war and a soldier supported by senior officers and having a member of the royal family as a lodger were unlikely to be found guilty. At the same Lancaster assizes Catherine Frazier, aged 15 years, was sentenced to transportation to New South Wales, Australia, for burglary; no assembly of gentility to speak for her.[364]

The fact that Colquitt was reinstated to his command of the *Princess* is further evidence of the importance of connections and influence. He certainly had a lighter side to his character. In January 1805 he and Major Edward Brooks (a key witness in the trial and declared close friend of Sparling) attended a masque ball and supper at Plumb's Hall near Liverpool; involving *"all the fashionables in the neighbourhood;"* the avenue was:

"....tastefully lined with ships colours and variegated lamps at the end of which were four porters clad in sumptuous array." [365]

The two military gentlemen made *"an admirable pair of country girls"*. Here we have another vivid if comical depiction of the primacy of society and connections. Then in supreme irony Major Brooke's himself was killed, in 1805, in a duel with Major Bolton, a barge companion of Prince William, in a dispute over wages for his job as a custom's 'jerk'. Another example of in fighting among the aristocracy and the aspiring sons of rich merchants, where in line with the treatment of duelists by the courts, Bolton was not convicted of Brooke's murder.

Prior to 'welcoming' John Crompton aboard the *Princess*, Colquitt's travails were not over. In February 1807 the ship made one of its few voyages out of port, to struggle to Plymouth Sound where Captain Colquitt was to be court martialed. The trial lasted seven days and took place on the Salvador Mundo flagship docked at Hamoaze, an estuarine stretch of the tidal River Tamar, between its joining with the River Lynher and Plymouth Sound.[366] The judge advocate was J. Biddel Esq. There were nine charges against Colquitt brought by a Lieutenant Peake. However, eight of the charges were considered to be *"gross falsehoods and founded in malice"*. He was found guilty of a ninth charge *"but not culpable"*. Colquitt was found guilty in part for a tenth charge for which he was only *"admonished"*. The trial was watched with great interest in Naval circles.

Colquitt followed the not unusual pattern of being a paragon of civic virtue but privately a harsh disciplinarian, which might be expected of a man overseeing the Liverpool Press Gangs. The admonished Captain sailed the *Princess* back to its domicile in the port of Liverpool. Having survived a trial for murder and a court martial, Colquitt eventually sailed into the sunset. In December 1809 he commanded *'The Persian'*, a frigate of 18 guns, to the West Indies. Surviving war and the risk of disease. He died, aged 71 years, in Hampshire on July 10th, 1847, having attained the rank of Rear Admiral. [367]

By October 1809, just prior to Colquitt's departure from Liverpool, John had re-engaged with the navy, this time the Merchant Marine. Samuel was anxious for his son and raced to Liverpool to search for him. He had mercantile links with Liverpool providing muslins, cambrics and ginghams to the houses of Penny and Roskell and Swan and Parker. In a letter to his other children, posted from Liverpool on the 10ᵗ th of October 1809, he was clearly having difficulty locating John and a companion. [368]The pair were thought to be aboard a ship named the *Chillam Castle*. The '*Chillam Castle*' was a frigate of 23 guns built in Hartley Pool in 1807, whose regular destination was South America. With a confidence matching John's bravado, the owners advertised that the ship was most likely to sail in a convoy, but could, if necessary, sail alone.[369] Writing from his lodging with a Mrs. Duckworth he was unable to find the ship:

"....due to the persistence of the low tide and though two young men had enquired of him at his lodging, they had not returned".

Neither could the dock master say anything of their whereabouts. Samuel speculated that they may have returned home in the knowledge that he was *"after them."*

Samuel's erstwhile partner William MacAlpine wrote from London on the 21st July 1808 reflecting on the behaviour of Samuel's sons and probably referring to John's first escapade involving Colquitt and sympathising with Samuel in a manner that demonstrated MacAlpine's appreciation of his character:

"The heavy vexation you mention for the loss of your son is truly affecting and surprises me beyond measure as from the example of sobriety you ever set before them and from the appearance of natural steadiness which I thought they all had in their nature. I really reckoned on them all as likely to turn out a treasure like you and all connected with you. I trust this will to be the case with the remaining, if they are as steady and as faithful as yourself. I flatter myself it will very shortly be in my power to do something handsome for both you and them."[370]

Samuel Crompton would have been painfully aware of the death of young Peter Ainsworth, of Bolton Le Moors, possibly the son of the bleacher and family friend Thomas Ainsworth.[371] Peter had been a midshipman on board the HMS Orpheus docked in Quebec when having accompanied his captain ashore, being short sighted and *"for the want of a railing"* he fell over the wharf into the sea and drowned.[372] Samuel was averse to his sons' military ambitions or desire to go to sea, considering these distractions from the pursuit of their trade. He would also have been fearful of the danger of military service at a time of war.

§

Samuel Crompton's sons fraternised with the likes of Sparling and Colquitt, whose story highlights the importance of connections and patronage. In turn Samuel's family expected him to exert his own personal influence and consolidate their financial future. Would Samuel Crompton have the necessary charisma and social/political leverage to achieve his aims? He would certainly have to overcome his natural shyness. While in Glasgow conducting a survey of the use of the spinning mule he was honoured by a complimentary dinner, but when the time came to attend, he *"bolted from the city."*[373]

The 1811 mule survey showed the prevalence of the mule relative to the spinning jenny, and even its dominance over Arkwright's water frame and the throstle (a modification of the water frame).[374] Thus Samuels good friends, the cotton manufacturers Lee and Kennedy thought that Parliament might offer him some recompense. There was a precedent as in 1809 Edmund Cartwright had received the sum of £10,000 for the invention of his power loom. If his family were to have the life they desired. If they were to be established in productive business and diverted from the sea and military service. If he was to overcome the hurt of others profiting greater than himself from his labours, then he must make his case to Parliament.

Chapter Thirteen

The Campaign Begins

*In the **whispers** which the officers about him (Kutusof) exchanged, and which my witness heard, there was no knowledge or even hint of what was to come.*

Hilaire Belloc, The Campaign of 1812, 1925

The first stirrings of a campaign for a reward for the mule were an appeal to the influential Sir Joseph Banks, naturalist, botanist and patron of the natural sciences, who had the support of the King George III.[375] Samuel wrote to Sir Joseph on 30th October 1807, outlining his claims.[376] The letter was mistakenly addressed to the President of the Society of Arts (SA), rather than to the Royal Society (RS), of which Joseph Banks was president. Possibly unread it was subsequently forwarded to the correct body. This was an unfortunate error as an approach to secure a patron was a sensible strategy, but an appeal to the SA was flawed. The Society encouraged new inventions, but the mule had been in use for over 25 years, enabling them to state that it was not within their remit to grant an award.

Unfortunate was the prevarication involved, over a period of 4 years, in passing the letter between 4 meetings and a subcommittee. On the 23rd of December 1807, Dr Taylor, Secretary of the SA replied to an enquiry by Samuel informing him that he had never received the original letter. It was in 1811 that he finally received confirmation that no reward would be forthcoming. Rejected and bitter he responded indignantly to the refusal, only to receive a curt reply that the Society had few funds and relied upon private subscriptions only.[377] Moreover, he had not provided a diagram and specifications for the mule, and these were seen as necessary to support any claim. French presented a vivid metaphor:

"....another stone, and a heavy one, deliberately cast upon the cairn, which was fast becoming, in his estimation, a monument of national injustice and private misfortune."[378]

During 1811 Samuel began to tentatively build the networks of influential people to champion his case Not visiting Parliament at this stage, but writing to Mr. George Rose, Member of Parliament,[379] and a little later to the prominent Sir Robert Peel.[380] Characteristic of Samuel's atrocious luck, and people's reactions to both him and his claims, he was initially treated dismissively. There can be no doubt that the Manchester manufacturers, *'the Manchester gentlemen'*[381] as he later called them, were fully aware of the impact of the mule on the productivity of cotton manufacture, and its contribution to enabling large scale factory production. Manufacturers from Scotland,[382] willing to give testimonials, and some representatives of the Yorkshire Woollen industry,[383] were also convinced of the machine's merits. But it was clear that the significance of the invention was not generally understood by some leading members of Parliament, or for political, financial, or other reasons it was considered prudent to neglect its importance.

Permeating his letters to MPs, friends and family, during 1811-1812 are Crompton's motives for pursuing a reward. He thought it *"his duty to do so"*, not just to himself, but also his family, and not least for the honour of his country.[384] Febrile from the physical and mental strains of his efforts to lobby and persuade, these motives are repeated in the correspondence, like a rough calico rag engaged to wipe his fevered brow. He also wished to provide for his sons, William, James, John, George and Samuel junior, by establishing them in business. Thus, the quest for a 'just' reward was a family affair and should be judged, not only by the success or otherwise of Samuel Crompton, but also by the fortunes of his children. They were, as we have seen, too often a source of immense worry. In the case of his daughter Betty an abusive marriage and alcoholism, with John and James their escapades at sea, and in the case of George Crompton his eagerness for a commission in Wellington's army.

Samuel's first contact on this journey expediting *"his duty"* was Mr. George Rose, who he saw as best fitted *"to take this business forward."*[385] It is understandable that he would see Rose as a good first contact. Influential, even when out of office, Rose had nurtured his political influence by projecting himself as William Pitt's *"right hand man."* Modern descriptors might present his role as a manager of public relations and publicist on behalf of Pitt. He also held powerful positions during Pitts administration. He had been Chief Secretary to the Treasury and Vice President of the Board of Trade. He was a staunchly conservative individual who opposed abolition of the slave trade and Catholic emancipation. However, approaching the end of his career, he proposed a minimum wage for weavers, who by 1811 were suffering from the effects of the continuing war and the mechanisation of their trade through the spread of power looms.[386] Belying any simple characterisation of historical personalities Rose expended a great deal of political energy addressing the poverty of seamen and the distribution of prize money, showing a more benign aspect of his character.

Given Samuel Crompton's initial focus on improving the quality of the working lives of artisans in the cotton trade and having at times two of his sons at sea, he may have warmed to Rose. However, had he the power of premonition he might have benefited from the knowledge that in 1813 John Palmer, who in 1784 introduced faster mail coaches, superseding the use of post boys, was awarded £50,000 by Parliament, in addition to an annual pension of £3,000, already awarded by William Pitt. The second award was emphatically opposed by Rose. Perhaps George Rose's time as Chief Secretary of the Treasury had imbued him with a reluctance to service such claims on the public purse. He would not be easily persuaded of the merits of Crompton's application for government funds.

William Beechey's 1802 portrait of George Rose graces him with an avuncular aspect. Sporting a fulsome cravat he exhibits a studied contemplation, appearing prosperous with the inference that he is a steady hand for affairs of state and the management of treasury. However, there was a factious and irritable aspect to George's nature. He was described by Lord Liverpool (Prime Minister 1812-1827) as

"a very low man, and very ignorant in all the higher departments of business, and yet at the same time very presumptuous, and he is the very last man under whose management I should be inclined to act."[387]

Despite this negative view he served under Liverpool as Secretary of the Navy, a post he had held under Spencer Percival, who took office after the death of Pitt in 1806.

George Rose's diary reveals personal animosities. When Spencer Percival reshuffled government positions in 1809, Rose expressed unease at the possibility of serving with Lord Melville (Henry Dundas) and Lord Sidmouth (Henry Addington):

"If Lord Melville and Lord Sidmouth shall be taken into the Administration to give strength to it, my situation will be a most painful and distressing one. I

cannot now quit the Government, however it may be formed, for the purpose of affording support to the King; at least, until it has taken a settled form; and not even then without a fixed determination to give it every assistance in my power, in aid of the cause in which they are embarking. But my dislike to the two Viscounts last mentioned is insuperable: for reasons of a public nature well known to my family, utterly unmixed with any personal consideration whatever."[388]

Engaging with George Rose was going to be difficult. In his introductory letter Samuel Crompton outlined the nature of his invention, together with its impact on cotton manufacture and national prosperity. He stated that his object was to gain compensation for loss of the fruits of his labour. Rose responded tersely that he did not understand Samuel's letter. It is, he stated, obscure as to its purpose, *"unable to ascertain the subject of it."*[389] Moreover, he did not consider that he was the man to take the business forward. He had far too many other public duties to perform.

Samuel read Rose's reply with incredulity, certain that he had clearly expressed his case for compensation. Unfortunately, this may be another example of fates tendency to lead him into mistimed pleas. George Rose's diary for this period shows that he was trying to extricate himself from politics. Samuel may have been canvassing a man who was rapidly losing motivation and not ready to champion another, possibly lost, cause. For 1809 his diary noted that he had refused the position of Chancellor of the Exchequer on the grounds that at 66 he was too old. He cited public and undisclosed private reasons for rejecting the office.[390] Crompton was undeterred, and pressed Rose further, repeating his belief that he was the man for the job. He felt that he had expressed his case clearly:

"I wrote to you on the 22 nd with as much of an explanation as any paper could contain, though it was but a part of what I had to say I flattered myself it would be sufficient whereby you might form an idea of what was meant."

He offered to give a further explanation or attend a personal interview. However, Rose was not moved by Samuel's persistence, or his arguments. An interview he wrote was not necessary, because if he required any further explanation, he could speak to Sir Robert Peel who would be familiar with the invention. He encouraged Samuel to write to Sir Robert. However, if George Rose meant to deter Samuel Crompton from bothering him further, he was to be disappointed. Samuel replied that he had indeed written to Sir Robert but had not yet heard if he had had any conversation with Mr.

Rose.[391] At this point the trail goes cold, no more is heard of George Rose until Samuel goes to London in 1812, and physically tracks him down.

The suggestion that he contact Sir Robert Peel pointed Samuel on the road to the capital and Parliament. However, even being physically present in London might not secure Samuel Crompton an interview with George Rose. The radical journalist William Cobbett was the author of many attacks upon Rose and his sinecures, and favours granted to his son George Rose Junior.[392] In an amusing anecdote in Cobbett's Political Register for 1816, no doubt a little exaggerated, Cobbett described his followers as a *"prostrate herd".* He made the following observation of Rose and his admirers/suppliants as they meandered through London:

" *Upon one occasion I saw a whole posse of Noble men and Gentlemen following at his heels down the street, when he, as if he wished to exhibit them in their true light, went into a shop and remained there several minutes, and they actually stood waiting 'till he came out, upon which they resumed the order of their march."*[393]

Should Samuel Crompton take his case to London then he would have the data from the 1811 mule spindle survey in his armory. Surveying factories within a 60 mile radius of Bolton, and though by no means complete, it did indicate the overwhelming prevalence of mule spinning, accounting as it did for 90% of all the recorded spindles. Despite deficiencies in the collection of the statistics; for example, domestic spinning was not covered and not all factories were included, it was a remarkable result.

Statistics were compiled for sub districts, such as Wigan and Bolton. They provided evidence of the size of cotton spinning concerns at this time. Manchester with its 106,324,8 mule spindles, compared to 2700 water frame spindles,[394] had the largest reported usage, while the firm of T&G Murray was the largest establishment, employing 81,600 mule spindles.[395] Samuels exact and careful nature is apparent in his correspondence with an unnamed Scottish gentleman who presented himself as an *expert* on the cotton trade and was writing an entry for the *"Eden Encyclopedia".* Having provided some statistics relating to Glasgow, Samuel's perfectionism drove him to kindly requests: *"if you can renew the statement with any additions or alterations so as to be more correct either in general or particular."*[396] .

The 1811 survey was no unscrupulous manipulation of statistics to strengthen his case. Rather, it was an expression of Samuels strong, and as it transpired correct, sense of the dominance of the Hall i' th' Wood Mule, and by inference the profit accruing to manufacturers, none of which was going to himself. Surely Parliament and Sir Robert Peel could not ignore such compelling evidence?

Like Richard Arkwright, Robert Peel was an iconic self-made man of the Industrial revolution. He was a highly successful cotton manufacturer which qualified him to understand and promote Samuel's cause. However, Crompton would have remembered the visit of Peel's workmen to Oldham's to inspect the mule, and the offer of what he considered to be a paltry sum of money for the privilege. Moreover, Robert Peel was no doubt disappointed that he had declined to work with him, a partnership that could well have been extremely productive and solved the Crompton family's financial problems. However, regardless of any lingering animosity it was clear that Sir Robert was the key person to engage as an ally, or even recruit as the putative leader of the cause. Yet again there was a mishap. Crompton had written to Sir Robert on two occasions. Responding to his second letter Peel replied to say that he had never received the first.[397] Referring to *"the machine"* he noted that *"the country had derived considerable benefit from it"; but* condescendingly described the mule as *"a new application of the invention of others."*

Peel avoided responsibility, advising that he could not *"take the business forward"* and that Samuel should enlist the support of the MPs for the County of Lancaster. The two sitting members in 1811 were Colonel Thomas Stanley and John Blackburne of Hale. The honorable members for Preston; Samuel Horrocks and Edmund Hornby could also be added to the list of potentially useful supporters, also Robert Holt Leigh and John Hodson of Wigan. Of course, at the time, Manchester and Bolton had no Members of Parliament.

Samuel Crompton would be pressing a Parliament dominated by the landed gentry and aristocrats. Certainly Leigh, Hornby and Blackburne were prominent landowners and Colonel Stanley and his cousin Lord Stanley, who in 1812 took his place, were minor aristocrats from an influential Lancashire family.[398] However, Blackburne was a conscientious long serving MP for Lancashire with knowledge of the cotton trade. Horrocks of Preston was a wealthy cotton manufacturer being the largest employer in Preston; but being labelled *'the silent member for Preston'* he was unlikely to be a worthy champion. [399] Hodson of Wigan was another successful manufacturer, but during 1811, and a good part of 1812, he largely absented himself from Parliament.[400] Hodson's success was a sign of the rising importance of the manufacturing class. In the general election of 1802, he conspired with Leigh to oust Portland's aristocratic interest in the Wigan borough by defeating George Gunning brother in law of Orlando Bridgeman;[401] the candidate who had so humiliated Sir Richard Clayton in the election for Wigan in 1780. In Parliament Samuel Crompton would have to rely upon the Stanleys' and John Blackburne, with the reluctant Robert Peel perhaps used in an advisory capacity.

In May 1811 Samuel wrote to Colonel Thomas Stanley (1749-1816) enclosing a copy of a petition and stating that he intended to approach Parliament.[402] It is apparent from this correspondence that his expectations were beginning to grow. There was a developing sense of urgency. He already had some names on his petition, and he wondered if the matter could be brought before Parliament in the current session. Even more insistent was his correspondence with the Scottish textile manufacturers, in one case a Mr. Kirman Finlay.[403] He advised Finlay that, at this stage, he has gone so far with *"the business that he must continue."* There is a sense of no turning back, but also perhaps a little apprehension. He urgently sought the signatures on his petition of the gentlemen of Glasgow. He also seemed to be somewhat surprised by the position that he now found himself in:

" I also should feel thankful for any advice you can point out to me as I am a complete novice in business of this kind, if anyone had told me three years ago that I should attempt anything of this kind I could not have believed them and my only anxiety in the business is that it should be fully and truly stated to the public. I am not uneasy as to the result provided I can acquit myself of having done everything I might do."[404]

An encouraging 'Christmas present' in the form of a response from Mr. Finlay, dated 21st December 1811, stated that the petition had now been signed and was on its way through Mr. McGovern, by direction of Mr. Hennessy. [405] Confidential and urgent business correspondence often involved business colleagues, friends or family and travelled by devious routes according to who was visiting whom, or who was conducting business where? With the Scottish signatures in place, it was time to make haste for Regency London! There he would be away from the troubles of the North, with the so called Luddite riots having begun to leave their fiery trace from Nottingham through Lancashire and into Yorkshire. The continuing war was also debilitating trade, leading to impoverishment.

During his campaign Samuel Crompton's expectations of a just or a likely reward vacillated, but often settled on £50,000, an amount probably acceptable to the parading, socialising Crompton children. However, early in his campaign his friend John Kennedy warned him to be prudent in distinguishing between what he desired and what he could achieve.

"I have too high an opinion of your good sense and experience in the world to harbour a thought that you ever had a wish to be either a man or a mouse and know that you will think with me that it is much better to get 10,000 than make for more at the risk of getting nothing."[406]

Good advice but neglecting the importance to Samuel of the honour and recognition bound up with the size of any award.

It was George Rose who Nelson had beseeched, prior to the battle of Trafalgar in 1804, to put Emma Hamilton and his natural daughter Horatia in the care of the nation, a promise he was unable, rather than unwilling, to keep. Whether Samuel Compton could move Rose and other members of the political establishment to accept that the nation had a responsibility to him remained to be seen. The great Parliamentary orators Pit and Fox had gone, and the incomparable Thomas Sheridan was immersed in debt and alcohol. Was there at least one eloquent and persuasive champion for Samuel, who when the time came could convince Parliament of the justice of his claims?

Chapter Fourteen

Of Luddites and Distraction

*"A crash—smash—shiver—stopped their **whispers**. A simultaneously hurled volley of stones had saluted the broad front of the mill, with all its windows; and now every pane of every lattice lay shattered and pounded fragments. A yell followed this demonstration—a rioters' yell—a North-of-England—a Yorkshire—a West-Riding—a West-Riding-clothing-district-of Yorkshire rioters' yell. You never heard that sound, perhaps, reader?"*[407]

Shirley, a Tale, by Charlotte Brontë (1849)

Loyalty and 'Rebellion'

During the year 1811, and throughout Samuel Crompton's London campaign of 1812, ill fortune and tragic events were to impact upon the likelihood of a successful outcome. The country was in a worrisome state. Nothing was known yet of Napoleon's fateful decision to invade Russia, in the campaign of June to December 1812. Also, after 1809 the Emperor was passing the peak of his conquests. Nether the less the state of alert against domestic insurrection was high, with moral panic and repression rife. Add to this atmosphere the poverty engendered by the replacement of skilled workers by machines, a parlous state of agriculture with rapidly rising prices of corn, and the suppression of organised labour through the Combination Acts (1799/1800), then we can comprehend the origins of the political and economic maelstrom that followed.

On Thursday, May 30th ,1811, John Blackburne presented a petition to Parliament from 40,000 people in Manchester and its neighbourhood, *"praying for relief"*. Colonel Stanley also stated that he had in his possession a petition *"of a similar nature"* numbering 6,000 to 7,000 signatures, from the weavers of Bolton. A further plea was the *"Petition from the Weavers and Other Working Manufacturers of Chorley against Sinecures and Corruption."*[408]Noting increasing prices, and falling wages, the Chorley weavers objected to the excessive amounts of public money, and correspondingly high taxes, paid to 'place holders' who did not work for their reward. The accusers had George Rose and his annual salary of £3,278 for being Clerk of Parliament in their sights; though this was small beer compared to the £23,117 paid to the Marques of Buckingham as a teller of the exchequer.

Despite the force of their arguments the petitions produced no direct material benefit for the starving populace. [409]In the Parliamentary debate on the weavers' petition championed by Colonel Stanley, Sir Robert Peel suggested a grant of £100,000 for their aid, but Spencer Percival thought it *"impossible to afford any relief."*[410] The judgement of the subsequent subcommittee was that any monetary assistance would have unstated *"pernicious consequences."* This debate highlights the ambiguity of attitudes to the prevailing distress. The reports were placed on the table to be printed, more paper but no aid.

On Thursday the 26th of March 1812 there was a meeting of the Livery of London at the Guildhall. This was a gathering of trades people who were members of the ancient guilds, highlighting the 'respectability' of the agitators. They had met *"to consider the unprecedented situation of the country"*[411] asking for an enquiry into public abuse and the reform of Parliament; their resolutions *"enumerating distresses under which the country laboured."*[412]The aldermen progressing along the front of the hall to take their seats were cheered, or hissed, according to their presumed affiliation. The resolutions had been proposed by the linen draper Robert Waithman. He was a man of substance, but generally treated contemptuously, even by radicals, as a mere shopkeeper with little education.[413] William Cobbett thought him a *"mere coxcomb."* He may have been a self-important and ambitious man, but in the general election of 1818 Waithman was to become the first person from such relatively humble origins to be elected to Parliament.

There were some objections to the purpose of the Guildhall meeting on the grounds of lack of patriotism. However, the seconder, a Mr. Favell considered that any flattering address to the Prince Regent *"would be to ruin both Prince and people."*[414] After the heightened excitement of the assembly a number of protesters moved on to attempt the destruction of the London Exchange where a Mr. Bettle attempted to reason with the rioters, but was abusively ejected from the building and had his clothes tore off him.[415] On the

9th March, 1812, the resolutions of the London Livery were forwarded, with little subsequent effect, to the Prince Regent, at his levee,[416] by the Sherriff and the Remembrencer.[417] On the same day there were riots in Huddersfield *"in consequence of the dearness of provisions and the want of employment."*

In the north of the country Mr. Favell's concerns regarding flattering the Prince Regent were about to materialise. During 1812 the north country appeared to be in a state of rebellion. There was widespread rioting; in some cases, accompanied by the destruction of machinery and factories. It was against this background, and the appeals for aid, that the priority of Samuel Crompton's petition to Parliament was judged. The letters from Samuel's children, while he remained in London, related stories of the troubles fermenting in the Manchester and Bolton area.[418] In April 1812 a public meeting was called in Manchester by the burgesses[419] of that town, in response to a request by 154 signatories *"that were respectable gentlemen"*, to address the Prince Regent. The address was to pledge allegiance or as one newspaper put it *"ardent zeal for the support of his government."*[420] This was seen as a provocation by many who blamed the unpopular Prince for their misery. Several handbills were issued calling on people to attend the meeting and peaceably oppose the address. [421]

Samuel Crompton Junior wrote that on the 8 th of April 1812, a crowd had gathered in St Annes Square, Manchester at 7 o'clock in the morning, 4 hours before the scheduled address to the Prince Regent. The burgesses, having seen the inflammatory literature and the calls for virulent, if not violent opposition, prudently decided to cancel the meeting. Denied their opportunity to heckle and harass, at 10 o clock, a section of the agitated crowd clamored into the Royal Exchange and broke all the windows, chairs and tables. The demonstrators had elected their own Borough Reeve, the chief official of the town. It had been the official Borough Reeve who had arranged and then cancelled the address.

The protestors reaffirmed the resolutions of the London Livery at the Guildhall. One newspaper report suggested, contemptuously, that having passed the several resolutions they *"clapped their chopped (chapped?) hands and threw up their sweaty night caps."*[422] During the agitation one foolhardy individual suggested that the crowd's actions were ineffectual and illegal! This person had to retreat into nearby Mr. Satterfield's shop, a high class linen draper in St Annes Square.

The riot act was read, and the military arrived and restored order. Samuel Juniors letter to his father neglected some salient details of the extent of the destruction in the Manchester Exchange. The committee of the Exchange had refused to allow the upper story dining hall to be used as the meeting place, on the grounds that the swelling numbers of protestors would be too much for the wooden staircase to bear.[423] However, there was extensive damage. All the external windows were broken, and the reading room and its periodicals (*"the diurnal literature"*) set on fire. The chairs it was reported *"represent a lamentable wreck of property"*. All but two of the magnificent chandeliers were smashed and in a symbolic act the *"valuable"* bust of the head of Colonel Stanley, Member of Parliament for Lancashire and head of the Lancashire Militia, was shattered. Colonel Stanley was reaching the end of his political influence. What he made of the destruction of his terracotta[424] proxy, as he recovered from illness in London, is not known. He had always acted independently in presenting pro and antiwar petitions to Parliament, in addition to the petitions for aid, but his strong support for the continuation of the war, to which most of the rioters objected, was well known. Yet Colonel Stanley was no fawning supplicant to the Prince having voted against an increase in his personal allowance in 1795 and aligned with the opposition voting against the bill to make George Prince Regent in 1811.

On the day following the frenzied attack on the Manchester Exchange the supporters of the address met at the Police House to requisition another address, with Sir Robert Peel chairing the meeting. The belated declaration of loyalty to the Prince Regent obtained its signatures by slow more furtive means. The continuing war was a prime cause of the prevalent poverty, but also a generator of patriotic fervor. For example, one observer saw a lost opportunity in the Manchester disturbances to publicly rebuke Napoleon:

"Would that we had told the Arch-Vandal of the continent, ay, the whole world, that conscious of his successful career of murder rapine, and desolation, his menaces have been regarded as bubbles, and that sooner than sacrifice our independence at the wheels of his triumphal car, our privations should equal the misery of his famished and devoted slaves. Faction forbad it."[425]

Though there were examples of proclamations of loyalty to the Prince Regent which provoked further rioting, in other cases disturbances had the more visceral motive of poverty. In a Manchester affray it was reported that a general cry went up *"now is our time for a cheap loaf"*[426] When in April 1812, the manufacturers of Bolton published their own loyal address this was no mere proclamation of loyalty to the crown, though that was evident. They believed that stories of the Prince Regents desire to continue to prosecute the war were *"mischievous rumours."* Their declaration was a heart rending appeal for assistance. The manufacturers had great sympathy for the distressed state of the poor. Many smaller producers would be perilously close to this condition themselves. The address described the abject poverty of many people in Lancashire:

"Their pale and ghastly countenances - their squalid and ragged clothing - their houses emptied of furniture - their half starved and half clad children crying for bread, or begging with piteous moan from door to door for the dole of charity, which grieves and almost bleeds, that it cannot supply their wants, together with the wretched poor that fills our workhouses, or claim parochial relief."[427]

Along with general agitation for political reform and protests against economic distress there was the destruction of machinery, in some cases the torching of whole factories. The Luddite riots lasted for a short period of time, 1812 until early 1813, covering the period that Samuel Crompton was pursuing his cause in London. The objectives of Luddite activity varied. In the Nottingham area they involved disputes over wages, where in the presence of the Combination Acts there was no collective bargaining over pay. It was not the use of machinery per se that was objected to but rather the use of the machines by some employers to degrade wages and working conditions. In the north and Lancashire, it was the effects of new machines in spinning and weaving on employment. [428] For some the motivation for machine breaking was political; though the extent to which this was the case has been a matter of debate.[429] Regardless of intention, the extent of dissent and the Luddite disturbances generated a fear of insurrection among politicians.

Amid the riot and disorder in the north was Colonel Ralph Fletcher, mine owner, magistrate and George and William Crompton's commanding officer in the Bolton militia. To forestall what he perceived as revolutionary activities Ralph Fletcher considered any devious means to be fair practice. This 'philosophy' included the use of agent provocateurs, and the instigation of riots by the authorities. The creation of culprits from the malleable poor. There is a note in Home Office papers where Fletcher inveigles against *"female orators sporting the cap of liberty"* and Orator Hunt and thinks *"that under whatever pretext they may be called, they ought to be suppressed."*[430] When in December 1819 Parliament debated the extension of the powers of magistrates, it was the behaviour of Ralph Fletcher that was cited as an objection to the proposal.[431]

Fletcher was one of the officials present at the infamous Peterloo massacre in 1819. He was, and remains, a controversial figure, viewed as the epitome of public service and an emblem of civic pride, or as an oppressor of working people. He mirrors Samuel Colquitt in the contrasting aspects of his personality, civic virtue combined with ruthlessness. In March 1812 Samuel Crompton Junior informed his father that Colonel Fletcher was in London but wrote that there was no assistance that he could offer, as he had little knowledge of the trade.[432] The Fletcher family were coal mine owners not cotton manufacturers. But Ralph Fletcher was also involved in an infamous Luddite disturbance that directly involved the Crompton brothers, emphasising the immediacy of these disturbances for Samuel's cause. It was the distress of the domestic weavers of Bolton that underpinned a renowned and tragic series of events.

Insurrection Close to Home

Captain Dewhurst of Halliwell (1716-1806), in his book of sketches, drew and coloured a picture of Lostock Hall, Bolton Le Moors.[433] Built in 1563 it was a timber and plaster construction with moss bespattered grey slate roofing. All that remains of this grand building today is the gate house; an addition of 1591. As with many ancient mansions, the hall became a farmhouse in the eighteenth century, and being such a large and old property, fell into neglect and disrepair, so that by 1816 it had been almost entirely demolished. During the year 1812 there may still have been some glimpse of its former magnificence, with its ornamental chimneys, mullioned windows with dashes of colour. Some levels of the hall were corbelled[434] with overhanging roofs.[435] The surrounding bogland, known as the Red Moss, afforded views of sheets of water reflecting heavy skies and circling crows. The towering gatehouse, with its heraldic shield, abutted a naturally formed, pleasingly rough edged pond. The landscape was not one of the stylistic creations of the landscape gardeners of the great estates, such as Capability Brown, but as with the encircling moat, a gothic symbol of personal wealth and its determined defence. This area of bog and marled earth was the site of Catholic recusancy, with secret gatherings and a chapel hidden deep behind the wooden walls of the hall. In the eighteenth and early nineteenth century the area may have been suffused with a sense of menace.

In Dewhurst's painting there are two boys sitting on a rock by the pond, one bowing his head in what looks like gentle shame while a man, perhaps a gentleman farmer, points accusingly towards the towering hall. Or! perhaps he is relating the legend of Lostock Hall, and the boy is drooping his head in dread, or tittering disbelief. The legend involves two prominent families, the Andertons and the Heatons and is a story of foul dealing and financial ruin.

The Andertons lived in the old mansion house in the sixteenth century and had raised a mortgage from the owners of the property, the Heatons'. The legend says that on the day that the loan was due for repayment the Andertons bolted all the doors to the property. They refused to respond to the frantic entreaties of the Heaton family who had raced to the Hall, eager to claim their money. As midnight passed the mortgage was foreclosed, and the weary heckling Heaton's' rode away with empty purses, facing financial ruin. The rivers Douglas and Croal begin their rise as small streams in the bogland, to then reach back into the moorland hills. The legend has it that no horse would willingly cross these streams until the rightful owners of Lostock Hall, the Heaton's', were back in their ancient home.

The marled ground encompassing the mansion was the site of several farming and weaving families. This included the Bromilows (Bromileys, Bromly), farmers and weavers who grazed their sheep on the surrounding Horwich Moor. A will for Joseph Bromilow, dated 1789, indicates the importance of the looms for their welfare and demonstrates that, at that time, the lot of the weaver was a comfortable and prosperous one.[436] Joseph was able to leave 100 pounds in trust to his son George, and a large spinning wheel to his three daughters Betty, Alice and Ellen. One pair of looms was left to his son William, another pair to his son Peter. Falling short of a factory this was a large family enterprise. Bequeathing the looms to the male members of the family undoubtedly reflected the higher status of the weaver. The will included his two grandchildren as beneficiaries, and he felt confident in dividing the remainder of his estate into one ninths to include all the family.

In the early 1790s weavers sported fine clothes, private carriages, appropriated their own space in inns. They often displayed a symbolic five pound note in the brim of their hats, as they promenaded about the town. A weaver was a gentleman! In 1793 the Manchester Mercury published a list of thirty deserters from His Majesties Manchester Marine Corps, thirteen of which were weavers. [437] No other occupational group was so well represented; including spinners of which there was just one. Though the 40 shillings reward to anyone informing on the deserters may have rendered their escape precarious. However, this happy situation was about to change. The Bromilows suffered from the increased mechanisation of weaving that made their craft based skills redundant. A generation later in 1817 Joseph's son John Bromilow died intestate. [438]

On February 27th, 1812, Lord Byron rose to his feet in the House of Lords and made an impassioned plea on behalf of the stocking weavers of Nottinghamshire, a county he had just visited to witness the extent of rioting and machine breaking. While using the contemporary description of these acts as 'outrages' Byron nether the less argued that:

" The perseverance of these miserable men in their proceedings tends to prove that nothing but absolute want could have driven a large, and once honest industrious , body of people, into the commission of excesses so hazardous to themselves and, their families, and the community."[439]

Byron continued, pointing out that despite the heavy presence of the military, police and the. preparedness of the magistrates very few suspects had been apprehended save:

"A few men liable to conviction, on the clearest evidence, of the capital crime of poverty; men who had been nefariously guilty of lawfully begetting several children, whom thanks to the times! they are unable to maintain."

He further reflected on the new machines which had displaced so many workers and *"produced goods of inferior quality,"* pointing to the primacy of personal enrichment, rather than the welfare of the common people. Byron's speech and the petitions from Bolton and Manchester, along with the representatives of Lancashire, Robert Peel and Colonel Stanley were pressurising London politicians to take account of the poverty in the north.

These disturbances were not new, for example the destruction of Arkwright's factory at Birkacre in 1779. There was also an incident in Bolton, in 1808, known as the "Flash Fight". Fireworks illuminated the night sky to signal illicit meetings, or the start of an attack. The Reverend Bancroft, vicar of Bolton, was in fear of his life from the nightly clamour, violence, and threats to his person, thinking that *"his secular office was inconsistent with his pastoral care."*[440] The Reverend had been charged with reading the riot act[441] to a potentially riotous assembly. Indeed no one else seemed willing to do this. However, the potent mixture of reverence for the cloth, Bancroft's eloquence and the threat of the military becalmed the crowd.[442] The degree of organization guiding these riots was further refined during the later Luddite disturbances.

In April 1812, as Samuel Crompton paced the streets of London canvassing for his reward from Parliament some of the hand loom weavers of Bolton decided to commit an act of sabotage. Not this time a spontaneous outbreak of disorder to challenge the diplomatic skills of a Reverend Bancroft, but a carefully planned attack. There was a network of secret societies with oaths and bonds swore on pain of death. While some disturbances were no doubt spontaneous, planned events were more prone to manipulation by government agent provocateurs, so called 'black faces'. While George and William Crompton proudly paraded in their finery with the Bolton militia the Luddites marched and drilled in the sodden, hidden delphs of the remote areas of the local moorland, provoking the shrieks of scattering grouse rather than eliciting the applause of ladies.

Samuel wrote to his sons on the 18th of April 1812, describing his daily meeting with Sir Robert Peel and his daughter, and their walks through St James Park.[443] He was troubled by a letter from his errant daughter Betty. He remarked that he could not vanquish the concerns of a parent, so his sons should remember their responsibilities as brothers. George replied on the 28th of April to say that Betty had been cared for and had borne a son. If this was some consolation to Samuel, there was other news that would inevitably disturb him. George informed his father that " *we have some unpleasant commotions here*" a gross understatement of the disturbances prevalent in Lancashire at the time.[444] He described how Samuel Junior, along with hundreds of others, had been made a constable. A captain's guard had been mounted and George and his brother William had been called to a tour of duty. A *"great number of prisoners had been taken"* which he estimated as upwards of 40, with 12 committed to Lancaster castle. Many families had received threats to burn down their houses and were in fear of their lives. These included Mr. J. Ainsworth, Colonel Fletcher, Joseph Pimbley's business partner Peter Hewitt, and Joseph Ridgeway, all prominent men in textile bleaching and manufacturing, and some of Samuel's invited expert witnesses.

Prominent among the disorders was the burning down of the weaving mill of Thomas Rowe and James Dunscough, just two miles distant from Lostock Hall, in Westhaughton. In a meeting held at nearby Flapper Fold, Chowbent there was a call by a Mr. Sidlow to " *burn yon factory down.* "Sidlow was probably a government agent provocateur as in the aftermath of the destruction of the factory he was not arrested.[445] A Mr. John Stones proclaimed himself „*Oliver Cromwell*" and appointed captains. Stones was another government spy acting on the orders of Colonel Fletcher,[446] the master of intrigue and provocation.

In the buildup to the destruction of the factory there was a merry dance of comings and goings by the hussars, the constables and the militia. There was only rumour to act upon and an underestimate of the risks to the mill. The Scots Greys were called to the factory, but they retreated believing that for the moment the premises were safe, but as a precaution left some firearms behind for the use of the loyal members of the workforce. Then the militia were beckoned, to once again depart believing that all was well. Within the interstices of these comings and goings the prospective rioters found their way to the mill.

It was claimed that the assault was led by a disabled boy on crutches, an unlikely scenario, but Abraham Charleston was subsequently the focus of controversy and tragedy. The rioters set to work in a frenzy of anger and destruction. The mangled power looms were piled up on the factory floor and the women hand loom weavers danced singing, clogs clacking, around the tangled heap. At a critical point someone bellowed *"torch the factory"*. A young lad, John Bromiley, was dragged from the midst of the rioters by his mother, an act of maternal love that would save him from the dreadful retribution of the law. It is not certain that John Bromilow was a Bromilow of Lostock Hall, though that is a strong possibility. Certainly, the Bromilows typify the weaving and farming families that suffered from the movement of weaving into the manufacturing process.

The militia, including George and William Crompton, where eventually called out to quell the riot and arrest the culprits. They pursued the Luddite rioters along country lanes, through meadows, hedgerows and over the hills, through woods and pasture. They no doubt extended their fevered search to the bog lands surrounding Lostock Hall. We can imagine, consistent with the legend, that their horses baulked at crossing the rivers Douglas and Croal. The Anderton's had not returned to Lostock Hall and the weavers were desperately pursuing their own 'birthright'. However, the rioters were no match for the militia, and they were soon captured, transported to Lancaster castle and imprisoned to await trial by a special tribunal.

Sir Richard Clayton interrogated some of the witnesses to the events. He dispatched a self congratulatory letter to one of the presiding judges, Justice Simon Le Blanc (1758-1816).[447]Le Blanc had been involved in some cases where he assisted working people,[448]but he was renowned for adopting a severe stance when presiding over the Luddite trials. The second justice for the special commission was the equally implacable Sir Baron Thompson. This lethal double act was regularly used for Luddite trials, in both Lancashire and Yorkshire.[449] Richard Clayton stated

".... no personal exertion was spared on my part, and by temperance added to firmness, I have had the happiness of preserving the public peace, not a single breach of it."[450]

So, within his own jurisdiction he had preserved the peace. However, the reaction to this destruction of the mill was very different to the treatment of the rioters who burned down Birkacre in 1779, when the Quarter Sessions adopted a measured and humane approach to the disturbances.[451]

The offenders expected hard but not unduly severe punishment. They had not accounted for the continuing war and the fear of revolution, not to mention the lobbying power of an affronted manufacturing class. Of those tried for setting fire to the mill 4 were found guilty and received the death penalty, 11 were acquitted - including John Bromiley whose mother had restrained him. Eleven prisoners were charged with taking an illegal oath, the majority transported to Australia. The executions were even more heart rendering due to the fate of Abraham Charleston, a mere 16 year old, though his age was disputed. It was argued that he was merely 13 years of age. His cry for his mother on the scaffold echoes shamefully down the centuries. Just a hint of the humanity evinced by Byron might have saved Abraham Charleston.

When on Friday July 10th, 1812, Parliament discussed how best to preserve the public peace the Westhaughton incident was cited. Lord Castlereagh moved for the extension of parliamentary powers, including the right of local militias to enter premises and search for arms. The Member of Parliament for Bedford, Mr. Samuel Whitbread raised a compelling objection to the proposals.[452] He stated that of the 40 persons who met on Deane Moor prior to the disturbances 10 of these were members of the local militia *"disguised with blackened faces."* Whitbread objected strongly to this form of spying and claimed that one of the militia men had proposed the burning down of the workhouse. When challenged because of the possible loss of life the militia man is reported to have said.

"Oh, the devil care for that" "let us do all the mischief we possibly can."

The tumult in the North of England provided the distressing and at times violent back cloth to Samuel Crompton's entreaties to Parliament. His sons, under the command of the notorious Colonel Fletcher, were involved in maintaining order in circumstances where Samuel himself was likely to have some sympathy with the plight of the weavers. The consequences of technological change had moved beyond his simple hope for the betterment of the cottage worker's lot. The key figures involved in Crompton's campaign, such as Colonel Stanley and Robert Peel, were at the heart of parliamentary debate and reaction to these events, with George Rose a symbol of place men and corruption. There had been opposition to disbursements of money to the poor on the grounds of a growing fear of insurrection and revolution, which along with the barrage of petitions arriving in the House, must have challenged any spirit of sympathy, sapping any generosity for other causes. Samuel Crompton's leverage was not that of the well connected Colquitt. He would now, more than ever, need the support of the Chancellor and Prime Minister, Spencer Percival.

Chapter Fifteen

The Campaign of 1812

Though faith had feinted when assailed by fear, Hope to the soul had **whispered**, *Persevere!*

Edward Shore, by George Crabbe, Tales 1812

The Swan with Two Necks

On the 13th of January 1812 Samuel Crompton arrived at the Swan with Two Necks Inn, Lad Lane. The coach journey from Manchester to London had taken three wearisome, bone shaking days. He was exhausted and experienced a degree of fatigue that would cling to him throughout his enforced stay in the capital, as he trod the streets of what he termed *"this overgrown place".*[453] This was the beginning of his concerted attempt to appeal to Parliament. Sir Robert Peel had advised him to set out his case and secure the support of the Members of Parliament for the county of Lancaster, each knowledgeable about the cotton trade and Samuel's contribution to its prosperity. So, Samuel Crompton, diffident, but with the eagerness of a self-righteous injured man settled down in the Swan with Two Necks to promote his cause: for *"the honour of God, the good of my neighbours, my family and myself."*[454]

The splendid Swan Inn, on Lad Lane near the junction with Milk Street in Cheapside, boasted a grand enclosed central yard. Embracing the burgeoning night and day traffic of coaches and horses, the space was enclosed by railed galleries giving access to the rooms. Given the density of building around the inn it had the unusual feature of stabling the horses underground. Meanwhile, the galleries and the courtyard were a vibrant melee of people seeking rest, doing business, or congregating for onward travel. Gazing down on this activity the effect of the galleries was to suggest the framework of a Jacobean theatre, and it was from this 'stage' that the Crompton letters provide the 'comedy' and the 'tragedy' of a script detailing his pursuit of those he called *"the great ones of the* earth."[455]

William Hone in his 'pithily' titled *"The Everyday Book: Or Everlasting Calendar of Popular Amusements, Sports, Pastime, Ceremonies, Customs and Events, Incident to Each of the Three Hundred and Sixty Five Days, in the Past and Present Times,"* noted that the Swan with two Necks was a corruption of the swan with two nicks. [456]Two nicks had been made on the beaks of the Kings swans. Hone chastised publicans using this name stating that the *"ignorant landlord hoisted this foul misrepresentation."*[457] This matter was raised by Sir Joseph Banks himself at the annual meeting of the Antiquarian Society in 1810.[458] In contrast to Hone, Banks, the author of the *"Ladies Museum"* preferred to refer to the *"ingenuity of the painter"* in having a sign with two necks emerging from a single swan. [459]

The succession of landlords of the Inn on Lad Lane may have been ignorant of the debates concerning this piece of folklore. Artistically inclined or not they were certainly commercially astute as the inn was the premier location for the transport of people and parcels to and from London and the North. According to *"Crosby's Merchants and Tradesman's Pocket Dictionary: By a London merchant assisted by several experienced tradesmen,"* a passenger could travel from the Swan with Two Necks to Northampton and then to Market Harborough, Leicester, Loughborough, Derby, Ashbourne, Leek, Macclesfield, Stockport, Manchester, Bolton, Chorley and onwards through several more stops to Carlisle. [460] Britton in his book, *Beauties of England and Wales*, thought that the inn was an excellent one, being furnished with every convenience for travelers. Moreover, *"It is much frequented by gentlemen belonging to the Manchester trade, and others, from the North of England."*[461] The Swan with Two Necks was a node in a transport system reaching eagerly into the heartland of the cotton manufacturing districts and beyond, feeding an insatiable London market and supplying an expanding export trade.

So remaining connected to the North of England, with ready access to the postal system, business contacts, gossip and information Samuel Crompton began his campaign. It was not an easy process. Restless and impatient, but never in his letters straying from his natural propensity for detail and care, he was constantly set back. Colonel Stanley was ill and confined to his bed[462]. Sir Robert Peel was not in town.[463]Lever *"had left yesterday for Bolton."* Also noticeably absent for long periods of time were the representatives of the constituencies of Lancashire.[464] On one occasion the House of Commons could not *"muster a house"* and had to be adjourned.[465]

There was an early indication of what he might expect from Parliament. Mr. Lee was eager to manage Samuel's expectations. The government he claimed, *"simply has no money so he should expect very little.*[466] However, constantly in Samuel Crompton's mind were the previous beneficiaries of government largesse. In 1732 Sir Thomas Lombe, his patent having expired, received a Parliamentary award of £14,000 for his silk throwing machine. Samuel asked his children to research into this case. [467]

To match Lombe, or gain any significant reward, he would need to establish a group of influential contacts. The Crompton papers contain a list of such prominent individuals, and their addresses. The list includes William Wilberforce, Sir Robert Peel, General Gascoyne and Samuel Whitbread together with the two Stanley's Colonel and Lord Stanley.[468] No doubt there were some individuals on this inventory of celebrity with whom he felt more at ease with than others.

The process of seeking a reward from Parliament for an invention, or a notable contribution to the national good, was invariably complex. There were several demanding stages to pass through. A petition had to be composed, and several drafts of that would follow, working with an experienced clerk at the Houses of Parliament (a Mr. White in this case). Hopefully this was perused by the influential figures who would support your cause. Then a committee must be convened to listen to witnesses, consider the petition, and publish a report. Of course, the witnesses must be recruited and organised to be in the capital at the correct time and to say helpful things; not an easy task when most of them are busy manufacturers residing in the north of the country. An unexpected turn of events, or in the case of Thomas Ainsworth the onset of gout where he could not travel *"but at the hazard of his life"* could upset any plan.[469] Then with arguments marshalled and 'warriors' mustered, Parliament itself must finish its proceedings for the day and turn itself into a committee of supply, to act on the report and grant or deny an award. So much to possibly go wrong. In addition, you most certainly needed a champion, a member of Parliament of some eloquence, charisma and strength of argument to emphatically seal the case and ensure your deserved reward.

The family were not passive observers of what was going on in London. They acted as promoters of the cause, research assistants and go between for Samuel and the Manchester manufacturers. They also expressed concern for their father's health and wellbeing. Particularly in the later stages of his time in the city, which he considered over long, he suffered from excessive tiredness and loss of appetite, occasioned by the physical effort of tramping the streets of what Boswell referred to as the *"Ocean of London."* He flitted from one potential ally to another, visiting the Houses of Parliament, where he would 'haunt' the lobby. There was also the mental fatigue caused by unbearable uncertainty, constant prevarication and delay. Samuel missed his children greatly and would often say so, being particularly concerned when George succumbed to illness.[470]

The Crompton correspondence parades us through this labyrinthine process and all its demands and frustrations. Though Samuel Crompton arrived in London in January 1812, it was not until 24th June that his hopes and ambitions were finally addressed by Parliament. Consequently, he continued to incur great expense, wanting at one point to purchase a new suit, but having to make do with his current level of dishevelment and exposure to the elements:[471]

"...the black breeches I had are as rotten as a pear and I have no other even the pockets are so rotten that I have had to make new ones."

Daily living expenses were another nagging concern and as early as the 21st of January 1812 he wrote to the manufacturer Mr. Yates to seek his support and added: *"please to give me an answer by return of post as I am here at an expense and would wish to stop as soon as possible."*[472]

Early in the campaign we have the re-appearance of George Rose MP. In a letter dated 15th of January 1812 there is an amusing example of Samuels persistence.[473] Having been put off and advised by Rose to make an appointment for the following morning, he attended the arranged meeting, eager to launch his campaign, arriving on the doorstep at Palace Yard, Westminster, one hour early. Mr. Rose, not surprisingly, was very busy! Samuel was not to be deterred. He followed Rose to a church service, at the Abbey Church, and listened to a sermon. Then he followed him to another church, St Margarets, and listened to yet another sermon. Replete with sermons and a surfeit of spiritual guidance he followed Rose back home where, with perhaps a little irony, he told Samuel that he may call upon him at any time. Trudging after George Rose who was no doubt searching for sanctuary, in the manner of the Cobbett's anecdote of the trailing supplicants, and enduring two sermons,' appeared to pay off. Rose - one assumes sincerely - expected to speak to the Chancellor of the Exchequer and Prime Minister Spencer Percival that day. How optimistic Samuel Crompton must have felt to be one step away from the powerful and controlling Spencer Percival, who could promote and possibly decide his case.

Bringing Things to Perfection

Samuel Crompton, having spent his day tramping the streets of London, would return to his small room; a sanctuary surrounded by the bustle of the Swan with Two Necks. There, in the eye straining, flickering candlelight, he wrote his almost daily letters to his sons and supporters. In this he was meticulous, carefully noting the time of the correspondence, straying into few personal matters and at times betraying a keen sense of privacy and concern about confidentiality. How does Seddon *"know that he is in town."*[474] Keep this secret. *"Tell no others but the Manchester gentlemen."*[475] His anxiety is apparent throughout, as is the shifting tide of his hopes and expectations. Yet all is not solitary confinement in Lad Lane and the letters allude to at least one instance of *supping* with a friend, a potential witness for the committee, Richard Ainsworth bleacher, son of Thomas Ainsworth. [476]

On his occasional visits to London George Crompton accompanied his father to various dinner parties. Given the emphasis upon conversation and 'performance' at these events Samuel Crompton's experience must have been excruciating. George expressed disappointment at his father's reticence and reluctance to press his case over dinner, and on other occasions. In contrast to the dashing and loquacious George, we can imagine Samuel sitting sullenly at the table, dreading the next address to his person. Without appetite, shifting his food about his plate, hoping that time would race unnaturally forward to draw a curtain across the evening. Contemplating his predicament, the candlelight illuminating the animated features of his dinner companions may have a harsher glare than the comforting solitary light in his room at the Swan with Two Necks. Samuel preferred communicating by correspondence or one to one business conversations with trusted friends.

Meandering through Westminster Samuel would have strolled down St James Street, there to endure the torment of walking past the bow window of Whites Gaming Club. Loafing on an exclusive table in this window, exchanging witticisms and caustic observations, would have been Beau Brummel, Lord Alvaney, and their aristocratic Dandy friends. A cardinal entertainment was to comment on the attire of passersby. One can imagine that the vision of this simple ill clad north country man would have excited some derision. Whites was a club where gentlemen would wager £3,000 on which of two trickling rain drops reached the base of the window first.[477] More money changed hands in bets than Samuel Crompton might yet receive from Parliament. The sarcastic observers were not even beholden to the inventor for the quality cloths that made up their clothes, as their preferred material was fine Irish linen. Perhaps they wagered on how long the poor man's trousers might stay up before reaching the end of St James. He would be viewed as a Newcastle collier ship coming into port rather than a resplendent frigate. This perception of Samuel Crompton would be material to his chances of success and the expectations of others regarding the reward he would be satisfied with. This was another aspect of Regency society that militated against him. However, the new manufacturing class, who were less engaged in such foppery, might better understand his worth and achievement?

What Samuel needed was evidence of the impact of his invention and the extent and vigour of the support for his claims. He worked tirelessly on these matters. In his first letter to Spencer Percival, he enclosed a history of the Hall i'th' Wood machine, a draft of the required petition, and the 1811 survey detailing the extent of the mule's adoption throughout the cotton and woolen industries of the North.[478] Moreover, when the time came his friends from the North would not let him down and they would offer more than ample evidence of the significance of his invention. Gathering a body of informed and influential witnesses was, along with other matters - as Samuel reflected - *"a herculean task."*[479] From the very first day in London he was asking his friend Kennedy to suggest *"intelligent"* people to support his case.

On his second day in the capital Samuel had been frantically meeting with influential people. He wrote that he saw a Mr. George Rennie, an *"engine man"* and a *"very intelligent man known to the Prince Regent."*[480] He also met several members of Parliament and agreed to meet a Mr. Giddy, the following day, in the Swan with Two Necks. This was the scientist Davies Giddy who offered advice, particularly mathematical, to Trevithick, James Watt and Humphrey Davey. Giddy was pivotal to contemporary scientific circles[481] and was a useful person to engage with, though Samuel noted *"What may arise I cannot yet say."* He also met with a Mr. Johnson concerning the petition, and of course his letters refer to Lee, McConnel, Kennedy and Ewart, the Manchester gentlemen. He gave permission for the Manchester men to see his letters and also asked his sons to encourage suggestions of *"an intelligent man or two"* to act as witnesses. Thus, the correspondence and frenetic meetings and arrangements began. His letters are a constant reminder of his exhausting programme. For example, Mr. Seddon asked him to call if he is that way, but he *"really has no time to spare."*[482]

Samuel was particularly concerned that Peel and his business associate William Yates[483] should be united in his cause.[484] He considered Robert Peel of critical importance to his campaign,

"....it is astonishing how much authority Sir Robert Peel has in all things relating to the cotton trade."[485]

He had written to Yates on the 21st of January asking him to forward a letter of introduction to Sir Robert Peel.[486] Another key actor in Samuel's campaign was Lord Edward Stanley; known as 'tongs', on account of his tall, thin, long limbed figure, combined with a large head. In addition to his military career,[487] both with the yeomanry and the full time army, he was a naturalist and a collector of zoological curiosities. Lord Stanley appears as one of the more optimistic protagonists in Samuel's cause. For example, in a letter dated 30th January 1812 Samuel Crompton wrote of Lord Stanley *"attacking"* the Chancellor of the Exchequer Spencer Percival. *" He has wrote to him twice and twice attacked him going into the house,"*[488] a comical illusion given Stanley's height and demeanour. This was in the early days of the enterprise, and one wonders if over the long course of this campaign sufficient enthusiasm was sustained by his erstwhile supporters. In a letter dated 10th March 1812[489] Samuel bemoaned:

"....it is very tiring that after all my anxious care, not to have some evidence at the critical moment to come forward but I fear that they are weary with my story. it would have not have been so very much but perhaps it is what they have not time to spend on."[490]

There are more echoes of the great financial strain of his prolonged stay in London. He pursued money owed to him by Mr. Peter Markland of Stockport, due from the 1802 Manchester subscription for the Mule, this under the guise of wishing to complete the list of supporters of his current petition, or as he put it assisting him in his *"arduous task."*[491] In other letters he wrote that he was keeping within expenses as best he could and suggested that if he should need some money his children might get an *"order from some friends."*

It was not until the 7th of March 1812 that Samuel wrote that he expected the Parliamentary Committee to be convened, on the Thursday of that week, or the Monday of the next. In a final round of consultations Mr. Blackburne was pleased with the steps that Samuel had taken, and Robert Peel offered his last piece of advice.[492] Samuel, clearly obsessed over the detail required for the committee to allow them to comprehend the significance of his invention. He appealed for the witnesses arriving from the North to bring with them *"some examples of spinning as those he has are defaced through having been carried about so long."*[493] Samuel's moment of truth was drawing closer. Anticipating the climax of his campaign he rallied his 'troops'; *"hoping you are all well and each attending to his post."*

As the time arrived for the committee to meet, Samuel had some notion of the rewards that he would find acceptable, unacceptable, or indeed insulting. Gone was his earlier humility were almost any contribution would be seen as an act of kindness, replaced now with a more steadfast expectation of around f50,000.[494] This shift in his expectations may have arisen from the drawn out nature of his quest, and the implicit and at times vocal support that he received from the highest placed individuals. The proposed committee was a notable collection of prominent parliamentarians including Spencer Percival, Sir Joseph Banks and William Wilberforce. Samuel had every reason to believe that his petition would be favourably received. He had been treated with kindness, at times with enthusiasm. What would the outcome be?

Back in Bolton and Manchester his sons were eagerly awaiting the results of their father's earnest efforts in London. His letters echoed the encouragement of leading parliamentary figures, including the apparent sympathy of the Prime Minister Spencer Percival. Prosperous cotton manufacturers and bleachers were willing to testify in his favour. His family would have reasons to be optimistic. However, Gilbert French reported that the children did not believe that he had done enough.[495] If this was true then they did not consider the physically demanding task he had faced together with the frustrations of his ill health, plus the intermittent absence from Parliament and London of some of the key people in his campaign. His letters abound with fruitless trips to Parliament. He also wished his case to stand on its own merits - an honourable vindication - rather than its success depending upon entertaining or cajoling individuals.

In March 1812 Samuel met with Spencer Percival. [496] He was pleased with the meeting, which Lord Stanley, Sir Robert Peel and others attended. Commenting on the petition, he thought that Percival *"did not appear hostile to it"*. Again, he was phlegmatic, perhaps disingenuous, writing that whatever the result he would be satisfied. He thought that if the petition, memorial and arguments of those present at the meeting were not enough to *"capture the attention of government"* then *"I know not what is."*

Spencer Percival was a difficult character to deal with. Though personable and charitable he was a pathologically single minded, self-righteous individual.[497] Arguably, the unbreakable resolve of this deeply unpopular man ultimately achieved victory over Napoleon. Parliament and the country wished to extricate British forces, led by the Duke of Wellington, from the Spanish Peninsular. Seeing beyond the military defeats Percival insisted the army stay, something which proved to be of great strategic significance later in the conflict. To get Spencer Percival on your side meant that victory was assured.

The Committee Meets

On the 6th of March the petition was presented, and a committee appointed.[498] On Wednesday the 18th of March 1812, the Parliamentary committee convened to deliberate on and determine the merits of Samuel Crompton's mule. In the chair was Lord Stanley. The first person to speak was the imposing and influential Sir Robert Peel. He hinted at Arkwright's fortune, amassed from the benefits of the water frame, pointing to the deficiencies of his machine. It could not spin *"weft of any kind, or of producing twist of very fine texture."*[499] This short testimony was then followed by the hapless Mr. John Pilkington, who had advised Samuel to offer his invention for public subscription, with the disastrous results that followed. Here, at least, Pilkington had the opportunity to make amends. He noted the extent to which cotton production was carried out in the United Kingdom using mules, emphatically citing the inadequacy of Samuel's first subscription. George Lee then stated that a second subscription of 1802, having raised no more than £500, had still not adequately compensated Samuel Crompton for the benefits of his machine.

In a cameo performance there was a brief statement by James Watt of the house of Bolton and Watt who noted that about two thirds of the steam engines that he had manufactured had been *"erected for spinning cotton has been applied to turning spindles upon Mr. Crompton's construction.»* Two thirds was an alluring rule of thumb, as it appeared again in the evidence of Mr. Ainsworth, attributing two thirds of the growth in the present trade to the application of the mule. George Daniels, the eminent historian of the Lancashire cotton Industry considered the written report of the committee to have been constructed after the event, rather than being a contemporaneous record of proceedings.[500] In particular, the questions were general and related to information that Samuel had already furnished, including his 1811 survey of the use of the mule. Nether the less the evidence for the impact of the engine appeared clear. There had been a rapid growth of markets for cotton on the continent and domestically.[501] Cloth was now exported to the East, rather than imported.

Though in early February George Lee had encouraged Samuel to have modest expectations, on account of the sorry state of government finances,[502] Lord Stanley was expressing very different sentiments. After the meeting of the committee on the Wednesday, 18th March, he approached Samuel and gave his hand *"the most hearty shake it ever had in this world, his eyes blazing with delight."* Samuel meanwhile was feeling ill and suffering from a loss of appetite. He could not, regardless of Lord Stanley's enthusiasm, shake off a fatalistic view of events. *"So many times,"* he opined he had *"brought things to perfection only to be disappointed."*[503] George Lee continued to be pessimistic and informed McConnel and Kennedy that Mr. Houstoun[504] had intimated to him that Spencer Percival had envisaged a moderate reward, of the order of £2,000. George Lee had objected that Lancashire would not be happy with the award of such a sum. Lee also worried about Samuel's simple north country appearance and the possibility that this had prejudiced the committee, who would see him as being satisfied with a small amount.[505]

By the 24th of March 1812 the committee had produced its report ready for printing and discussion by the House. On the 8 th of April Samuel Crompton made a last respectful appeal to Spencer Percival to support his case. [506] To establish an acceptable minimum sum of money in Percival's mind he wrote:

"I hesitate not to say if I had given (sic) £50,000 for the full enjoyment of what I alone had laboured for and which in justice I had a right to I believe I would have made it more than ten times that sum for myself and family and am certain that my countrymen have made it more than 500 times that sum of value to the national interest."

He informed Percival of his troubles when developing his machine, and how:

"I was literally besieged in my house and hunted when abroad as if some strange being had appeared on earth."

To anticipate the results of his appeal Samuel Crompton retired to Kensington to the stay with his musical friends the Harwoods, where that welcoming family might calm him.[507] He could only wait. His future now lay with the House of Commons.

Chapter Sixteen

The 1812 Overcoat

*"Mr. Brougham had closed his examination and Mr. Stephen was in the course of his cross examination of the same witness, when at about quarter past five o clock, a report of a pistol shot was heard in the House and Gallery; it did not at first interrupt the business of the house, a rush was heard between the door and bar and cries of order. A **whisper** ran round that somebody was shot."*[508]

There is a story, difficult to verify, which may contain an element of truth, that signifies the ill timing of events and the harrowing frustration that Samuel Crompton experienced. It was the ultimate snatching away of opportunity, the most artful slap in the face possible, for this fate battered inventor. Samuel had good reason to believe that the Chancellor of the Exchequer, and de facto Prime Minister, Spencer Percival was a trusted supporter of his cause. On the 11th of May 1812, in the lobby of the House of Commons, Samuel Crompton was chatting with Sir Robert Peel and Mr. John Blackburne, when the Prime Minister approached them. Samuel showed characteristic shyness and reserve. Fearing being drawn into any speculation regarding his award he drifted away, leaving Parliament to decide his fate.[509] Percival was thought to be clutching a parchment on which was written three sums of money. He is reputed to have asked *"What would Crompton like 5,000, 10,000 or 20,000 pounds?"* Not quite what Samuel would have wished to hear, given his hope of £50,000.

Samuel Crompton had not retreated far down the steps outside Parliament when he heard the stomach churning report of a pistol. Spencer Percival had been shot. Lying in a pool of blood, eyes wide with disbelief, he whispered to the MPs, parliamentary officers and petitioners surrounding him; *"I have been murdered."* He had been assassinated by John Bellingham, a ship broker of Liverpool. Bellingham's frustrations originated from a struggle to obtain compensation for his perceived ill treatment over a business deal with the Russian government. He had been imprisoned in Russia, ostensibly on false charges, receiving no assistance from the British ambassador, Lord Granville Levinson Gower. Gower was taking an eighteen month holiday at the time, leaving the matter to his equally unhelpful assistant Sir Stephen Sharp.[510]Pathologically single minded and self-righteous Bellingham believed that he would be seen as a benefactor to the nation and exonerated from any wrongdoing. [511]

Once again Samuel's progress had halted. Percival was reputed to be on his way to the chamber to argue for the £20,000 reward. The committee of supply was postponed. He reported his personal inconvenience. If Bellingham had not committed this crime, *"I believe I should be on my way home."*[512]The murder shocked and saddened Parliament. Lord Chief Justice Eldon was reported to have been emotionally devastated.[513] On the streets of London, and in other parts of the country, the response was very different. Demonstrations were rife, along with street celebrations and the obligatory vitriolic pamphlets. Spencer Percival had been deeply unpopular. He was blamed for the continuation of the war. His 'Orders in Council'[514] that inhibited trade were seen as a cause of poverty and repression.

London was in an anarchic state. The fear of insurrection was keen enough to distract the minds and colour the temperaments of the politicians, diminishing the prominence of the ever pressing Samuel Crompton and his invention. There were riots in Whitehall, and outside Newgate prison, all celebrating the assassination. London was militarised with the yeomanry and the Horse Guards patrolling the streets. Initially scuppered, the transportation of Bellingham to jail, by carriage, was greeted with applause, with wild attempts to shake his hand and congratulate him. The Members of Parliament were sent back to their respective counties to suppress any further insurrection. The priority of the government was to establish order, with the Prince Regent being cited as the next target for assassination.

Strangely, Samuel made no mention of the disturbances. Granted that a letter cannot cover all matters, and his chief purpose was to communicate to his sons the progress of his campaign, it is still an odd omission. His prime concern was the four months he had spent in the city. He wrote that he did not *"know whether he can make the clothes he has hang together until he gets home."*[515] He had thought about returning home and then coming back to London, but even at half the price of the ten or twelve pounds fare *"the difference would be a new suit of clothes."* However, he was not indifferent to the demise of Percival. Stumbling upon the funeral procession, he followed it for two miles.[516]

In the aftermath of Percival's assassination Samuel still had confidence that he could secure a generous award. *"Mr. Houstoun says that we must persevere, we are sure to do well at last."* He wrote, *"indeed everyone that I know sings the same song."* However, ultimately his fatalistic disposition got the better of him. *"What comfort is there in this to rest upon but hope, and what has hope to rest upon while it is just hope it is nothing more than hope not realised."*[517]

On the 14th of May, just two days after the assassination, trekking through Hyde Park in a *"grand and tremendous thunderstorm"* Samuel Crompton was intent on business as usual.[518] He was back at the House of Commons where they were discussing their support for Percival's family. He wished to know when the committee of supply would now convene? The ever tolerant Mr. Blackburne informed him that the House had been concerned with *"solemn"* business, but that the speaker had been consulted and the matter would be addressed at the first available opportunity. Lord Castlereagh, a politician at least as, if not more unpopular than Percival, who was acting as interim Prime Minister, was consulted.[519] His advice was to wait until another Chancellor of the Exchequer had been appointed.

It is difficult to know how Crompton's persistence was taken. There was a curious and unexplained incident where the parliamentary Clerk, Mr. White approached him in the lobby of the House and berated him. Samuel, he said *"had deceived him more than any man he ever met with in the whole course of his practice, and he has done the business for the county of Lancaster more than 32 years and also for many other counties."*[520] Lord Stanley also approached him three times. There is a suspicion that in his lingering Samuel appeared too needy, reinforcing the stereotype of a simple artisan who would be satisfied with little.

§

The execution of Bellingham, scheduled for the 18 th of May 1812, understandably excited a great deal of attention. Whether you were a sympathiser, an outraged citizen or merely the curious with a taste for public executions it was the event to attend. Lord Byron left a ball early! at 3 o clock in the morning, to watch Bellingham's demise, with his old school friends Bailey and Maddox. They observed events from the windows of a house adjacent to Newgate Prison; a service for which the proprietor no doubt received a handsome remuneration.[521] At the time Byron was being feted throughout London for his poetical masterpiece *Child Harold*, and in his words he *"woke up one morning and found himself famous;"* an epigram equally applicable to Bellingham.

The aristocratic political diarist Charles Cavendish, Fulke, Greville (1794-1865), later secretary to the privy council, wrote in his memoirs how he and a fellow student at Christ College, Oxford, though subject to a curfew, jumped out of the window of an apartment to meet a chaise and four, galloping into the pitch black night to witness the execution. Then curiosity sated, raced back to college to avoid discovery.[522] However, overall attendance at the execution was considered disappointing for such a momentous event[523]. It was raining heavily and the authorities, fearing civil disturbance, had put out notices discouraging people from joining the crowd. There had been tragedy at a previous execution. In 1807 Owen Haggerty, John Holloway and Elizabeth Godfrey, were executed for murder and robbery. Some individuals in the dense, agitated, possibly drink fuelled, crowd had feinted or collapsed, leading to the crushing of 100 people, with 27 fatalities.[524]

William Cobbett, despite being incarcerated in Newgate for over 22 months, was able to present a detailed description of the act of assassination, the trial and the execution.[525] In an account published in his radical publication *'Cobbett's Political Register*[526] he sought to correct the false reporting of what he termed the *"hired newspapers"* offering *"a correct view,"* not just to the country, but to the world.[527] His report feigned correspondence with his friend James Paul,[528] of Bursledon in the State of Pennsylvania. He noted that a letter was likely to be intercepted, confiscated or at least read and copied. So, he preferred to communicate through print, in the knowledge that the message was more likely to arrive through:

"...some one of the thousand channels which there is no power capable of blocking up."

The key differences between Cobbett's view and the reporting of the *"hired press"* was reference to the extent of discontent in the country, and the degree of support for Bellingham. Cobbett's evidence was an inference from the presence of a significant military force in the capital, but also stories that would have been relayed to him in Newgate. His description of the Horse Guards is bluntly menacing. They are :

"......a troop of soldiers who ride monstrously big horses, and are armed with swords, pistols and guns - a troop of these were sent for and the mob or populace,[529] *called them murderers."*

There was a standoff in Westminster with the Horse Guards confronting the stubborn populace, who remained there until midnight. Cobbett also described the celebrations in some parts of the country. Nottingham was the scene of jubilant crowds, church bells ringing in celebration. The City of London experienced an outbreak of graffiti on its walls, encouraging the rescue of Bellingham.

Despite the inclement weather, and the risk of disorder, Samuel was interested enough to observe the execution. He wrote to his family, describing the unfolding drama.[530] He was not abroad quite as early as Lord Byron, or Greville and friend, but he woke at 4.00 o clock, then again at 5.00 and finally at 6.00, indicative perhaps of his restless nature. It is not clear if he had planned to attend the execution, he seems to have stumbled upon it. The letter he writes was simply to use up a 'frank' and he has no particular business to write about. This despite the symbolic and tragic act he witnessed.

Samuel was strolling by Westminster when he saw a parade of the richly plumed Horse Guards. Believing that *"the act"* would take place in Westminster Palace Yard he was surprised to see no evidence of the *"dreadful apparatus."* The scaffold was instead being erected at Newgate. William Wordsworth made a similar mistake, suggesting that the authorities may have disseminated misleading information regarding the venue. In Wordsworth's letters to his wife Mary, he constantly alluded to the instability and fragile nature of the times,[531] with the King ill, the self-absorbed Prince Regent unpopular and widespread riot and unrest. He cited Bellingham's crime as a manifestation of the discontent. Cobbett certainly reported that popular prints were directing people to the Palace Yard and saw the change of venue as evidence of the authorities fear of insurrection.[532]

Samuel Crompton arrived at the wet and poignant scene just as Bellingham was chatting to the curate. A moment earlier the calm, collected, as ever sartorially elegant Bellingham, had spoken to the Sheriff and the clergy. While in the antechamber awaiting his fate, he expressed some remorse for the killing of Percival and in characteristic style expressed his deep sympathy for Percival's widow, saying that there can be no one sorrier than he for her loss. So, until the very end Bellingham saw his act as necessary, if unfortunate and tragic in its consequences. From where Samuel stood the curate appeared to bless Bellingham. Then the final act of denouement was committed while Bellingham was not expecting it. Samuel noted that it was the general opinion that the whole procedure was conducted with great humanity.

There were significant differences in reports of the size and behaviour of the crowd attending the execution. One newspaper suggested that attempts to *"hussar"* Bellingham were put down by shouts of *"Silence, Silence!"*[533] Cobbett adopted a different view. It was reported to him that there were thousands in tightly packed attendance. He wrote that the crowd universally expressed support through cries of *"God Bless You,"* repeated several times. The Lancaster Gazette, in contrast, attributed this cry to *"just a score of persons."*[534] In the aftermath of the execution, when Bellingham was finally cut down, there was an unseemly auctioning of his clothes, including the distinctive great coat that is apparent in his portrait. The coat sold for 10 pounds.[535] A story circulated that after *"being laid open"* Bellingham's heart continued to beat for another 4 hours, attesting to the steadfastness of his character. The latter tale might cast some doubt upon Cobbett's sources and his general account of the execution, but there is clear evidence that there was significant support for Bellingham. We may never know the truth as to the size of the crowd, or the dominance of any one vocal faction. Cobbett would invariably exploit the potential for antigovernment propaganda. Equally the press would be circumspect in what it reported.

Samuel wrote, *"I came back they had just cut him down, after that I came here, and wrote this and though it does not concern us, yet it is much to be feared."*[536] He sought reassurance from Mr. White who considered that the new chancellor *"whoever that would be must attend to every agreement that Spencer Percival made."* Crompton's mind was focused entirely on his cause rather than the tragedy of Percival's death and the pathos of Bellingham's fate. He bemoaned the fact that it had taken two months *"since the report was submitted, to complete one hour's business.* "Like Bellingham he considered himself a subject of cruel treatment. How ironic that he witnessed the execution of the man who had shot Spencer Percival because the government did not recognise his right to compensation for the indignities he had suffered in Russia. Samuel Crompton was also appealing for compensation for his indignities, through the unrecognised contribution of his invention to the national good.

Great Expectations

Eleven days after the execution of Bellingham, the mishaps of Samuel's youngest son John (1791-1864) remind us of the continuing war with France. John having escaped the command of Captain Colquitt and evaded his father on his second retreat to Liverpool in 1809 had continued to serve in the merchant marine. While sailing home from South America his ship[537] had been captured, near Bermuda, by two French frigates and a sloop of war.[538] The French had plundered the ship and scuttled her. The forlorn sailors were deprived of their belongings and garb other than just enough to protect their modesty. While they were kept prisoners *"many weeks"* the marauding French frigates captured another ship off Cadiz Then judging them to be more trouble than they were worth, the English captives were *"sent home with joyful hearts."* Arriving in Plymouth John wrote home for some money, which was duly received.

The French frigates Ariadne, Arachno, Herald and L'Andromache variously combined to capture, plunder and destroy English vessels in the West Indies. During early 1812 the Mameluke, which may have acted as the prison ship for the English sailors, also sailed with the Herald and L'Andromache to destroy 13 American and 11 English vessels.[539] In early May 1812 the captain of an American schooner, based in the sugar island of Antigua, was boarded by a party of sailors from these ships. The captain observed several English prisoners which he understood to have been taken from a brig from Antigua, which the French had captured and burned.[540] John may have been one of those sailors. Around the time that John Crompton was arriving at the capital's docks the Ariadne and Andromache of 44 guns each, and Mameluke brig of 16 guns were destroyed by the British ships the Growler and the Northumberland, this at the cost of five men killed and twenty wounded on the Northumberland; there is no record of French losses.[541]

Arriving exhausted, from Plymouth, at the Port of London, John made his way home to Bolton on foot *"with just a few shillings in his pocket."* Samuel's Kensington friends the Harwoods were surprised that his eldest son had not sought the further assistance of his father's business acquaintances in London.[542] Perhaps this very proud young man thought that his presence would be an embarrassment to his father and hinder his efforts in Parliament. Harwood asked Samuel if he did not approve the spirit *"which led him to persevere in the profession he has once chosen."* Samuel was reputedly at the docks in London when John arrived. His son exhibited such a miserable condition that he did not recognise him. [543] Preoccupied with the deliberations of Parliament, disturbed by the riots at home, the pall of Percival's death, it is no surprise that Samuel did not spot John disembarking.

When the time arrived for his case to be presented to the House, Samuel Crompton still firmly believed that he merited an award of at least £50,000.

Writing to Mr. White he used a rather belabored engineering analogy of bringing the metals and materials together, and not expecting *"a tinkling toy"* in return. [544]The letter betrayed his anxiety. He hoped that White had ensured that everyone involved had complete knowledge of the case; *"that the workmen (the politicians) are well informed of every necessary portion of materials."* He considered that *"every man should be at his post aiding and assisting in every way possible way that it may sound far and wide the honour of the British name."* He did not consider that the parlous state of government finances should be an obstacle to receiving his reward.

"....to talk of the poverty of this nation sounds like ridiculous nonsense in my ears, the immense sums that are raised and by what means and if £50,000 is a serious national object they are at liberty to set as they please."

He would also he stated, *"be very happy to return to his family and his usual employ."* The scene was set for Parliament's deliberations.

The Mules Fall Silent

The new Prime Minister was Robin Banks Jenkinson, Earl of Liverpool (1770-1828) who was renowned for his suppression of radicalism, both in 1812 and after both the Revolutionary and Napoleonic wars. He was considered an even tempered and prudent man, though a little slow to come to decisions. Walter Bagehot thought him an *"extreme moderate."*[545] Described as an ungainly and awkward figure, there were several complaints of him while he headed the war office, including by Charles Castlereagh, Lord Castlereagh's brother, and the Duke of Cumberland who *"very much disliked Lord Liverpool being at the War Department."* [546] The former complained that Liverpool would declare one thing in public while the next day saying something completely different in his private correspondence.[547] For Samuel Crompton such indecision could be a further obstacle to his endeavours.

Percival's replacement as Chancellor of the Exchequer was Nicholas Vansittart, Lord Bexley (1766-1851), who had to deal with the country's high levels of taxation and debt. A patient and kindly man the new chancellor subsequently introduced an exotic array of taxes including charges on horses, male servants, carriages, dogs, agricultural and trade horses. Bexley probably considered that Crompton would have been better served by having applied for a patent. Certainly, in the aftermath of Percival's assassination Lords Liverpool and Bexley had much on their minds and were not primed for largesse.

On the 24th of June 1812 Lord Stanley, Whig and Foxite, Head of the Lancashire Grand Jury and later to be a supporter of military action at Peterloo; the increasingly deaf member of one of the most powerful families in Lancashire, lived up to his reputation of being an ineffective parliamentarian. The speaker of the House of Commons having left the chair, the House was reconvened as a Committee of Supply, empowered to grant moneys to petitioners, in this case Samuel Crompton. Lord Stanley presented a potted biography of Crompton's contribution to the Lancashire trade and his difficulties in gaining any remuneration.[548] While sympathetic in tone, the reading of this speech reveals a lack of passion. It omitted some of the most powerful arguments presented by the witnesses attending the specially appointed committee Absent was the presumed enthusiasm of Percival for his cause and no mention here of the mule survey. It was as if the spinning mules lay silent.

Where oh where! Samuel Crompton and his supporters must have thought, was the compelling statistical evidence that the mule had enhanced the cotton trade and added to the wealth of the nation, not to mention the coffers of the Exchequer? What of the ardent statements of support made by leading textile manufactures of Lancashire? Then the galling timorous request that *"a sum not exceeding £5,000 be granted as a remuneration for his invention."* Samuel had placed a great deal of faith in Lord Stanley and the other Parliamentarians and must have felt betrayed. He was depicted as a poverty stricken individual forced to attend upon Parliament for some recompense and support. Though Stanley alluded to the genius of Crompton and the advantages of the mule being *"almost incalculable"* he described him as *"in that class of community, a common manufacturer, and having nothing to depend on for his subsistence but his daily labour"* and therefore he had been unable to purchase a patent. The subscription having failed he was *"compelled"* to petition Parliament. The episode evoked the sense of an act of charity not a reward.

The motion was seconded by Mr. Blackburne. Mr. Giddy proposed that the award be offered without any fee or deduction, which was accepted, though not subsequently honoured. So much for the vigorous handshakes, expressions of delight and keen anticipation. Though to be fair to Stanley he may have had a clear awareness of the political climate and the sense of what was realistically achievable. Of course, in 1812 £5,000 was a significant amount of money. However, relative to Samuel's expectations, his desire for recognition, comparison with other awards, and fervent desire to secure a prosperous future for his family, it was a profound disappointment. In a letter written to his children from Kensington, dated 26th June 1812 he expressed his regret regarding the amount of money awarded and presented his opinion of the leaders of the country who had let him down so badly. [549]

"I have striven every possible way to awaken the leaders of parliament to a sense of disgrace."

" I have gone the length to many of saying that I would not pledge myself to accept of a mere mockery of remuneration. I had had enough of that and that me they could not dishonour, all the disgrace lay with them, but all to no purpose, and it has ended as I expected..."

In public Samuel demonstrated humility by visiting several of his supporters to thank them. He called upon the ailing Colonel Stanley, who was still in danger of losing his life. However, in private, he was seething with resentment. Eventually he had to undertake the arduous journey home to Lancashire. He must have been relieved to relinquish the pressure of canvassing and traversing the city and welcomed a return to more familiar surroundings. He described his journey as *"pleasant and having the agreeable company of a Bolton man."*[550] However he was still bearing the fatigue of his time in London and was ill. He missed the canal boat from Manchester to Bolton and after staying with friends in Salford, had to catch a later sailing. Jane Harwood was particularly upset at Samuel's sudden departure from Kensington. Apparently, she *'had no warning.'*[551] She shed tears and declared that *nothing should have kept her from home if she could have thought that you were going.* At this point Samuel may have been insensible to the frustrations of others, or even his own inconvenience, as he travelled humiliated through the bleak northern evening to face the recriminations of his family.

The extent of Samuel Crompton's resentment is apparent in the arguments that followed over the deduction of fees and expenses from his award. On 22nd October 1812 he wrote to George White at the House of Commons to question why £47. 17 shillings and 4 pence had been deducted for inserting one clause into the Appropriation Act.[552] He was so agitated that he suggested that he might not yet accept the remainder of the money. He also revealed how he thought that he had been judged by Parliament.

"It always seemed to me that the leading men in government did not consider the case but the man who they ventured to suppose had never had the command of a thousand pound which is a sad mistake, or they would never have said give the man £100 a year it will be as much as he can drink."

The deed was done. He now had to think how best to secure his own future comfort and the prosperity of his family.

9. Sir Richard Arkwright

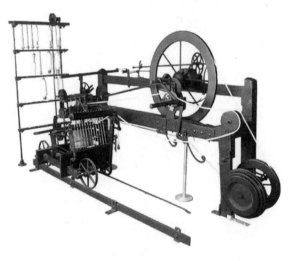

10. The spinning mule

11. Parson Folds

12. Lord Chancellor Eldon

13. 'Brothers in Law' by Robert Dighton

14. George Crompton

15. George Rose MP

16. Sir Robert Peel

17. John Blackburne

18. Lostock Hall by Captain Dewhurst

19. A flattering depiction of the Prince Regent

20. The Swan with Two Necks, Lad Lane

21. Spencer Percival

M.ʳ WILLIAM COBBETT.

22. William Cobbett

Part Five

1813-1827

Disharmony and Persistence

Chapter Seventeen

The Shrouds Over Which Ariel Whispers Breathe

The lucid Squadrons round the Sails repair:
Soft o'er the Shrouds Aerial **Whispers** *breathe,*
That seem'd but Zephyrs[553] *to the Train beneath.*
Some to the Sun their Insect-Wings unfold,
Waft on the Breeze, or sink in Clouds of Gold.

Alexander Pope, The Rape of the Lock a Heroic Comic Poem.

Pope's poem *'The Rape of the Lock'* was an indictment of the folly and vanities of eighteenth-century society which he saw has having departed from more heroic and epic concerns. It tells the story of Belinda who, attending a court party, was outraged by the theft of a lock of her hair. The poem argues for humour, tolerance and concern for more weighty matters. There is evident anxiety for the changing times. The imagery is of fine garments and the interplay of colour and ethereal light; a fitting lyrical picture for the bleaching and dying of cloth.

"....Dipt in the richest tincture of the skies, Where light disports in ever-mingling dies. "

Certainly, Samuel Crompton would have wished to refocus the interest of his sons on business and away from ubiquitous credit, folly and vanity. Commitment to a bleaching business was one way to achieve this. Bleaching was an attractive investment for Samuel's £5,000, less much resented expenses. Two of the highly successful manufacturers who gave evidence to the committee considering Crompton's petition, Mr. Thomas Ainsworth, of the house of Ainsworth and Co and Mr. Joseph Ridgeway, of the house of Thomas Ridgeway and Son, were bleachers.

The history of bleaching has a strong association with crime and its presumed causes in decadence, and departures from sober Christian practice. In 1786, James Holland was executed on Bolton Moor for croft breaking, with the spinners and weavers of the area pressurised to watch and learn! Captain Dewhurst of Halliwell recorded in his diary on the 27 th of September 1786:[554]

"To Manchester. Dined with Mr. Howarth. Saw the body of Holland who was executed, dissected at Mr. White's by LP and young White."[555]

Mr. White was the eminent Manchester surgeon whose daughter had Married Sir Richard Clayton of Adlington Hall. So, from being the object of an intimidatory display of the consequences of assaults on private property James Holland supplied further, if involuntary, public service, by contributing to medicine. The poet James Orrell[556] marked the occasion of the execution with a published verse in which he captured the temptation and consequences of croft breaking, but also expressed the compassion of the observers:

"The tempting muslins did allure thy eye, Not finished until they passed the whister's hand, Through the long dreary night exposed they lie, In beauteous order whitening all the land............"

"Bound in the car, that slow and solemn moves, Thy near approach to death the crowds all mourn, With tears exclaim (and heaven such grief approves), The road thou goest, thou never wilt return...................."

In 1796, William Pimbley, a brother in Law of Samuel Crompton stole 10 yards of muslin, in an armed raid on the bleaching croft of Abraham Entwistle of Rivington. He was sentenced to twelve months hard labour. He was lucky to avoid execution, as just two years later in 1798, Mr. John Eccles was hung for breaking into the same croft, and that of a Messrs.' Tipping in Horwich Vale. On the scaffold Eccles confessed all and attributed his behaviour to not reading his bible and bad company.

"Thus in the space of about three months, I was reduced from a state of decency and credit, to commit this rash action, which must now be atoned for with my life; all which sad calamities I attribute to the effects of drunkenness, neglect of divine worship, and most of all to the seduction of abandoned company: May the merciful God enable the numerous working people in my neighbourhood to be content with their condition in life, to cultivate the blessings of an indulgent

Providence, and to praise him for the means he affords them for living comfortably.[557]

Samuel's sons might have been advised to heed the moral lessons promulgated at these gruesome events and note how easy was the fall from *"decency and credit."* They might also have been wise to consider the contents of an unsigned letter written to their father from Calais in 1801. The correspondent reflected on the morality of the French during the revolution, and the burning of churches. The writer considered that *a moderate diet, regular hours and steady conduct are the testimony to morality.*[558] The Crompton's, while not entirely rejecting bad company, did at times adopt steady hours and regular conduct. Their father certainly sought to imbue them with discipline and sobriety, involvement in a bleaching enterprise might help.

By the close of the eighteenth century the technology of bleaching had changed radically.[559] The term *'crofter'* stood as a reminder of the rural origins of the activity. The larger manufacturers no longer required swathes of land near a stream, the key requirements of atmospheric bleaching. The industry had moved increasingly to the use of chemical processes. The advances further challenged the moorland skylines as great bleaching factories, powered at first by water wheels and later by steam, rose to prominence.

Samuel invested his reward in an existing bleach works - in need of much repair and modification - located in the moorland settlement of Darwen. The croft was rented from Mr. Robert Hilton and was named Hilton's Higher Works, Spring Vale and the 'Whitehall Bleach Works.'[560] The Crompton's enthusiastically embraced the new bleaching processes. One document in the Crompton papers sets out a recipe for bleaching; liquor, which was a composite of water, vitriol and salt etc. *"to be united for 4 days if possible."* When wanted 1 gallon should be added to 5 gallons of water, this then *"answers in general for all kind of cloths."*[561] The surviving accounts give examples of the pipe work and other fixtures bought in by Samuel and his two sons James and George with whom he was in partnership.[562] The croft breaker William Pimbley, who in 1796 had narrowly avoided execution, now assisted with the work of modifying the bleach works.[563]

The new Crompton's residence was Low Hill, Bury Fold, Darwen, an house where Samuel gained some contentment. His troubled spirit craved the distraction of this new business, and he gained some peace of mind from gardening. However, it was October 1813 before the required construction work on the croft could begin.[564] There had been much preparation of legal agreements and documentation for the transfer of ownership of the enterprise. Meanwhile, he continued with his spinning and manufacturing business along with his other sons Samuel Crompton Junior and John the runaway mariner. He also entered the partnership of Richard Wylde and William Crompton. However, in early 1813 there were family troubles concerning James and George to resolve, with John and Samuel junior also having their difficulties.

The 'Harmonious' Family!

There is a mezzotint by the caricaturist Robert Dighton, entitled *"the harmonious family (circa 1794)."* It depicts a motley group of facially contorted family members, each intent on playing their own instruments, at the expense of true harmony. A metaphor for the economic and social pressures on customary relationships. There is an argument that the Georgian period saw a move from the importance of the consanguineal family (groups of descendants or blood relatives) to the narrower conjugal family[565] (husband, wife and young children). The problem for Samuel was how to achieve the family cooperation among his sons that had featured in his own upbringing. The truly harmonious family was perhaps a chimera. His Swedenborgian religion offered little guidance, other than forbearance, and reassurance that in heaven family groupings were based upon spiritual compatibility and not blood relations.

In April 1813,[566] bleaching was far from the mind of James Crompton as his ship docked in Pernambuco, on the Northeast Atlantic coast of Brazil, a rainy region with a tropical marine climate. The temperature would have been approaching its summer plateau, hot and humid. The most likely port was Recife. The name Pernambuco means the place of the Brazil wood tree (Caesalpinia echinata), a wood that produces a brilliant red dye.[567] James would have gazed at the jagged coastline and the volcanic archipelago of Fernando de Noronha with the buildings of Recife displaying the crisp, bleach white facade of colonialism, its magnificent new developments reflecting the prosperous sugar trade. The streets would be bustling with sailors seeking transient refuge from the 1812 Anglo American war. American and British mariners would pass by each other in the silence appropriate to being in a neutral state. Their ships were anchored side by side but unable to *"take each other."*[568] Some of the mariners may have been prisoners, decanted onto land, too troublesome and expensive to transport back to the captor's home port.

Since June 1812 the United States had been at war with Britain over its insistence that it had the right to seize American ships to check for military supplies that might aid the French. These were the so called Orders in Council that had made Spencer Percival so deeply unpopular. The orders were a series of decrees made by the Privy Council. Ironically, they had been suspended by Lord Castlereagh (16th June 1812), just two days before America declared war on Britain. On hearing of the suspension (12th August 1812) President James Madison continued with hostilities, because the reaction of the British to Americas declaration of war was unknown. The war lasted until February 1815.

James's ship the *"Margaret"*[569] had been sailing in waters frequented by American privateers. American schooners captured British merchantmen, only to be recaptured, and the Americans also deposited onto the rocky shoreline.[570] As James noted *"the Americans are very hot on this coast."* He judged the capture of an American Schooner by the Lyon of London just the day before they arrived as a *"very near escape of being took".*

James and the crew were waiting for a convoy and hoped to be sailing for England by the end of the month. His letter to his father is touching. He apologised for the sweat that was pouring from his face onto the parchment, and he looked forward to returning home to see both family and friends. He would trust to the *"Margarets heels,"* and he anticipated that he might miss seeing George, who was trying for a commission in the army and if successful would have to go abroad. James set sail in a convoy from Pernambuco on the 2nd of June[571] and entered the port of Liverpool on the 3rd of August, 8 weeks later.[572]

Meanwhile, George was assisted in his quest for a commission by Thomas Ainsworth, the bleacher, who made several trips on his behalf to army headquarters at the Horse Guards. George may have been motivated by his elevation to Captain in 1811, in the Bolton Regiment led by Colonel Ralph Fletcher.[573] Knowing Samuel Crompton's objections to George's military ambitions, and his desire that his sons be established in business managing the Whitehall Bleach Works in Darwen, then Ainsworth was a reluctant but industrious emissary.

There had been victories against the French on the Iberian Peninsula where they had suffered a major defeat at the battle of Salamanca. Napoleonic troops were embattled and tied down by guerrilla warfare in Spain. For a brief period in 1813 there was an armistice where both sides regrouped. Despite

Napoleons 1812 debacle in Russia, the possibility of further military action and personal peril was still high.

Regardless of his father's wishes George was determined to exploit Samuel's network of business associates and Lancashire emigres, combined with a direct approach to the government and the military bureaucracy in Whitehall. He even attended Parliament, experiencing his father's frustration at the absence of the members for Lancashire. On one occasion he stayed in the House until it had adjourned at 7.00 in the evening.[574] He did receive some encouragement. Lord Stanley had intervened to present his application to Colonel Henry Torrens, private secretary to the Commander in Chief, the Duke of York. He replied to Lord Stanley stating that Mr. George Crompton was *"noted for a commission"* and that the Commander in Chief would *"be glad to give your request every favourable consideration that his numerous engagements will admit."*[575]

While in London, during 1813, George resided at Wisemans in Kensington. Close to the Royal Palace this village suburb of the capital pulsated with celebrity, artistic talent and the representatives of political power.[576] Not yet overwhelmed by the building boom of 1817, the area would nevertheless have been growing rapidly. Matching the view of Georgian London as the epicenter of style and fashion Kensington would have suited George perfectly. He would have dressed and behaved to reflect the elegance that surrounded him; sporting *"the glittering textures of the filmy dew (Pope)."* A miniature painting of George, set in a locket, reveals his sartorial and military posturing. Though he looks aristocratic, he is disingenuously wearing the uniform of an officer of the Peninsular campaign.[577]

George used membership of the Bolton militia as the basis for his application for a commission in Wellington's army. We can picture him relaxing in Anderton's coffee house, tavern and hotel in Fleet Street, enjoying his whiskey, brandy and wine, while drinking in the elegance of the bon ton and the bustle of commercial exchange.[578] Perhaps writing to his father expressing fond wishes and detailing his days business. Anderton's was one of the many London Coffee houses considered respectable if *"not quite so splendid"* as the larger hotels and inns.[579] The patrons of Anderton's may well have matched Georges political inclinations as Cobbett reported the meeting of the inhabitants and householders of the parish of St Dunstan on the 29ᵗth of June 1810, where they objected to a published declaration in favour of reform by their vicar Rev. Richard Lloyd; earnestly recommending him.

"....to confine himself, henceforth, to the discharge of the duties of his vicarial office and to remember that the most exalting and exalting attribute of a minister of the gospel, is to allay the irritations, to soothe the animosities, to extinguish the prejudices of his flock, and to cultivate, promote and confirm the evangelical doctrine of peace and goodwill towards men."[580]

Despite George's best, and ostentatious, efforts he was unable to obtain an audience with the Duke of York. An army agent, Mr. Robert Deighton, situated in Horse Guards Parade, confirmed that the Duke could not see him, this despite the rather obvious inducement of a *"brace of moorland birds,"* supplied by Thomas Ainsworth. [581] Mr. Deighton did warn him that there were 2,000 on the waiting list for commissions, the Commander in Chiefs patronage was now limited, and all regiments were abroad. The Duke of York had attempted to modernise recruitment in the army and provide training for cavalry officers, adding to the existing arrangement for artillery and engineers.[582] Ainsworth wrote that the army was increasingly *"recruiting its officers from the schools."*[583] However, Castlereagh, while secretary of state for war (1807-1809), had also reorganised the army and used local militias, as a pool for recruitment, which would have encouraged George. [584] Recruitment to the officer class was based a little less upon influence and patronage. In 1809 a special commission accused the Duke of York's Mistress, Mary Clarke, of using her influence upon the Duke to sell lucrative commissions. It was not clear that Frederick Duke of York would have been much moved by George, Samuel or any of the 'Manchester men'. George may have been tempted to simply enlist for the army, but in a chilling warning Deighton through Ainsworth advised him not to volunteer. Volunteers he wrote :

".... go by the name of "Glory Panters" and are "but in the ranks with a musket, till some are killed off to make room for them."[585]

Samuel's concerns were suddenly well founded. However, as usual, the Cromptons were let down by their ostensibly influential associates. Georges commission was not to be.

While George Crompton sought his commission and James Crompton was sweating profusely in Recife, John Crompton having returned home from his own maritime adventures was making Samuel Crompton Junior's life a misery. They were both engaged in the cotton spinning business. John, it seems was exerting a mocking control over his younger brother. Samuel Junior followed the family tradition and ran away, this time to Dublin. There is in the letter to his father describing his predicament, an insight into the difficulties of members of the same family working together in the new small commercial firms characteristic of the early stages of the Industrial revolution. [586] The letter presents an example of the personal reasons for the dissolution of partnerships. A weaver's family with a smallholding had little choice but to work together in harmony. However, the emerging, more formal business relationships, allowed the possibility of exit.

Dublin was not such a remote place for Samuel Junior to seek refuge. There were many business dealings and personal contacts with that city, through the cloth trade. Indeed, Samuel Junior sends his letter to Bolton via the care of a mutual acquaintance, a Mr. Cullins. He was clearly distressed and opines that he would prefer home if he *"had been permitted to enjoy it in peace"*. He stated that unlike his brother he *"has not used harsh language in a commanding tone"*, and it seems from John, *"I have received only insult and bad language, indeed it was evident that he delighted in anything that would make me miserable."* The business was clearly faltering, and Samuel Junior wrote of losses and bad debts to which must be added the liability of John's intemperate nature. It is tempting to explain John's cursing in terms of his experiences at sea. William IV famously acquired a seasoned vocabulary while serving in the navy. Whatever the explanation, Samuel Junior hoped that his father *"would not think badly of him,* "and endeavour to find him some profitable employment back home in Bolton.

By October 1813 George appeared to have given up on his quest for a commission. James had returned from South America and was able to join George in the management of the Whitehall Bleach works.[587] George appears, on this occasion, to be less frivolous and quite business like in organising the preliminary work on the site and drawing up a draft lease for the attention of his father and an attorney.[588] He judged their new Darwen home to be a *"very pleasing place"* which he thinks they *"will have no inclination to leave."*[589]However, the early days of altering the works and setting up the new business did not always proceed smoothly. One letter expressed disappointment that an uncle could not attend at the site through illness,[590] probably William Pimbley, croft breaker.

The Darwen Bleach works was not a commercial success, being auctioned off in 1819.[591] A coal pit was sunk under the works which polluted and impaired the supply of the spring water used in the bleaching process.[592] Samuel then had to engage in a long and expensive legal action against the proprietor Hilton.[593] French adds the incompetence of George Crompton as a further reason for the failure of the enterprise.[594] In fact George quickly opened another bleaching business at Hoddlesden Vale in 1819[595], which by 1822 had also failed.[596]

The business activities of Samuel Crompton's sons again emphasise the importance of partnerships and how fragile and short lived they could be. For example, the London Gazette between 1802 and 1822 has at least eleven entries relating to the dissolution of partnerships, largely in muslin manufacture, involving members of the Crompton family.[597] Even while in London seeking his commission, during 1813, there was disquiet regarding a possible lawsuit and imprisonment. George's correspondence indicated the stress that these fleeting associations could create.

" *....I have already spent 3 to 4 years with no purpose, but the ruin of my health and I defy them to add sorrow to what I have borne for them, what they will do hell and the devil cannot conceive anything.*"[598]

Perhaps, therefore there was another reason for George to wish to sign up for the regular army, escaping lawsuits and creditors. However, it is one dissolution on the 17th of May 1812; the partnership of William Wright, George Crompton and Thomas Morris that would be especially unpleasant for George Crompton and lead to further anguish for his father. The truly harmonious family was yet to assert itself. Samuel's cause seemed forgotten, and poverty beckoned.

" *This day, black Omens threat the brightest Fair, That e'er deserv'd a watchful spirit's care.*"(Pope)

Chapter Eighteen

Georges Unpleasant Affair

*First, **whispering** gossips were in parties seen.*
Then louder Scandal walk'd the village-green
Next babbling Folly told the growing ill,
And busy Malice dropp'd it at the mill.

George Crabbe, The Parish Register, 1807

Escape To the Capital

Sometime during 1814, an anxious George Crompton was once again, on the run, clambering onto the coach from Manchester, following his father's route down the ill made pothole ridden Great Northern Road to the capital. Unlikely to be indulging in polite conversation with the more genteel passengers enclosed within the carriage, but sharing, the at times rain sodden, upper *'estate.'* Still drawing on his credit with enough time on his journey, through the sleepless night, to contemplate his father's meagre reward. Worrying about how in his absence his brother James, now returned from South America, would manage the Darwen Bleach works. George was being pursued for debts arising out of a failed partnership and facing the strong possibility of imprisonment.

Even the broadest outline of Georges legal dispute is difficult to delineate as there are no extant court documents. Rather the circumstances must be inferred from the details of the correspondence, mostly between Samuel Crompton Junior and his father.[599] Old friends of the Crompton's are involved, with Thomas Lever visiting the attorneys Branford and Murray to discuss *"your sons unpleasant affair."*[600]. The contentious partnership was between William Wright, George Crompton and Thomas Morris, forming the firm of Wright and Crompton, muslin manufacturers of Bolton. According to the announcement in the London Gazette the partnership was dissolved on the 27th of May 1812.[601] But in 1814 the acrimony festered on.

George owed Wright money, but instead of discussing how it might be paid back he had George arrested. Lever considered Wright's behaviour *"infamous"* and *"shabby,"* particularly given that George had such a poor time of late, and the association had been unproductive. Wright claimed that George had signed a document admitting liability to a debt, carried forward from their late partnership. Such was Lever's low opinion of William Wright that he believed that if George did sign such a document, then *"he has been tricked in some way."* Lever's advice was to call for someone *"man enough"* to talk to Wright and persuade him to take a different course of action. He advised Samuel not to appear anxious, else Wright would „*stiffen*" in his resolve. Someone though must becalm this irascible character. George Crompton for the moment avoided prison and was on bail.

Branford and Murray, attorneys, wrote to Samuel Junior noting that the partners had agreed that a Mr. Boardman should arbitrate on all claims and disputes, and make an award between them. George, they claimed had signed a paper to this effect on the day of the dissolution of the partnership. However, he continued to argue that he signed no such document. Samuel's business partner Richard Wylde also offered fresh advice: While George was free on bail in London the bail money might be lost. However, bail money could be protected (exonerated). If this was the case then George should stay in London and defy them to come for him, and with the bail money not lost he would be able to *"bring them to better terms."*[602]

George's uncle Joseph, probably Joseph Pimbley, had called on Samuel Junior and proffered some advice.[603] He recommended that George accept liability for any debts, declare himself bankrupt, and willingly go to prison. Joseph recounted how he had sent several persons to prison for debt, and he had found no attorney willing to try and argue for the payments of debts on the debtor's release, even though they had assets and property. In other words, by going to prison George would effectively relinquish his debts and perversely preserve some dignity.

Samuel Junior pressed his father to seek legal counsel. There was a need to clarify that if George did go to prison the value of his future assets would not be reduced by any outstanding debt. Meanwhile, Wright stated that he knew little of the matter. It appeared that it was Morris who was the more belligerent, seeking *"what the court allows and nothing less."* George hiding in London, broke his usual habit of placing his address on letters he sent to his brother, simply stating London. Samuel Junior remained in Darwen, resolving to tell anyone who visited the croft asking for George *"that he had gone away,"* and that they were not sure when he would return. [604] Not the start to the management of the bleaching concern that Samuel Crompton senior had hoped.

George attempted to manage the Darwen Bleach Works at a distance, or at least queried James on its problems and progress. Many improvements had been made and he wished to know what they were.

"Have you put in the lead pipes for the supply of the Bowk house?" "Hopes he has done with the frogs and other things that used to be troublesome? Hopes the dry house now comfortably fitted up and capable of doing a large quantity of work?"[605]

Dapple, presumably a horse in the employ of the bleaching works, was doing well and *"becoming a firm favourite."*

It was not long before the musing and coffee house socialising ceased. In August 1814 George Crompton was incarcerated in the Fleet prison. His prison sentence was two months or less, a period compatible with the policies of the newly formed Court of Insolvent Debtors. There had been a shift in attitudes and the law relating to insolvency. The Insolvent Debtors Act of 1813[606] allowed the defendant to submit themselves to gaol for two months, during which time their case would be heard by the court and a schedule of debts constructed.[607] If on relinquishing their assets they were sufficient to pay the creditors then they would be released. However, the process was ambiguous and exploited. Asset values were often understated. Unscrupulous debtors submitted themselves to imprisonment to avoid paying off their debts. It may have been this murky area of dubious accounting and zero scrutiny that Joseph Pimbley referred to when advising George to take his punishment.[608]

George was discharged from the Fleet on 13th October 1814.[609] The Fleet was the prison of *'choice'* for debtors. It was considered the best prison for the Winter, being warmer than its companion prisons the Marshalee and Newgate. With a little money life need not be too hard. An anonymous clergy man, writing in 1853, but covering his importunity dating from 1808 produced a veritable Cooks tour of the debtors' prisons. In the Fleet there was a coffee room, a dining area, an inn of sorts with its own sign, a chandlers shop, two other shops and an outside area for the playing of racquets.[610] For those who could afford the upkeep, your family could accompany you into the prison, or you could take lodgings within the Fleet rules, a distinct area just outside the prison walls.

A "Kiss A Piece"

While George Crompton was serving his sentence in the Fleet, he had the pleasure of befriending Mr. Joseph Nightingale. Nightingale was a Lancashire emigre. He was born in Chowbent, the gathering place of the handloom weavers who burned down the Westhaughton weaving factory in 1812. There are several brief biographies of Joseph Nightingale which in-between the dating of his birth (1775) and the date of his death (1824) note his employment as a teacher in Macclesfield, his production of an estimated 50 books,[611] and his persistent and final illness. One biographer noted:

"He was of a kind disposition, lively imagination, and possessed a cheerfulness that never deserted him till the last. He suffered long from a severe disease, during which and in the concluding scene, he was well supported by the hopes and consolations of religion."[612]

Joseph Nightingale was an errant Methodist minister who straddled stoic, disciplined methodism and Georgian liberality. He was a nonconformist nonconformist! In 1807 Nightingale published his epistolary book *"A Portrait of Methodism"*. In the preface to that book, he anticipated trouble.

"If I appear to have been too personal on my remarks on some living characters, among the Methodists, it has arisen from my utter detestation of bigotry and intolerance and from a desire of distinguishing the precious from the vile."[613]

The response in the *'New Register'* was to accuse him of:

"....foaming all the trash and absurdity amongst this sect that he has ever beheld and having depravity at his heart".

Nightingale subsequently sued for libel and Lord Elinborough ruled in his favour, awarding him damages of £200. Given that Ellinborough was a major establishment figure and Nightingale a nonconformist then this was a tribute to his impartiality, though he may have favoured Nightingale's challenge to Methodist orthodoxy.

Nightingale's surviving letters to George, his *'favours,'* in the Crompton papers, though at times taking a bizarre turn, are entertaining and informative. While George was in London evading arrest Nightingale was writing his latest piece of work. No less than the history and significance of the bazaar, with reference to one that had just opened in Soho Square.[614] The book encompassed two letters to George Rose Esq. who if he considered Samuel

Crompton's letters obscure would surely have been perplexed by the purpose of this book. Positioned as a work of Political Economy it expounded the advantages of having a marketplace under one roof, including its aesthetic appeal. The book even elaborated on the rules, including what time selling should commence (10 o clock). There was a suggested form to filter out inappropriate individuals. In particular, he saw the bazaar as providing improving and highly appropriate work for women. There was an emphasis upon the nurturing of enterprise, to the extent that some descriptions sound like the modern concept of a business incubation center.

Joseph Nightingale may have had Samuel Crompton's treatment in mind when in *The Bazaar* he wrote:

"There is not, perhaps, in the world so much mechanical ingenuity as in this city. I am and have been myself acquainted with several persons who have stood in need of. nothing but of having their extraordinary genius made known to reach the highest eminence of wealth and distinction. They have toiled in their obscurity and starved in the midst of inventions which would have done honour to the age and country in which they lived. Some of them have' fortuitously attracted notice in time to become ornaments to societ ; others have died exhausted in. the unequal struggle ;and some, less blessed, still pine in despised poverty and neglected wretchedness. Of such matters, I have had ocular demonstration, and there is not one man of observation in London who could not adduce many examples of a similar melancholy kind."[615]

George and Joseph Nightingale had a mutual acquaintance, Mr. Thomas Smallwood, who was the clerk to Thomas Lever, a Bolton merchant who had a warehouse in Milk Street, just running north from Cheapside, London. Thomas Lever had dissolved his partnership with James Lever, possibly his brother, in muslin manufacturer, Bolton Le Moors in December 1812,[616] presumably now focusing on the London business.[617] Lever had been prompt in exploiting his friendship with Samuel Crompton. Immediately after Samuel had received his £5,000 from Parliament, he had requested a loan of £100 secured by bills.[618] Both George and Smallwood also shared a common interest, the practice of shorthand, and it was Joseph Nightingale who taught them.[619]

In a letter dated October 31st, 1814, Joseph Nightingale revealed his fondness for George Crompton. [620] George had taken the stagecoach to Manchester, and heaven forbid it had been raining. The poor *'Captain,'* the nickname that Joseph and his family gave George, would have been soaked. In this letter Joseph exercises his poetic nature to the full. The family speculated as to the adequacy of Georges great coat - *"ejaculating a prayer for the strength of your double milled coat"*. They dammed with indignant anticipation the probable aggressive refusal of the coach driver, and guard, to let George enjoy shelter inside the coach.

".......you must have caught a violent cold and indeed "between fire and water troublesome bundle (confound it)."

Joseph playfully expressed his powers of reasoning, deducing that George had arrived home, from the known receipt of a letter that he had entrusted him to deliver. Kisses are granted on George's behalf, there are cuddles in profusion.

"Mr. Smallwood left us yesterday to cuddle his wife as he is duty bound."

The sad paucity of any very affectionate or personal letters in the Crompton papers is fulsomely compensated for by Nightingale's writing. The personal insights render these few letters precious in reflecting upon the character of George, and implicitly his father.

Amusingly, as if in real time, the writing of one letter was interrupted when a Mr. Rylan entered the room and self-consciously took up the pen. He found it difficult to know what to say beyond expressing concerns that George having left London should find himself in a bleak place like Darwen, lacking entertainments and sociability. He expressed the hope that Bolton would offer him more. Meanwhile the Reverend Nightingale retreats to cuddle *"Mrs. Mc"* for George and to deliver a kiss. He promises to dispatch more kisses to the *"ladies templar"* who are to arrive that evening; a metaphor for strong women implying the female adjutants to the warrior priests, the Knights Templar. This was a franticly busy and cultured Georgian household, with the Micawber like Joseph Nightingale, with his classical allusions and spurting sentimentality, at its epicenter.

Finally, the author of *"English Topography: A Series of Historical and Statistical Descriptions"*[621] promised a trip to Manchester.

§

Samuel Compton had travelled to London to arrange George's discharge from the Fleet. In a later practice piece for his shorthand George related a story of how his father, Smallwood, Nightingale and himself had met in the coffee room at the Bull Inn. Having placed a £5 note, given to him by Mr. Lever, in the brim of his hat, he had quite forgotten about it, until it fell out some twelve weeks later on the 6th of September 1814.[622] Perhaps an example of Georges absent mindedness, or more likely a cavalier approach to money? The correspondence between George and Nightingale often has samples of shorthand as a postscript displaying their expertise and disguising personal messages. Smallwood and George assisted each other in their learning and practice of this then rare accomplishment, critiquing each other's work. On one occasion Smallwood suggested that George exhibited the fault of most learners in not making his curved letters round enough but requested. [623]

"....you will oblige me by serving me with the same sauce, for I have as much need for improvement in the art as yourself.[624]

In a letter dated 16th November 1814, after George had left the Fleet and London, Nightingale expressed mocking relief, using shorthand, that George had departed and vacated a bed with the room subsequently occupied by two, sometimes three families.[625]Joseph Nightingale was not sure how they would have managed had George not left. However, he was sorely missed, for his playing the piano at *"their little parties"*. Together with the newly married Mr. Thomas Smallwood they intend to drink to George's health, with the best red port that *"we can lay our lips upon"*. Of course, there is the usual hectic flow of affectionate kisses, meeting the lips more rapidly than the red port. George is thanked for his *"Kiss a Piece"*, with Joseph having some difficulty delivering a kiss to a Miss Eliza but managing to corner all the rest.[626] Meanwhile, Mrs. Nightingale is once again in a fit, swearing that if George does not write soon *"we must never write to you again."*

Joseph Nightingale experienced a further episode of imprisonment in the Fleet, being discharged on the 24th of June 1815[627]. He was accused of not paying £75 for a plate from a Mr. Holland. Nightingale had sold the plate to an Alderman Goodbehere for £32, this while still owing the money to Holland. This was considered, along with a similar transaction involving a watch, to be an act of fraud.

The letter in which he celebrated his discharge from prison is addressed 60 Old Bailey, a location 'within the rules' of the Fleet. [628] The more prosperous prisoners could obtain lodgings within a certain distance of the prison (within the rules). Old Bailey was a road within this sanctioned area. The Sergeant of the court stated how Nightingale's expenditures, while living within the rules, appeared disproportionate, suggesting ill-gotten gains. This reflected a tendency to be extravagant that he shared with George.

On release Joseph effused on the pleasures of freedom.

« *...you know how sweet the air smells, how bright the sun shines, how charming is all nature under such circumstances as mine"*[629]

On leaving the *"rules"* the Reverend Nightingale moved himself and his family to 42 Skinner Street.[630] Skinner Street was near to the Marshalee and Fleet prisons as well as the Old Bailey.[631] It was also near Fleet Street, a teeming parade of inhabitants inspecting the cluttered book stalls and impertinent print shops; and close to Paternoster row which hosted the primary booksellers of London. In Skinner Street one could find the representations of Georgian elegance and entertainment in the form of a clock and watch maker, Ham and a manufacturer of pianos, Monro & May pianoforte Makers at number 60;[632] but most of all it was the literary heart of London. The street was inhabited by William Godwin, radical writer and bookseller, who was visited by an array of contemporary writers and poets including Shelley, Lamb and Cobbett. Despite being a neighbour there is no evidence that Joseph Nightingale had any significant social interaction with Godwin who lived at number 41. His religious leanings would not have fitted well with Godwin's atheism.

George Crompton would never be a part of the more radical political and literary world of fashionable London. [633] Rather he was allied with a particular group of lesser literati that had connections outside the capital. They were northern emigres who fraternised with manufacturers such as Thomas Lever, who the true 'Romantic 'intellectuals of the day would despise for their focus on profit and wealth. No associate of Colonel Ralph Fletcher could be seen as a supporter of radical causes, or over liberal thinking.[634]

Samuel Crompton had despaired of London as *"this overgrown place"* and Cobbett described it as a great *Wem* (or boil). Crompton's distaste arose from the tedium and fatigue of traversing the metropolis, a practical man's view of the city. Cobbett's perspective was a form of existential crisis. London was corrupt and its distractions antithetical to the spread and development of radicalism. Godwin also, saw the capital as a dangerous place. Yet at the same time it offered the excitement of theatres and pleasure gardens and most of all an invigorating and productive intellectual atmosphere. However, the social intellectual and distance between the recklessly gambling aristocratic members of Whites and Almacks and Godwin and his politico literary circle was equal to that between George Crompton and the London intellectuals among whom he mingled but did not mix. However, George Crompton and Joseph Nightingale were united in their Georgian optimism, love of life, but most of all in facing the ever present risk of impoverishment and incarceration for debt.

George Crompton's absence from Darwen, and his imprisonment, hampered the management of the bleaching enterprise. For the Crompton family the 1820s involved a series of misadventures, unsuccessful partnerships, plus the usual roguery. The flooding of the Whitehall Bleach works in 1822 was a significant blow to Samuel's business plans. Other business activities included a partnership as a cotton merchant with Richard Wylde, which had been in operation since at least October 1812.[635] Wylde had been supportive of George's legal dispute, but misfortune also attended this shared enterprise. Crompton and Wylde were major suppliers of cotton wool to a large concern, Delph Mill in the Dingle in Turton. The Mill was not managed well and had large loans owing to Crompton and Wylde, secured on its machinery. The mill was flooded when a weir burst its banks, sweeping away the security for the loans. Wylde, Samuel and William Crompton purchased another concern at Wilderswood in Horwich and they supplied the machinery. However, on the 18th of December 1822 both Samuel and William retired from the business. [636]

Around the time that George returned home on that rain sodden trip in 1814, French states that Crompton's *"children were dispersed."*[637] Certainly their inclinations and adventures had made establishing them securely in business problematic, though the rabid movement between partnerships was not untypical of the times. Samuel continued as a muslin manufacturer in King Street creating new patterns and attempting to improve the weaving of elaborate coloured designs.[638] Again, he was plagued by people stealing his ideas and producing goods more cheaply, using inferior materials, so that he never could compete. Gilbert French noted that the designs were pirated *"by his near neighbours and pretended friends."*[639]

The beleaguered inventor could not forget his ill use by Parliament, and the cotton manufacturers of Bolton. By 1823, given the misfortune attending his business activities and the passing of 11 years since the award, he might yet consider appealing to Parliament again. There was a least one person who thought that he should, an enthusiastic but vulnerable young journalist, John Brown. However, to effectively press for a second reward Brown would need the co-operation of George and the other Crompton children.

Chapter Nineteen

Brown: A Cause Resuscitated

"...the society of the workhouse was not very well calculated to delight the mind of a volatile child. He saw givers destitute of charity, receivers of insult, instead of gratitude, witnessed little but murmurs or malicious and slanderous **whispers.** *»*

From the Memoirs of Robert Blencoe by John Brown

Third Time Lucky?

This book began with the story of the fascinating collection of business documents discovered under the floorboards of the premises of McConnel and Kennedy. Also, the last minute reprieve of Samuel Crompton's business and personal correspondence by Mrs. Irving of Blackburn. These documents have proffered important information and insights into Crompton's campaigns and his relationship with his family. The narrative continues by reflecting, with some frustration, on documents that have been lost.[640]

In the year 1824[641] Samuel Crompton was approached by a young man, a Mr. John Brown, editor of the Bolton Chronicle, who he soon befriended. John Brown was eager, animated and apparently outraged by the injustice that Samuel had suffered at the hands of the manufactures of Bolton and the Parliament of 1812. He pledged not only to write a biography of Samuel Crompton, but also - given a new and hopefully more sympathetic Parliament - to launch a further campaign for compensation.

Samuel was 72 years of age and in the twilight of his life, no doubt eager to relate the story of the mule to a sympathetic young listener. Ostensibly, Brown would have been best suited to write Samuel's biography, as he was already working on an history of Bolton.[642] He would be familiar with the salient aspects of Samuels invention, its impact on the cotton industry and Crompton's personal struggles. They were both in the habit of walking over the moor to Hall i' th' Wood, where Samuel would relate the story, he presumably never tired of telling. [643] This was a ramble that he often undertook alone, visiting the old hall, remembering his travails, also the blissful, if at times vexing, episodes when he lived there with his wife Mary. We cannot know the full range of topics covered in his conversations with Brown, on their meandering over the rough moorland tracks, but perhaps he recollected the inquisitive and calculating intrusions into his privacy. He would almost certainly have talked of the *"great and the good,"* for whom he felt gratitude but also profound disappointment.

Of the Lancashire Members of Parliament who Samuel Crompton had pressed and canvassed for his reward in 1812, the formidable 'placeman' George Rose had died of his long standing illness (d.1818). The enfeebled Colonel Stanley had died on Christmas Day, 1815 while convalescing at Bath. John Blackburne had become increasingly confused and *eccentric*.[644] The Whig Lord Stanley was an active, if ageing member of Parliament. He remained an ardent campaigner for Lancashire and local causes but faced relentless criticism from both radicals and Tories for his support of the magistrates in the Peterloo massacre of 1819. Meanwhile Sir Robert Peel Bart had retired from Parliament in 1820. His son Robert was progressing an even more successful Parliamentary career. Though disdained for his lack of *"family and connection,"*[645]Peel junior was admired as a man of independent means, immense practical ability, and at times great oratory. It would be this Robert Peel that John Brown would have to convince to support Samuel Crompton in his resurrected campaign.

Brown obtained a large quantity of Samuels's personal correspondence relating to the 1812 appeal.[646] He began his work in earnest on the 7th of May 1825, writing to the firm of Hick and Rothwell,[647] iron founders, engineers and millwrights, to request them to sign a memorial for a further petition to Parliament. His arguments echoed the injustice of the paltry compensation granted to Samuel.[648] If only Samuel Crompton had had *"a single genuine friend to speak for him"*[649] he claimed, matters might have been very different. The role and responsibility that Brown was assuming for himself was clear. He felt that he would not fail Samuel Crompton. What is intriguing was Brown's suggestion that he had in his possession documents, that no one had seen before, that would ensure the success of any second application:

"......*suffice it to say that I am in possession of a master key and of requisite to vindicate the honour of the Nation from the blot thus inflicted.*" Moreover, he was "*the only person to whom they have ever been exhibited.*"

It is difficult to verify his excitable claims, but Brown waxed lyrical over the beneficial consequences of a successful outcome. There would he says be a "*fragrance over Bolton Le Moors.*" However, as usual, the auguries were not good. On the 21 st of April 1824 Brown had been visiting Samuel at his home in King Street when he fell down the outside steps, breaking his collar bone in two places and spraining his ankle.[650] It might be thought that anyone with a detailed knowledge of Samuel's past failed attempts at compensation and possessing even a modicum of superstition would, at this point, have halted the enterprise. Brown however appears to have been even more determined to succeed and make up for lost time. By the 9th of July 1825 he is in the metropolis expressing the familiar lament that there was an absence of key MPs in the House.[651] He wrote that he preferred Parliament to prorogue, rather than have the project falter through some «*trivial objection.*»

Meanwhile, departing from Samuel's desire to restrict the petition to within the boundaries of Bolton Le Moors, Brown sought the signatures of London's eight leading engineers plus the "*interested and friendly*" Charles Rossie.[652] He produced a thirty two page pamphlet entitled: '*The Basis of Mr. Crompton's Claims to a Second Remuneration From Parliament for his Discovery of the Mule Spinning Machine.*[653] The text was critical of the lackluster performance of Lord Stanley in presenting Samuel's 1812 case to the House. This was a risky strategy as he would be actively seeking Stanley's support. Certainly, Brown was correct in his criticisms of Stanley's speech. For example, it was incorrect of him to claim that Samuel required money to bring his invention to perfection. Of course it was subsequently developed by other mechanics and engineers, but as Brown noted, by the time of the first subscription in 1780 the basic principles and practice of mule spinning were demonstrably complete.

Given that Brown had long conversations with Samuel and privileged access to his private documents, then the tone of the pamphlet's narrative may reflect Crompton's feelings about the inadequacy of Stanley's presentation. Brown noted the omission of any detailed points made regarding the impact of the mule on the cotton trade and the reversal of the net direction of trade with India. He cited the array of detailed statistics from the mule surveys of 1811. Brown also wrote fulsomely regarding Samuel Crompton's character, declaring that he *"stands before the country with clean hands and a clear conscience."*[654] He implied a comparison with Richard Arkwright, stating that *"there was no indirection or chicanery in Mr. Crompton's conduct."*[655]

In his pamphlet Brown reflected upon Crompton's sensitivity to accusations of impoverishment. He challenged the proposition in Edward Baines *History of the Cotton Industry (1824)* that he had suffered great *indigence.* Samuel was thought to have been deeply offended by this remark. Brown wished to focus upon the natural justice of the claim, and the benefits of the mule, rather than any dire financial need on Crompton's part. Though at times experiencing poverty Samuel was able to avoid destitution. In 1824 his Bolton friends, and others, presented him with an annuity of £63 a year. The same benefactors commissioned his portrait, the idea being that sales would supplement the annuity income. Unfortunately, the engraving was not popular and did not grace the walls or hearths of many homes; rich, middling or poor. French explained the lack of interest as the shame of facing the image of the man who 'everyone' had so ill-treated.[656]

Emphasising the contemporary neglect of Samuel Crompton, Brown chastised a Mr. Guest, author of the *Compendious History of the Cotton Manufacture*[657] who said little about the inventor and did not highlight the inadequacy of the award of 1812. Guest gave an equivocal compliment regarding the spinning mule. He suggested that the machine produced far superior yarn to Arkwright's water frame, but that the export of this cloth was undermining British exports of muslins who lost out to those produced by the lower paid Continental weavers.

'*The mule has thus been auxiliary to the prosperity of foreign, and generally hostile nations....at the same time, has proportionately impoverished and injured its own.*'[658]

Of course, there were multiple causes for the decline in trade post 1820; and it would be difficult to argue that finer yarns - with their prodigious contribution to the National Treasury's coffers during the Napoleonic war - ought not to have been made possible. It is understandable that Brown dismissed Guest's work as neglectful and negative. Overall, cries of dismay and barely suppressed outrage suffuse Brown's document. It pulsates with anxious claims of the mules positive impact.

The renewed campaign reflected the 1812 offensive in being belaboured and protracted. It was 8 months after his arrival in London, on the 7th of March 1826, that John Brown wrote to George Crompton to say that both Lord Stanley and Mr. Blackburne appear to be acting in *concert*.[659]

In an amusing aside - reminiscent of Samuel Crompton's experiences - he related how having approached the quirky Mr. Blackburne, in the House, he was directed to apprehend the retreating Lord Stanley. Brown pursued him up the stairs[660]. Lord Stanley, at this stage of his life, was no quick and tricky quarry, but the episode echoed Samuel's experiences in relentlessly being avoided or referred to others. Here was a young man, an irritant but pursuing a cause that they could not entirely ignore. Lord Stanley, eager to continue his panting, strenuous trip to whatever meeting awaited, assured the hapless Mr. Brown that he had an appointment with Mr. Huskisson (Chancellor of the Exchequer under the administration of Lord Liverpool) the coming Friday. What memories Brown's pursuit of these individuals must have evoked. Stanley and Blackburne would have been acutely aware that they were dealing with a more insistent, less reserved individual than the peculiarly reticent Samuel Crompton.

The Crompton family were also wary of this 'interloper,' who seemed to have secured the affection and trust of their father. He was particularly presumptuous in his communications with George, who was still bleaching in Darwen.[661] George Crompton had argued with his father and there was a rift. The reason for the altercation is unknown, though it may have been sustained by a continuing resentment of Samuel's lack of success in obtaining a substantial Parliamentary reward. However, given George's reputation for inefficient management there could have been other frictions. Brown was clear that he would only keep George informed, regarding his activities in London, if he became reconciled with his father, a gentle blackmail. He even suggested that a Mr. Thomas Chapman could mediate between the two of them.[662] This was an arrogant and controlling posture to adopt in relation to a mature son, who had himself been part of the 1812 campaign. One can only assume that Brown's motives were a keen affection for Samuel, and the sense that any further involvement with George would be a betrayal of Crompton senior's trust.

Despite the familiarity of Brown's letters George, and other family members, were not well acquainted with him. James Crompton wrote to George, from Hyde in Manchester asking:[663]

"I cannot tell what his ideas mean nor what he would do" ....*"who is this Mr. Brown; do you know anything of him?"* Then portraying the natural cynicism of a businessman: *" or do you know what per cent he will expect providing he succeeds?"*

Brown certainly wanted a quarter, or a third, share of any profits from the sale of Samuel's not overly successful, personally designed, washing wringers.[664] He was probably not motivated by money in his pursuit of Samuel's cause, but the family had valid concerns. James Crompton would like to have seen the pamphlet and the petition. He was concerned that the papers held by Brown might go missing. George replied:

"All I know of Mr. Brown is what Mr. John Taylor[665] told me and who seemed not to form the best opinion of him and what sister Dawson said which was quite the reverse."

John Taylor had written to George suggesting that his father had never given Brown permission to apply for a further grant. In June 1825, Betty Dawson had received some small financial aid from Brown,[666] in the form of a guinea.[667].The guinea was subsequently enclosed in a letter to her father, who was convalescing in Harrogate. Her letter explained how Brown was waiting to find ways to go to London. She also expressed concern for her father's health suggesting that he should desist from taking long walks.

There was one influential person in the campaign of 1825/1826, who, apart from the elusive Huskisson, could give Brown access to the Cabinet. Nicholas Vansittart's (1766-1851) was created Lord Bexley of Bexley in Kent on the 1st of March 1823. It was logical for John Brown to approach Bexley. He had been the longest serving Chancellor of the Exchequer in British History, though by the time that Brown canvassed him he was a cabinet member of Lord Liverpool's administration by virtue of having the Chancellorship of the Duchy of Lancaster. So ostensibly he was a Lancastrian ally.

Bexley had been appointed Chancellor of the Exchequer on 20th May 1812 to replace the assassinated Spencer Percival. He had therefore played a part in Samuel's 1812 debacle. Bexley was a very different character to Spencer Percival. He was a mild mannered, moderate man, with a wide range of charitable and religious interests. He had been criticised for his lack of knowledge of economics and finance. He had also been responsible for the introduction of the previously noted curious array of taxes. However, the problems facing Brown were Bexley's lack of connection with the cotton industry, the passing of time since Samuel's award, and the possibility that his political position in cabinet was under threat.[668]

On the 27th of December 1825, John Brown was granted an interview with Lord Bexley, which he minuted.[669] The meeting was characterised by Bexley's silence, presumably respectful, as he listened to John Brown outline the early history of the mule. He recounted Samuel's trials and tribulations, including John Pilkington's poor advice to reveal the secrets of the spinning machine and seek a public subscription. It was a narrative that Bexley was no doubt already familiar with. After the meeting Brown seemed pleased with proceedings and reflected:

"Lord Bexley listened very attentively - said little, but I thought my representations made an impression upon his mind."[670]

Bexley did ask if the mule had increased in value since 1812, to which Brown replied, tentatively, that he thought that it had, with twice the number of spindles and an increased importance to the cotton trade.[671]

Lord Bexley, having listened politely, indulged in the now customary ducking and diving. His Lordship pointed out that he was currently out of office. If Brown wished to write a memorial, with accompanying documentation, it should be sent to Mr. Huskisson. If Huskisson approved of it, he would pass the appeal on to Lord Liverpool. Bexley appeared to be exasperated with Brown when he reminded him of a conversation with John Blackburne in Hyde Park, during 1812. Mr. Blackburne had informed Bexley that he had seen Spencer Percival's papers proposing an award of £5,000. Bexley had exclaimed that *"this was nothing"*. However, he *"insistently"* pointed out that this was not the whole of the conversation. He had meant that had Crompton applied and received a patent for his invention he would have been far richer, possibly to the extent of 50 or 100 thousand pounds. As if to further irritate him, Brown reminded him that he seconded the approval of a further award to Dr Jenner in 1807.[672] He objected that this had been an altogether different matter, as Jenner had abandoned his medical practice to develop inoculation.

Lord Bexley offered advice as to the contents of any testimonial but was clearly reluctant to engage in the bid himself. However, Brown left the meeting convinced that he could ultimately gain his support. There can be no doubt that Lord Bexley's kindly and calm manner saw him through this interview, which he may have found uncomfortably probing. He was at a stage in his political career when such a cause may have been onerous to him. It was clear from the minutes that he was extremely reluctant to become involved. There was the fear that it would encourage further second applications from disgruntled beneficiaries of government largesse. The interview was a vignette, of Crompton's experiences of 1812, encouragement without fulfilment. Despite the lack of progress Brown was eager to be positive in his letters to Samuel.

"....you are much indebted to Lord Stanley and Mr. Blackburne, but Lord Bexley has been your sheet anchor (all underlined)."[673]

If on the first occasion it was Bellingham's assassination of Spencer Percival that had undermined Samuel's campaign, on this second attempt it was possibly illness. On the 17th of March 1826 Brown reported that Lord Bexley had been taken ill in the House of Lords.[674] Other travails were that the King (George IV) was ill, and that Parliament had been dissolved. Writing on the 22nd of April 1826 Brown reported that Lord Bexley had retired to the country to recuperate. Though he had managed to gain the attention of Bexley there is no evidence that Brown's petition was ever seen by Parliament.[675] He had the unenviable task of writing to Samuel to point out that Lord Bexley was unable to pursue the matter any further, without losing his influence in cabinet, and that there was little hope of success. He concluded his correspondence with the proclamation:

"Adieu my friend, not always may the oppressor prosper."[676]

On the 7th of July 1826 Brown reported a meeting with Mr. Blackburne and Lord Stanley. Given the speed at which business was typically pushed through Parliament by Ministers - indeed Brown reported on this haste in an earlier letter[677] - then this faltering campaign was beginning to have an increasingly languid feel. There were promises of yet more meetings, and getting Huskisson on board, suggesting that the earlier promise of Stanley to consult Huskisson may not have been fulfilled. For this eager, possibly obsessive, young man, convinced of his case, the delays must have been cruelly exasperating. The experience of Samuel Crompton in dealing with politicians, at once eager to please but reluctant to act, was being repeated.

The political state of the country, in the mid 1820s, was unstable. After, the general election of 1825 there were four changes of premier after Lord Liverpool: Canning, Goderich and then the Duke of Wellington. The political establishment would not have been receptive to any secondary claims on government funds. Sir Robert Peel Junior was under mounting political pressure. In 1827 he moved away from the right wing of the Tory party in objection to Canning's pro Catholic leanings.[678] Peel emerged as a specter that haunted Samuel's failings and was described by Brown as Crompton's *"primitive enemy"*, undermining him in *"every department of the executive government."*[679]

Consistent with his age, and declining health, Samuel was phlegmatic in his approach to this resuscitated campaign. Not wishing to place too much hope on a project that had caused him so much anguish and disappointment in the past. There may have been several reasons for his insistence on restricting the signatories to the memorandum to Bolton Le Moors. He may have been aware of the increasingly parochial nature of his fame. Or he simply felt that that national and parliamentary support was unlikely. He may have nurtured a desire to receive a local apology through recognition, not so much for his invention but for his shabby treatment. If Samuel was guarded and pessimistic regarding Brown's efforts, then he was prudent to have been so.[680] This was another example of unfinished business that characterised the life of this excitable young man. He commenced but did not complete his series of volumes of *the History of Bolton*, and he had no success in gaining further remuneration for Samuel Crompton.

The Unwitting Reformer

Brown's attempt to reinvigorate Samuel's cause was perhaps doomed to failure. Of course, there were the usual misfortunes such as Bexley having failed *"from the want of power"* and being unable to act without *"losing his own declining weight in the cabinet.* "Also, in 1825 the environment and times were not propitious. Though post war trading conditions had generally improved, there were dips in economic activity in 1822/23 and 1823/24. In 1825, after frantic speculation in canal, railway and particularly cotton stocks, there was a banking crisis.[681] The Manchester Courier and Lancashire General Advertiser, for Saturday 24 December 1825, reported that 22 banks across the country had suspended payments.[682] The closure of two banks in Brighton had produced a *"bustle and confusion that could not be described.* "The cotton trade suffered, as integrated overseas markets meant that a crisis in any one of them transmitted to the rest.[683] For weavers a post war drop in wages never recovered, and their employment prospects were hindered by the more widespread adoption of the power loom. These were challenging times for masters, employees and domestic workers. Baines considered the commercial crisis of 1826 as the *"final calamity."*[684]

James Crompton, who had been imprisoned in Lancaster Castle for debt during 1823, was a keen observer of the slump in cotton manufacture. In August 1825 he considered that bleaching had been slow due to the accumulation of stock in the warehouses and factories, with all factories in Hyde (Manchester) working a four day week.[685] He lamented:

"America seems to be carrying on cloth manufacture and printing in great spirit and will do a deal of mischief in the trade."

James was not averse to emigrating to America himself. By late 1825 the economic situation had deteriorated rapidly. A Mr. Ashley informed him that things have never been worse and that if matters did not improve:

"....all the factories in the neighbourhood (Manchester) would be standing very soon."[686]

James had observed a personal advertisement in the Manchester Guardian, placed by an acquaintance, Mr. Lomax, who was seeking a position and was not averse to going abroad. It seemed that many impoverished workers, sometimes the factory owners themselves were considering taking their trades and their capital to America. He further lamented that working days may soon be reduced to 3 days a week and *"various well known names"* in the textile industry were experiencing difficult times.

In Darwen George Crompton confirmed James's observations, noting that *"we have nothing new here except an extension of poverty and distress,"*[687] He reflected upon the conditions prevailing in 1812 and compared them to those obtaining in 1826:[688]

"There appears a fatality in the application to parliament on account of my father on his first application in 1812 the country was full of discontent and Luddism and the unfortunate event the death of Mr. Percival and at this time the commercial and money matters are in the most distressing state possible...."

George observed that in the manufacturing districts the labouring classes were in *"unprecedented distress"* with less than half working, and wages at a low level of £5 per year. He considered that the masters were no better off than their workpeople. George had visited the parish offices to inspect the accounts and judged them to be terrible. The expenditure on the poor just a few months previously was £10 a week but was now £40 and rising. There were 800 labourers in the Parish of Darwen and nearly 400 families with little Parish relief to sustain them. He did not know when matters might improve but *"God grant soon is my daily prayer."*

Economic conditions did begin to improve during 1826. However, in May of that year, in Manchester, a group of *"a few hundred boys"* broke away from a peaceable demonstration of 3,000 people to destroy power looms in several mills. They set on fire the mill of Mr. Hugh Beaver in Jersey Street, by throwing burning rags of cotton through the windows of the lower story.[689] The disturbances were eventually quelled by the constabulary and the military. The protestors expressed their frustration with politicians, when at the main meeting a request for a further petition to Parliament was treated with disdain.

"....we have petitioned long enough, will you let me eat at your table until the answer comes."

The riots lasted several days, fortunately with no fatalities, or major casualties other than two members of the mounted Cheshire yeomanry. One was hit by a '*brickbat*'[690] and another, struck by a projectile. His bridle reign broke, resulting in the horse falling on him, though he recovered well. The riot act was read when the rioters assembled outside the factory of Peel, Williams and Co; the largest engineering firm in Manchester,[691] founded by George Peel cousin of the first Baronet Sir Robert Peel. So economic distress and social disturbances were yet again a backcloth to Samuel Crompton's desire for recognition.

In addition to the inimical economic environment of 1825 so much had happened since the release of the secrets of the spinning mule for public use in 1780. In the aftermath of the Napoleonic wars cotton spinning had expanded its capacity enormously. Though small establishments were the prevalent form of enterprise there were a growing number of larger factories. Manchester had 104 cotton spinning mills, some of which employed over 1,000 operatives. Steam power was more prevalent with 110 steam engines employed in the town. Weaving was powered by steam with an estimated 20,000 steam looms in Manchester alone.[692]

The country no longer faced the spinning shortages of previous generations. Now the focus was on the loom and weaving. Though his invention was partly responsible for these developments, even in those quarters where it was initially appreciated, its significance may have receded from public memory. However, an ungrateful nation might be reminded of the importance of the mule, even if it had evolved beyond the original machine. For example, the so called Roberts' machine (Self Acting Mule), invented by Richard Roberts in 1825, removed the need for the manual operation of the 'engine.'

Given this background John Brown was bound to fail in his Parliamentary campaign. However, there is one critical and moving legacy left by Brown. He published a pamphlet; an interview with a mill worker called Robert Blincoe. Though Brown had a propensity to abandon his schemes and despair, it might have been a great comfort for him to have known that his detailed and moving account of the life of Robert Blincoe, [693] first published in 1824, would be a weapon in the armoury of the union agitator John Doherty[694](1798-1854). Doherty cooperated with the industrialist, philanthropist and social reformer Robert Owen (1771-1858) to introduce the ten hour bill (1847) to limit the working hours of children.[695]

Robert Blincoe had been escorted from the workhouse in Nottingham to work in woolen, then cotton mills. He was subsequently subjected to outrageous abuses.[696] The promise of riches and undreamed of comforts were frequently used to entrap the wretched young inhabitants of the workhouses into the employ of the mills. Gold watches, and being allowed to ride the masters horse, being examples of this material mirage. Blincoe was able to provide a full and rich account of this and other practices. The treatment of children, and adult workers, in the mills was seen by political agitators such as Hunt and Doherty as akin to slavery. They were in fact critical of abolitionists such as Wilberforce[697] for not addressing what they considered to be slavery on home ground.[698]

John Brown was a sensitive and well-meaning young man who bore an acute sense of injustice that would have connected deeply with Samuel's personal anguish. His apparent inability to carry some works to their conclusion, for example his unfinished history of Bolton, may reflect a depressed or bipolar personality.[699] Certainly John Doherty writing in the preface of Browns Memoirs of Robert Blincoe suggested as much:

"He united within a strong feeling for the injustices and sufferings of others, a high sense of injury when it bore on himself whether real or imagined and a desponding when his prospects were not good."[700]

Given the challenging economic background and political obstacles, resuscitating Samuel Crompton's cause was not a project that would best suit a melancholy young man, no matter how enthused he might have been in his more productive moments. Brown seemed to seize upon conspiracy and the need to find fault in others. For example, he blamed the Society of Arts for neglecting Samuel's case in 1811, while ignoring, or being unaware, that Crompton had forwarded his appeal to the incorrect address.

As his fervour dwindled, and hope receded, Brown slipped inexorably into a dark recess of self-doubt and misplaced guilt that he had failed Samuel. John Brown did not blame Samuel Crompton for the more inhumane features of factory production. In his life of Robert Blincoe, the injustices of employment in the mills were interpreted as aspects of individual behaviour, rather than anything intrinsic to the factory system itself. No matter what John Brown's thoughts might have been on these issues, the injustices and travails of the world, contributed to a sense of personal grievance, even darker than that held by his kindred spirit Samuel Crompton. This led to his death, by his own hand,[701] in the unforgiving great Wem. He died alone in his lodgings in the chatter full square of coffee houses and inns at number

8 Palace Yard,[702] scene of the decoy by the authorities of Bellingham's demise in 1812, a place of execution, military gatherings and popular assembly. Not like Goethe's Werther the romanticised suicide of a hapless lover, or the death of the despairing young doyen of the romantic poets, Thomas Chatterton. The threads of Brown's hopes and dreams, his '*azure shrouds,*'[703] lay snapped and tangled as the burgeoning factories dominated, romanticism was challenged[704] and the industrial sky blackened.

John Brown considered the paltry reward of 1812 as *"the ruin of a previously industrious and united family,"*[705] though we must judge this to be an idealised view. But if Samuel Crompton's dreams and aspirations for his family were to be realised, and his reputation salvaged, then it would now depend upon the further endeavours of his sons. Meanwhile, Samuel Crompton was seriously ill. He was as physically worn, from his disappointment, as one of his old over coats; and he did not have long to live. How far was his quest for at least some recognition to remain a search for unattainable treasure, with his honour just another casualty of the merciless unfolding of the industrial revolution?

Part Six

1825-1917
Charity and Guilt

Chapter Twenty

Of Boggarts and Dreamers

*"There lay Mrs. Hale - a mother like herself - a much younger woman than she was, on the bed from which there was no sign of hope that she might ever rise again. No more variety of light and shade for her in that darkened room, no power of action; scarcely change of movement; faint alternations of **whispered** sound and studious silence; and yet that monotonous life seemed almost too much!"*

Elizabeth, Gaskell, 'North and South'

Riches Hidden and Lost

I recall my grandfather's cottage, a small eighteenth century terraced property, once a crofter's home. Cosy, but cramped, the extended family would gather there on a Saturday morning for tea and gossip. The diminutive parlor was perpetually inhabited by scores of flies, invading from the neighbouring poultry and pig farm on which he had a part time job, recording the number of eggs laid, gathering them in and clearing the detritus from the base of the cages. The flies buzzed wildly around the room, causing no apparent distress, at times a source of the sometimes cruel pleasures of childhood, as they were mercilessly swatted. The poultry were battery hens showing how even this natural process had been mechanised. Despite this science, the place was the site of some superstition. I was prone to warts on the back of my hand, that in an earlier age might have led to accusations of witchcraft and evil. A presumed cure was to rub the warts on a pig's back. My mother would walk me down to the farm and encourage me to vigorously rub the offending lumps across the course skin of a singularly unimpressed pig. In truth it worked!

The cottages were named Gorton Fold in Horwich, surrounded by old stables where the saddlers had done their work and the site of a long since demolished water powered cotton spinning factory. It utilised the local brook, a small stream where on a hot summers day the brown trout could be seen to rise gulping to the surface for a brief sojourn before darting nervously out of sight between the dancing weeds. Some of the cottages followed the Lancashire tradition of having the date of their construction, and the initials of the very first owners cum builders, impressed into the stonework. One has the year 1714 and the initials WHE featuring in a bold wobbly tar black script.

Gorton Fold is one of those mystical legacies of the industrial revolution, showing no extant physical remains of textile manufacture, but thought by Baines to be the very first source of cotton production and the factory system.[706] A child like painting of the fold, circa 1825, shows the blending of agriculture and manufacture, with the cows grazing on the enclosed pasture. Either side of the field a three story Mill and a barn face inward; stone overseers glaring down at the workers cottages.

During the 1950s and 1960s, gazing out of the bedroom window of the cottage onto the cobbled stable yard, with its ageing buildings used as garages for the few who owned cars, the old wooden doors looked little different from the days of horse drawn carriages. There can be a dreamy picture that we have recourse to when we are shocked by a bereavement. It is looking out onto the busy courtyard that I think of when I hear of someone's death. My grandfather died in that bedroom, saying goodbye to the old stables that evocatively depicted a world in transition and the business of life; the haunting memories and mental woundings of war and momentous change passing with him. It is in this way that I imagine the deaths of Joseph Pimbley and Samuel Crompton.

In January 1817 Joseph Pimbley died in his cottage at "The Cross" in Anderton. George Bibby, a yeoman farmer, wrote to Samuel in Bolton to invite him to the funeral.[707] The presumably modest procession was to leave Joseph's house in Anderton on the Saturday, from there to proceed to the Parish Church at nearby Standish. There is no record of whether Samuel attended the funeral, or if the sun peeped through the clouds on a frosty morning, or if rain and storms pelted Joseph's wooden coffin and churned up the muddy roads.

On the evening of April 10, 1816, Mount Tambora in the Indonesian archipelago had erupted for a second more violent time, having done so 5 days earlier. The eruption excited British gun boats into the phantasmagorical pursuit of imagined pirates and devious enemies. The atmosphere was filled with a fine dust, spoiling crops and unsettling the weather. For the Northern Hemisphere the result was two wet cold *"lost summers"*. However, January 1817 was generally a mild month. The funeral cortege left the Fold called 'The Cross', a collection of diminutive cottages likes those at Gorton Fold. One onlooker, if local lore was to be believed, would be the *"Boggart."* The story is a fitting metaphor for Josephs and Samuel Crompton's lives, and other economic casualties of the industrial revolution.

On a crossroads for Rivington Pike, Horwich and Blackburn there is an extant moss strewn Celtic cross with its head stone missing. Known as the haunting place of the headless man, it was the focal point for the legend of the *"Boggart"*. Joseph Pimbley and his family lived in the cottage directly facing the cross. On misty mornings, or in the deceptive twilight, they may have glimpsed what they thought to be the ghastly apparition. The cross has an history of being passed around local industrialists adding a sense of antiquity and stability to their properties.[708] It supplied a timeless artefact, becalming the dramatically changing landscape, and their turbulent lives. The bleacher Joseph Ridgeway first removed the 'monument' from its original site and placed it outside his home. When Ridgeway died, Lord Leverhulme, the soap magnate acquired the cross for his 'bungalow' in his Rivington pleasure grounds. In 1946, the cross returned to its original spiritual home in Anderton.

The legend originated in the reign of Henry the VIII during the dissolution of the monasteries. There was a Catholic priest named Father Bennet who lived at Lady Chapel, a ruin now submerged under a large reservoir.[709] Reputedly, there was an escape tunnel connecting the chapel with the priest's home, and a convent at nearby Roscoe Lane. Given the likelihood of the chapel being plundered by King Henry' soldiers, Father Bennet decided to hide the churches valuable artefacts in the tunnel. The riches comprised a silver cross, a pair of gold candlesticks and opulently bejeweled chalices. The legend tells that while hiding the valuables, the priest vanished, presumed dead.

Father Bennet's congregation were perturbed when he neglected his religious duties. A Mr. Dick Fisher reported his absence to Cardinal Allen of Rossall, the immediate superior of the priest. However, the Cardinal, while expressing concern, offered no assistance. Disappointed, Dick galloped the thirty miles back home. While passing the convent, he thought that he saw

Father Bennet crossing the Green to his house. The priest was acting strangely and was, inexplicably, wearing a leopard skin coat. When hailed the good father disappeared into thin air. So unfolded the story of the haunting of the cross, which was thought to conceal the entrance to the tunnel. There were several stories relating how the priest died. One that he was over ambitious in his digging, suffocating as the heavy sodden soil fell in on him. Another that he was attacked by robbers. Yet a further colouring of the legend, was that the treasure was stolen not by King Henry, but by an envious colleague.[710]

The Boggart, and the various accounts of the fate of Father Bennet, reflect the salient causes of economic failure, a rapacious state, misadventure, crime, and betrayal by business partners. Joseph Pimbley and the Crompton family are exemplars of the cycles of success and failure and the pursuit of an elusive fortune. The lost treasure of the Boggart legend stands as a warning of the perils of coveting and protecting wealth. At the end of a life, we can take stock of what has been accumulated, but not the pain and distress expended in acquiring, or losing it.

The Whispering of Wills

During 1825, while John Brown was preparing the case for a second reward, Samuel Crompton had been ill for some time. He had taken to convalescing on the Isle of Man and in Harrogate, where he reported some improvement in his health. In June he wrote from Harrogate to his family, by way of his daughter Betty Dawson. Betty had been acting, rather incompetently, as his housekeeper.[711] Samuel noted his uncomfortable journey and complained of the coaches being full of people returning from the Manchester races.[712]

"...he .had not been able to write at all my hand trembled so on account of the fatigue of my journey."

Tellingly, he admitted that this discomfort could have been avoided if he had not had to wait for two days to receive the balance of an account, a remark that betrayed his poverty. He wrote that he may not be able to afford to stay beyond the end of the week, unless Betty can forward funds, by Sunday at the latest.

Not for Samuel Crompton the grand hotels of upper Harrogate, such as the Dragon with its patronage *"by the great families of the three Kingdoms,"*[713] or the sumptuous Queens Hotel with its ballroom, 40 lodging rooms, billiard room, 15 coach stands and stables for 46 horses.[714] Rather the comfortable, if simple, private lodging house of a young couple John and

Elizabeth Downham, at number 7 York Place, in the less fashionable, if still respectable, lower Harrogate. He perhaps shared his accommodation with the retired professionals and annuity holders, together with fellow invalids visiting to take the waters.[715]

Samuel had made previous visits to Harrogate and appeared convinced of the healing powers of drinking from the pumped sulphur springs and bathing in the spa water. In an earlier visit to the Isle of Man in July 1823, he noted that his cough was significantly better, but:

"I know not how it is that so many people have interest themselves concerning me, indeed they all consider me to be old and very weak, but I cannot tell how they see this." [716]

He considered that in Harrogate *"the waters have a most wonderful effect."*[717] The infamous Dr Solomon inventor of the supposedly all powerful, all curing *Cordial Balm of Gilead,* offered his advice to bathers in spa towns such as Bath, Matlock and Harrogate.

"From the observations the author has had frequent opportunities of making at Harrogate, Brighton, Buxton, Worthing, Blackpool, Cheltenham, Ramsgate, Southampton, Bath, Hot-Wells, Bridlington, Scarbro', and many other watering-places and sea ports, he is warranted in recommending the Cordial Balm of Gilead, as the safest and most effectual medium, by which the vessels of the human body can be perfectly prepared to sustain the severe shock the whole system is made to undergo, by sudden immersion in the cold bath."[718]

Imbibe the *cordial balm* or prepare to drown! In fact, given the discovery in the 1810's that it contained a half pint of brandy, drowning was the more probable outcome. Whether Samuel Crompton engaged with this quackery is not clear, though he undoubtedly sampled a *'mystic poultice'* prepared and sold by a fellow Swedenborgian, Mr. Samuel Dawson a Bolton surgeon and herbalist.[719] Revealing is the fact that the fabricator, and ingenious marketer, of the 'miraculous' *Cordial Balm of Gilead* made an immense fortune, signified by a sumptuous property and estate, Gilead House, in Liverpool.[720] Wealth again followed business acumen and effective personal marketing, independent of the promulgators merit, or the intrinsic worth of any invention. Though Solomon died in 1819, with his reputation tarnished, his *Guide to Health* was still valued enough to have a new edition printed in 1827.[721]

If the waters of Harrogate did have any beneficial impact upon Samuel's health and wellbeing it was short lived. On the 26th of June 1827 he passed away in his home in King Street Bolton. The Bolton Chronicle published an obituary the following January which had been replicated throughout July in various other regional newspapers, including the London Chronicle. [722] The shared piece gave a potted history of his invention, including its impact on national wealth. His failed attempts at gaining a significant financial reward and his death were touchingly reported:

"....Mr. Crompton unsupported by influence or patronage, was left in the remnant of his days, to struggle under disappointments, losses, and fatigue both of mind and body, till he sunk quietly and almost unnoticed into the grave....... Mr Crompton died in King street, in this town, on the 26th ult, in the 74th year of his age, leaving four sons and one daughter."

The funeral was attended by his sons and grandsons, plus a pantheon of Bolton manufacturing notables, including Dobson and Rothwell engineers and mule manufacturers. Also present was Benjamin Hick, a successful civil and mechanical engineer who had made several improvements to the steam engine and invented new scientific instruments. Hick must have ruminated, as Samuel was interred, upon the theft of many of his own inventions then in profitable public use that had not been patented. Other prominent mourners were Thomas Cort, James Taylor, Benjamin Dobson, Pitt Hewitt and Thomas Howell. [723] So not quite so unnoticed as suggested by his obituary, which nevertheless created the correct impression of a life of fatigue, neglect and the absence of 'effective' patronage. French noted that Crompton's home in King Street was not large enough to accommodate the reception for everyone attending the funeral, and several neighbouring houses opened their doors. [724]

Samuel Crompton's death was mourned, and his life celebrated, by those merchants and manufacturers who had supported him in his struggles. The generation of cotton spinners who had spurned him and paid no recompense for the benefits of his freely given invention, we might suppose would sooner have forgotten his name. In the years just prior to his death he was judged as having the appearance of a broken man.[725]French commented :

"Some of our local readers may yet remember the tall but somewhat bent figure of the quiet old man, as he slowly and thoughtfully paced the streets of Bolton thirty five years ago."[726]

The grave was marked by a simple stone with the inscription:

"Beneath this stone are interred the mortal remains of Samuel Crompton of Bolton, late of Hall-i'th'-Wood, in the township of Tong, inventor of the spinning machine called the MULE, who departed this life the 26th day of June 1827, aged seventy two years."

Despite numerous attempts to find appropriate words for the tombstone it culminated in an error. Samuel had been 74 not 72 years of age.[727] Even in death he was robbed of the credit of two years of life.

§

The power of the last will and testament to illuminate a life, attitudes and relationships should not be underestimated. Neither should it be neglected as an instrument of revenge, or the literal last word in any argument. The bleacher Joseph Ridgeway bequeathed funds to the Parish Church of Horwich, to be released on the retirement of the Reverend Hewitt, with whom he was in dispute. However, this weapon was an imperfect one. Following Joseph Ridgeway's death his wife, who considered herself generally ill-treated, ignored his request for his statue to be placed in the front of the church, and instead commissioned one of herself.

Joseph Pimbley's will mirrors the legend associated with the place of his death. It requests the distribution of wealth that did not exist. The usual grandiloquent introductory wording of wills encompassing the general categories of property, wealth, bonds etc. belied his financial decline. He departed life leaving a sum of under one hundred pounds.[728] One of the executors to the will was John Smith colliery agent reflecting Joseph's association with coal; but the days of small scale ventures excavating coal pits were on the decline and coal mining concerns were becoming larger more sophisticated operations.

Samuel Crompton's will is a simple affair. Recognising that he was sick and weak but of sound mind, he expressed concern that several accounts and outstanding debts should be paid.[729] His house and garden at Over Darwen were left to his son George, who was an executor along with his brother John Crompton. The household furniture was to be sold. Remaining monies to be shared between all his children. No substantive wealth here, real or imagined. There was to be no material recompense for Samuel's sons and daughter, no inheritance to reflect their father's achievement or his anguish for their welfare. His will left very little but debt. The worries about his children and grandchildren that preyed on his mind, when writing from Harrogate in 1823, remained unaddressed.

"I feel as if was loaded with care for all my children & their children (sic)"[730]

Samuel Crompton's sons had been manufacturers, and even during the worst of times they perceived themselves this way. They could obtain credit, survive incarceration, and even shipwreck. Though generally beleaguered they had at times, a glamorous existence. Members of the militia, they interacted, through their father's reputation, with the political grandees of Lancashire, and to some extent with the great and the good of the country; though in truth the patronage was nonexistent. The world having expressed regret for the treatment of Samuel Crompton, might move on, but his family would still fight for justice. Perhaps a further yearning for the Boggart's treasure?

Chapter Twenty-One

Of Trotting and Trotters

*"We did hear a **whisper** of a distinguished Lancaster Belle, who chose the mysterious character of "The Invisible Girl."*

Lancaster Gazette 10th Feb 1827, On the Lancaster Fancy Dress Ball

Bumpy Terrain Is No Joke!

In the early 1960s, as a callow youth, I was employed in a local cotton mill.[731] Owned by the Taylor family, Victoria Mill was reputed to have been the largest manufacturer of towels in the British Empire, and second largest in the world. All that remains today is the bold stone doorway, set in a fragment of the mills red bricked facade, like a giant fireplace fronting the main road, enticing the glimpsing imagination to fill in the void. My memories are of the whacking of the power looms, but also the unenviable coughing and spluttering of those workers who crawled beneath the machines to sweep up the dust and fluffs of cotton. Yet as in all such things they were sustained by humour. The Bolton tradition of practical joking called *"trotting"*, singled out by Gilbert French, thrived in the mill. [732]I was subjected to the customary errand of the naive, sent to the factory storerooms for a 'can of steam', or a 'tin of elbow grease'. French bemoaned the lack of evidence of *'trotting,'* noting how it could tell us much about the customs and manners of the time, to which he might have added insight into the robustness and resolve of the benighted Lancashire textile workers.[733]

There is a painting by Selim Rothwell (1815-1881), illustrating a group of prosperous gentlemen, of the middling sort, joking and drinking in a tavern. Two of the men, strangely, thrusting their feet into buckets of possibly icy water. This is a depiction of trotting acted out in its reputed place of origin, the Swan Inn, Bolton. It suggests that the typical location for trotting is the tavern, and its nature the consequence of drink and high jinks. No doubt there were informal gatherings of friends and more formal clubs and associations who practiced this 'art', though the nature of the practical joke in this case is hard to fathom. Perhaps a pretended cure for the gout, an endurance test, or an artistic flourish to represent the levels of insanity to which the trotting and the *trotters'* antics could be elevated. The gathering maybe a club or society, these being a marked feature of the eighteenth and early nineteenth century social landscape. The societies encompassed the reformation of manners, literature, self-education or more hedonistic activity, such as the consumption of roast beef. Though in 1805 the editor of the Staffordshire Advertiser was irate, not having received a promised letter from the Idle Club.[734]

Samuel Crompton had found solace as a member of the *'Blue Key Club.'*[735] The group met in the afternoons in the Millstone Inn, Bolton. Its members where primarily the more elderly small scale cotton manufacturers from the town and surrounding moorland villages, mustering to gossip, discus politics, and of course drink, though by all accounts moderately. It was designated the 'Blue Key Club,' because having locked up their premises, and retired to the Inn, they would place their extremely cold keys in the fire, then in their ale, a consequence of which was that the keys turned blue. Samuel also frequented the informal *'Black Horse Club'* that met at the Black Horse Inn. [736]There he conversed with his supportive manufacturing friends, Rothwell, Kennedy, Hick, and Isaac and Benjamin Dobson. Samuel was remembered when attending the club meetings as being taciturn and taking just a small drink of beer. It was considered, that though he said little, when he did talk it was good sense.

It seems unlikely that Samuel Crompton would have engaged in trotting or be anything other than circumspect in his humour. French does relate one instance of his sardonic disposition. On hearing of the marriage of Napoleon to the Austrian Arch Duchess Marie Louis in 1810, he quipped *'good god, do we want a breed of em'*, evidently Napoleon's intention. Posthumous attempts to appraise the character of Samuel Crompton pursued the pseudo science of delineating the nature of the bumps on his head (phrenology). Gilbert French demonstrated great zeal to establish his *'exact'* character by hiring a well known phrenologist, a Mr. Bally of Manchester. He did not analyse the inventor's actual skull, but rather a plaster cast commissioned by Crompton's friends. Mr. Bally reported his results in a memorandum dated

15th June 1853. French noted his Italian origin and indifferent English. Bally was unaware of whose bust he had examined, and through the medium of at times comical English reported that he had found *"a development with good perceptive, and rather large reflective."* In addition, *"fully good domestic economy"*. Pointedly, Mr. Bally also noted *"mechanical invention"* as a facet of the skull owner's character.[737]

Though Mr. Bally was perturbed by the bumpy and imperfect cast of the skull - the interesting point being which bumps he discounted and why - the results of the exercise correspond with anecdotal evidence of Samuel's character. His sons noted that their father was *"a singularly handsome and prepossessing* man."[738]Bally did not find evidence of a sense of humour. However, when the infamous Fowler Brothers analysed the facsimile skull of the author and humorist Mark Twain, very much alive and skeptical, they found *"a cavity with no opposing bump."* This suggested that this talented and entertaining man had an absence of any sense of the comical.[739] From a modern perspective we may be suspicious of the phrenologist findings. We can liken them to the illusory accuracy of horoscopes; glimpses of what we desire in vagaries. However, it is revealing that Samuel Crompton was such a taciturn, and enigmatic character, that an experiment to determine his personality was considered necessary. Or was this exercise to result in a *'scientific'* confirmation of Crompton's genius to set before an increasingly indifferent world?

A lack of humour was not a characteristic of George Crompton. There is evidence of this in Nightingale's correspondence with George.[740] The writing is playful, mercilessly teasing the cigar and brandy loving "Captain". There is also an indication of George's sociability in the variety of organisations of which he was a member: commercial travelers society,[741] freemasons, yeomanry etc.[742] He even entered a wager with friends in Darwen that whoever should marry first should provide the others with a dinner.[743] He was a respected member of Darwen cum Blackburn society and the Conservative Association.[744] He married Sarah Lancaster the sister of a Blackburn Surgeon, Dr Lancaster,[745] though she died in June, 1822.[746] Invitations abounded, including to ceremonial marches and balls.

In February 1827, a few months before his father's death there was the Lancaster Ball. This was a major event of 370 people, largely in fancy dress or as the Lancaster Gazette put it:

"Times long past seemed blended, as by magic, with the time present."

The purpose of the Ball was to raise money for the suffering poor of the manufacturing districts, including the immediate neighbourhood of Lancaster. The sense of fun amidst poverty was amusingly represented by the feats of the older generation. According to the newspaper account:

"Old gentlemen and Ladies, stiff as palisades when they first stood up with their partners were seen gradually and unconsciously gliding through habit into an agility not natural to their apparent time of life; yet occasionally recollecting themselves and returning to the quant rigidness of their assumed character."[747]

The event fulfilled all expectations.

"....whether those who projected it with charitable views;[748] *or those who went merely to be amused; those who attended with the more ambitious aim of amusing others."*[749]

George Crompton, dressed as a Russian Officer, may have embraced all three motives. [750] Another guest at this grand event was a Miss Turner modestly choosing to abjure fancy dress.[751] This was likely to have been Ellen Turner, daughter of William Turner a prominent manufacturer and employer of George Crompton. She had recently suffered at the hands of a villain whose story portrays how fortunes could be made through duplicity and marriage, rather than invention and the further obstacles facing George as he planned a third appeal to Parliament.

The Laughing Abductor

In the Pantheon of *Trotters,* we must cite Mr. Edward Gibbon Wakefield, not a Lancashire man, but a practical joker none the less. Known for his *"frank and cheerful disposition"*[752] he was the son of Edward Wakefield of Pall Mall, a prominent land agent with an income of between £7,000 and £8,000 a year. Young Edward would have paid no regard to the advice of Lord Chesterfield to his son that to smile with humour was genteel, while laughing was for the vulgar.[753] While at boarding school in Edinburgh he resided with a clergyman and his family who exasperated by his relentless mirth, practical jokes and boyish mischief wrote to his father with an urgent appeal to take him back.

Edward Gibbon was familiar with intrigue and the importance of control over information. During the Napoleonic Wars he was the Kings messenger in Europe. It was with the arrival of peace after the Battle of Waterloo in 1815 that he sought further 'romance' and adventure. There is a fine line between the deception required of practical jokes and trotting and engaging in deceit for personal advantage, involving, as they may, similar skills. Edward Gibbon Wakefield exercised these complimentary 'talents' early in life, when at the age of nineteen he eloped with a young heiress, just fourteen years of age, Miss Eliza Ann Pattle a ward of Chancery.[754] A newspaper advertisement, June 1816, called for the apprehension of the raucous miscreant and sought advice as to the whereabouts of Eliza. There was a reward of 300 guineas, and the threat of contempt of court for anyone assisting Wakefield in his intent to marry her.[755] If caught, the paper ominously warned, the accomplices would appear before the Lord High Chancellor, Lord Eldon.

The elopement was a carefully planned affair, to the extent that Wakefield rented accommodation immediately across the street from where Eliza was under the momentarily neglectful supervision of her widowed mother. He even ensured that any pursuit would be futile by tampering with the mother's coach. His stealth reaped its reward. On the 24th of August 1816 he married Eliza Anne Pattle, only child of Thomas Charles Pattle Esq. of Canton, in Gretna Green. [756] On ascertaining the wealth of his father, and therefore Edward Gibbon's prospects, Eliza's mother accepted the marriage, which despite the conniving and intrigue, appeared to have been a love match.

Tragically, on the 3rd of July 1820[757] Eliza died, well short of her twenty ninth birthday when she would have inherited her father's wealth. Wakefield, though grieving, experienced the frustration of a lost fortune. The death also thwarted his ambition to be a Member of Parliament, for which he needed an estate. So, once again, Edward Wakefield applied his skills of deception when on the 7th of March 1826 he abducted another young heiress,[758] Miss Helen Turner, a minor and the daughter of William Turner of Shrigley Hall in Macclesfield. His daughter was one of the most eligible young women in the country. A highly successful calico manufacturer and printer Turner had a personal fortune yielding £5,000 a year. In 1840 he employed George Crompton to manage his mill at Ewood in Blackburn.

Edward Gibbon Wakefield was the pantomime villain in this second abduction, but the execution of the plan was a family affair. Edward Gibbon's stepmother[759] was meticulous in reconnoitering the movements of the Turner family at Shrigley Hall. She befriended a Mr. Grimeditch, a close acquaintance of the Turner's. On the day of the abduction the conspirators, having hired a shabby green coach from Warrington, headed for Miss Turner's boarding school in Liverpool. The Wakefields were accompanied by their complicit French manservant, Mr. Thevenot. On arrival they presented the owners, the Misses' Daulby, a forged letter from a fictitious Dr Wilson. The letter described Ellen Turner's mother as being in a state of *"near paralysis,"* in need of the comforts and attentions of her daughter. Believing that her mother was critically ill Ellen accompanied the group to the Albion Inn, Manchester. She was confined to a room to await the supposed arrival of her father.

The elegant and persuasive Edward Gibbon Wakefield, with all the seductive arts of the well-honed cad convinced Miss Ellen that due to the failure of the banks her father was ruined. However, he could yet be saved if a loan for £60,000 could be advanced by his uncle, a Mr. Wakefield banker of Kendal. The advance would be considered secure if only she would marry him, Edward Gibbon. Understandably, the timorous child, prior to making any commitment, wished to see her Pa, Pa, but this was deemed impossible. He was in Yorkshire to where they must hasten to meet him. Instead, the wretched rattling green coach jolted to Carlisle, close to the alluring Gretna Green and the liberal Scottish marriage laws.

When the group arrived at a Carlisle coaching inn the frail looking young lady, who was clearly of some consequence, and the over cautious behaviour of her companions excited the suspicions of bystanders. Or as the Sergeant prosecuting in the subsequent court case put it:

"Gentlemen, you know whenever a coach and four arrives at an inn it generally attracts the observations of those persons who are often loitering about inns; so, it did in this case."

So, escaping the lingering inquisitive eyes of *"those persons loitering about inns"* the abductors raced to Gretna Green. There Ellen Turner was married to Edward Gibbon with *"a drunken blacksmith, and a French lackey (presumably Thevenot) as an attesting witness."* The dastardly deed completed the gang headed for London, to stay at a hotel in fashionable Hanover Square. Hanover Square was the location of St Georges Church the chosen site for the marriage of many fictional aristocratic heroes and their true loves. Though in Maria Edgeworth's novel *Patronage* [760]when the ill-fated Sir Percy married Arabella there was:

"....a long list of fashionable friends, who, as Lady Jane Granville observed "would not have cared if the bride had been hanged the next minute"[761].

Meanwhile, Wakefield's' father warned him that news of the abduction was abroad and that if they did not flee the country at once they were bound to be apprehended. It was not long before a report of the events reached William Turner, who with his brother, the duped Mr. Grimeditch, and one other gentleman pursued the Wakefields' to France, fast enough to catch sight of the couple strolling along the promenade in Calais. They confronted Wakefield who responded with threats of violence, refusing to *"relinquish his lawful wife."* The antagonism and shouting resulted in the group facing a French magistrate who deemed the marriage illegal, though this would have to be established by an English court.

On the 23rd. of March 1827, Wakefield and his brother were interred in Lancaster Castle and their trial began. They pleaded to have proceedings moved to the Kings Bench in London. They argued that they would not receive a fair trial at Lancaster due to accusatory material published in the Macclesfield Courier. The objection was denied on the grounds of the publications extremely limited circulation. For the defence there was the redoubtable Mr. Scarlett, for whom there was some concern as he had been ill the previous week, and he entered the court looking wan and weary. Scarlett attempted to establish the legality of Edward Gibbon Wakefield's marriage to Miss Turner, asserting that she had willingly married him:

"He would call witnesses to prove, that from the first moment Miss Turner was in the greatest spirits; that she was on the most friendly terms with Mr. W. and sat on his knee before they arrived at Gretna Green, and that this intimacy and friendly feeling continued up to the last moment."[762].

This argument did not convince the jury. Wakefield was found guilty of abduction and sentenced to three years imprisonment in Newgate. Scarlett established that the abduction had not been forced, otherwise Wakefield would have been guilty of a capital offence. As for Miss Turner, having obtained her divorce and marrying the wealthy Mr. Thomas Legh of Lyme, she died on the 17th January 1831, in Berkeley Square, London, at the tender age of 17 years. [763]

It was during his interment in Newgate that Edward Gibbon Wakefield turned to writing books, mainly as reflections on the benefits and optimum policy for colonisation of Australia and New Zealand. He even created a spoof letter from Sydney in Australia, ostensibly written by a fellow convict, advising the end of transportation and commending the sale of land to prospective colonisers.[764]

Robert Torrens (1780-1864) was a leading Political Economist and a member of Parliament for Bolton during 1832-1835. Torrens and Wakefield campaigned for electoral reform which resulted in Bolton being granted two members of Parliament. Torrens was a follower of Wakefield's ideas regarding systematic colonisation.[765]He considered this as a way of avoiding a glut of capital at home.[766] Wakefield's publications had an enormous influence upon British colonial policy.[767]

Wakefield also challenged the deterrent effect of the death penalty, not surprising, given how near he was to receiving it. [768] His ideas provided a humane contrast to the arguments of John Scott, (Lord Chief Justice Eldon) and the Reverend Whitehead of Bolton. William Turner would have agreed with Wakefield, as he also opposed capital punishment.[769] Though Wakefield's book on crime and punishment was intended to be a statistical exercise the numerical material was interlaced with commentary on his time in Newgate and the nature of policing and criminality. Wakefield saw Newgate as the *"nursery of crime."*

Edward Gibbon never had his entrée into the higher echelons of British Society, so it was not surprising that he emigrated to New Zealand. During the 1830s he established *The New Zealand Company*, an investment scheme based on organising settlement in the colony. Neither did his reputation and criminal past prevent him from being elected, in 1852, to the New Zealand Parliament. However, the family continued to be surrounded by controversy. In 1839 his brother William was prosecuted for speculating in land designated for settlement. He had privileged knowledge of the planned arrival of migrants and the land allotted to them.

Colonisation impacted significantly upon the progress of the cotton industry in the early nineteenth century and throughout the Victorian era. The colonies provided captive markets for finished cotton goods, while supplying the raw materials for their production. It would have been more efficient to facilitate local manufacture in the colonial territories, but the priority of industrial policy was the protection of the domestic market and manufacturers.[770] During the 1850s over half of all cotton goods were exported. Based on this the industry expanded exponentially[771]. Beckert notes that by 1835 there were about 1500 cotton manufacturers which expanded to over 4,000 by 1860. Some of this growth may be attributed to Edward Gibbon Wakefield who while offering a villainous tint to the story of colonial trade shows how individual life histories interact with broader economic and social change. In his *'Art of Colonisation'*, Wakefield makes his view of colonial enterprise clear:

"My fancy pictures a sort and amount of colonisation that would amply repay its cost, by providing happily for our redundant people; by improving the state of those who remained at home; by supplying us largely with food and the raw materials of manufacture; and by gratifying our best feelings of national

pride, through the extension over unoccupied parts of the earth of a nationality truly British in language, religion, laws, institutions, and attachment to the empire.[772]

Wakefield, the 'artful trotter', is another example of the world for which Samuel Crompton had been so ill suited. A fortune made through subterfuge and marriage, not by invention and application. Colonisation, growth in cotton manufacture and the enrichment of manufacturers such as Turner, with attendant poverty, are the background to one last attempt by George Crompton to secure recognition for his father's achievement.

Chapter Twenty-Two

The Final Trott

I sigh for one& two & still I sigh
*For many are the **whispers** I have heard*

John Clare, Child Harold

George Crompton had varying business relationships with William Turner. In 1823 he wrote a letter to George admonishing him for purchasing a barrel of ale, in addition to the four he had already used.[773] He also complained that George had and allowed women to work in the rain, suggesting the supervision of agricultural activity. Turner refused to pay the women declaring *"that we do not make Hay in the rain."* There is further correspondence between Turner, and George relating to the Hollins bleach works, one concerning bowkings[774] and finished material[775]. The other containing instructions for bleaching power loom cambrics.[776] These commercial transactions would have involved Turners extensive calico printing works at Mill Hill, Lower Darwen. Turner and his family lived in Mill House until in 1818 they acquired an estate at Shrigley Hall, from where his daughter was later abducted. Mill house was reputed to possess an underground strong room to protect inventors in their modification of textile machines.[777]

George also became an employee of William Turner in 1840, when he took up management of the Fernhurst mill. Turner was a controlling man who monitored and interfered with Georges management of the factory. There is even a suggestion that he coerced George, albeit it gently, to move from the Hollins to the property close by the mill at Fernhurst. George was constantly rebuked for some fault or other in his management. Turner asked how is it that there are three payments, one to the joiner 29 shillings 4 pennies, one to a mechanic 27 shillings, and one to David 31 shillings 12 pennies, when he had said that there should be no overtime? He complained of low levels of spinning, noting that George has the power available to do better, much the same as other mills. In fact, his message threatened.

"For unless we can produce them as cheap as others, we had better shut up at once" and *"I again repeat if ever I find it in the same state, I shall make a change."*[778]

Turner may seem to be an old curmudgeon with a negative and controlling personality. However, the fact that he lived at a distance from the mill might have induced some anxiety, and a focus on perceived problems. He was also a popular MP for Blackburn from 1830 to 1841. There would be no modern day emphasis on beginning communications with something positive. No motivator, but a man concerned for the security of his assets. Whatever the case, George's employment as the factory manager did not last long. On July 17th, 1842, aged 65 years, William Turner died, while in residence at Mill Hill. His obituary stated that he was a member of the Windham Club, in St James.[779]

The Windham club was:

"a place of meeting for a Society of Gentlemen all connected with each other by a common bond of literary or personal acquaintance."[780]

George was unlikely to have been a member of this celebrious society. Given his comparatively lower social status it was no surprise that the nephew who inherited the mill, with a vow to cutting costs, perhaps also having a low opinion of George's management, sacked him.

Thus in 1842 George Crompton was unemployed.[781] The rest of the Crompton family were also in a humble state. In 1841 John was a warper in a mill in Great Bolton and his wife Mary a dressmaker.[782] When George decided to seek recompense for his father's invention, he sought a reward for himself and his two surviving siblings, John and Betty. Certainly, George Crompton revised his philosophy of life. A poetic fragment in the Crompton papers, depicts him as a hermit living in a moss covered cave entwined by ivy:

".......let the blessings of health and contentment be mine; and no cares shall disturb my repose."

Here he would be:

"But free from the ills that attend on the great, and far from all folly and strife."

While poverty may have induced a change of philosophy concerning material gain, it has its own dynamic around contemplating survival. George may have enjoyed exercising his poetic imagination, but there is evidence that he still harboured hopes and ambitions for some recompense for his father's invention. In 1842, we find George visiting London to replicate his fathers' quest. [783] There was by then an even greater interlude since the arrival of the mule. Also, the demise of William Turner meant the loss of another potential supporter of any appeal. One argument in favour of the 'project' was that, often, posthumous fame can flourish. No doubt one or two potted biographies of Samuel appearing in the popular press and magazines may have had nostalgic appeal for some potential benefactors in Parliament. [784] But 1830s and 1840s Victorian Britain was a period of high unemployment, extremes of poverty, civil unrest and the emergence of urban slums, with deteriorating working conditions for women and children. While emphasising George's need this background also diminished his likelihood of success.

So, with testimonials as to his character and general worthiness, plus a list of supporters of his petition, George set off for the capital. [785] He stayed at Gingers Hotel, Westminster, most likely named after Gingers publishers and book shop, that was previously established on the site. The brandy and cigars were less evident than during his visits of 1813/1814. The petition[786] was directed not to Parliament, but for the attention of the then unpopular, young Queen Victoria.[787] Compared to Samuel's and Brown's emphasis upon biography, epic struggle and economic consequences, the appeal adopted a personal tone. He wrote that he was now 62 years of age, one of three surviving children, a brother and a sister. James and William were now gone. George also pleaded that he was out of employment, due he said to *"the badness of the times."* Samuel Crompton had refused to beg and considered his campaign a matter of honour. He was offended by any hint of being driven by poverty. This was evident in his objections to Baine's potted biography of him, and Brown's criticisms of Lord Stanley's allusions to Crompton's lowly status. George's petition was not outright begging, but it was pervaded by a sense of the desperate.

Whatever the opinion of the late John Brown and the Crompton family of Sir Robert Peel (junior), George referred her Majesty to Peel for further confirmation of the role of his father's invention in establishing the primacy of UK manufacturing. He claimed that a few moments before his assassination Spencer Percival had emphatically stated, in the presence the Earl of Derby, and John Blackburne MP that his father was to receive £20,000, not the £5,000 granted. However, gaining further support for the petition in Westminster was to prove as elusive for George as it had been for

Samuel and Brown. Complaining bitterly of the cost of his transport to the capital he found it difficult to apprehend anyone in the Lobby of Parliament to discuss his petition.[788] This the same lobby veritably haunted by his father, and the site of the assassination of Spencer Percival.

In George's letters to his second wife, Mary (nee Dewsbury Wood, married 1834), we hear the familiar refrain of Lord Stanley being indisposed with an illness.[789] This was the son of the Lord Stanley who 'assisted' Samuel Crompton. He was Edward Smith Stanley 14th Earl of Derby, three times Prime Minister (1852,1858, 1859). George gained no pleasure from Mr. Bolling Member of Parliament for Bolton who had gone to Brighton. Mr. Hornby[790] deferred an appointment until the next day, experiencing a *"shock;"* having not received any letter from George from Blackburn. George does manage to catch the attention of the Duke of Wellington, while he was walking to the Duke's house, interrupting him on his way to Parliament.[791] *"His Grace"* asked that he call at the house to see if he could obtain an appointment. Once again procrastination at the highest levels. This constant chasing of prominent but elusive individuals was causing George frustration and physical discomfort very similar to that experienced by his father 30 years previously.

"....have taken off my boots as my feet seem to swell and makes me hobble over the stones sadly."

The past impinged on George's expectations. He was not this time intoxicated by the opiate of everyone's praises and false encouragement. He had met most of them he says,*" in past times,"* and though he finds his father much admired - *"though not as grand as he expected"* - he knows that it may mean nothing, and that *"this is the reality."* So, George's experience of Parliament reinforced his pessimism. He may have reflected on just how difficult this exercise had been for his father, tempering any remaining resentment. *"Lord Stanley is again out of town,"* what a familiar reproachful echo from the past. George wrote despairingly:

"I'm quite tired of this hanging on life always to be doing something too soon or cannot be seen is almost every answer" and : *"am so puzzled in this labyrinth of hopes and fear and expenses going that cannot be helped."*[792]

His unpleasant experience and overwhelming fatigue were compounded by a fearsome cold,

"......stopping in the parks and street to let the water run from my nose"[793].

How Joseph Nightingale would have joked and exclaimed *"poor Captain,"* and the ladies templar sighed and wept to see *"the Captain's"* weary condition, and the material poverty into which he had descended. Was Samuel looking down at George with paternal concern but thinking *"I told you so!"*

Then a moment of hope. George met with Colonel Wilbraham,[794] the private secretary to Lord Stanley.[795] He expressed relief at handing over his appeal to Wilbraham. He had satisfied his conscience by passing the documents into the hands of some authority. Now sick of the whole business he wished to move on. In celebration he treated himself to a roast beef dinner. To hand over the papers was enough, to have tried and to have the possibility of a meeting with Lord Stanley, maybe just maybe more interest in his case could be aroused.

Bootle Wilbraham MP was a fitting emissary for George. He had been liked by the late King George III for his anti-Catholic sentiments. His political disposition positioned him as an old fashioned conservative of the Pitt School. During his career Wilbraham opposed more bills, causes and legislation than he ever supported. He was alarmed at the likelihood of insurrection, enthusiastically supporting the magistrates and yeomanry involved in the 1819 Peterloo massacre.[796] George's role in suppressing the Westhaughton factory riots of 1812 may have elicited some admiration and sympathy from Wilbraham. He was also a local man with an estate and coal mining interests in Westhaughton.

In October 1842 Wilbraham wrote to George Crompton informing him that Sir Robert Peel had favoured him with the sum of £200, proffered through the áuspices of the Royal Bounty Fund.[797] This was to be divided equally between the surviving Crompton children; George, John and Betty.[798] A final whimper indeed. Or another insult by the Peel family? Certainly, a good portion of George's share of this gratuity must have been expended on his stay in London, travel and the roast beef dinner.

Sir Robert Peel was a zealot for financial economy, having an obsessive focus on balancing the national accounts. During 1842 he had addressed the countries financial position by reintroducing the unpopular income tax which had been abandoned in 1816. The landowning class in Parliament was in retreat, and Peel was pursuing his free trade agenda. With his financial preoccupations it was perhaps no surprise that the favour granted to the Crompton family was so parsimonious. The money was passed to George through the church, emphasising the charitable nature of the grant, going in the first instance to the Reverend Gilmour Robinson of Tockholes.[799]

A meeting was arranged between George, John Crompton and Betty Dawson at the Swan inn, Bolton, to discuss *"a little money that might come to them,"* resulting from his business in London. Poverty had forced a retreat into obscurity resulting in a loss of contact between the various members of the family. George asked Mr John Taylor of Blackburn to locate his brother and sister.[800]

So, the final act in this succession of appeals was played out in the Swan, the scene of Rothwell's zany depiction of the ice bucket trot. Consider the elements of trotting; the practical joke misrepresenting reality, this to trigger a reaction, remaining within the bounds of decency but nevertheless humiliating the victim. Thus, the unfulfilled promises to Samuel Crompton rendered him the victim of a pernicious trot. George's treatment and meagre reward for his efforts was perhaps the final most ungracious trot of all. Where to now for the recognition of the achievements of Samuel Crompton and the ambitions of his family?

23. John Bellingham at his trial in 1812

24. The Horse Guards (Captain Packe and Fenwick)
by Robert Dighton Junior, 1804

25. John Crompton

26. The assassination of Spencer Percival

27. The Court of Chancery, 1808

28. The harmonious family by Robert Dighton

DOCTOR SYNTAX MAKING HIS WILL.

29. Dr Syntax making his will by Thomas Rowlandson, 1820

30. Gorton Fold, Horwich, 1825

31. The Headless Cross, Anderton

32. The remains of Taylors mill

33. Edward Gibbon Wakefield

34. The art of trotting, Swan Hotel, Bolton, by Selim Rothwell

35. The 1862 Inauguration of Samuel Crompton's statue

Chapter Twenty-Three

Of Celebration and Regret

*"By and by the grimy night toilers, anxious for the safety of their homes, cycled to the outer districts and began to **whisper** tidings of what had happened. There were rumours of fires, demolished dwellings and crowded thoroughfares. People quickly formed their intention of not returning to bed, locked their doors and started for town."*[801]

Times long past, as if by magic, blended with the time present.

When on the 26'th of September 1916 Kurt Frankenburg, the 29 year old captain of the German Zeppelin L21, shivering in the freezing cold air of the airship's gondola, strained to see the barely visible terraced streets of Bolton, he thought that he was flying over Derby. No matter, there were incendiaries and bombs to be dropped before heading home to the Imperial German Naval Airship Service HQ at Nordholz near Cuxhaven. [802] Frankenburg and his crew of 12 had been seeking targets in the comparatively rural area of Rossendale, where the progressive bombardment had rendered some damage in the form of potholes and broken windows. One local school subsequently boasted a stuffed thrush, which they marked as the only casualty of the raid.[803] Rather less pleasing to the imagination were the four bombs dropped on the sewage works at Irwell Vale. One military hit was the track of the East Lancashire railway. Otherwise, the flight had the hallmarks of not entirely successful target practice. Heading for Bolton the craft was yet to wreak its most destructive havoc.

The L21 had been enticed to the town by the distant glimmer of foundry fires. The zeppelin traced an inner and outer ellipse, the form of the route was like two loose loops of cotton lying in preparation for a strangle strength knot. The craft passed over the densely populated area of Halliwell that contained the majority of the larger cotton mills. In the town the Soho Iron Works pressed on with its work for the war effort, illuminated but escaping attack. In fact, the craft passed nearby or directly over 14 major manufacturing establishments with all except one, the mill of Messrs. Ormerod and Hardcastle escaping unscathed. [804] The mill had a bomb fall through the roof, penetrating two stories of the building, its worst effects countered by a new water sprinkler system.

The fate of the Ormerod and Hardcastle mill had been very different during the hot summer of July 1818, when at 12 o clock midnight the spinning factory was destroyed by fire.[805] During 1818 there had been a spinners strike, supported by parades, subscriptions and training for the processions, together with the inevitable civil disorder.[806]The yeomanry was summoned to suppress a riot in Stockport, with numerous arrests and six rioters dispatched to Lancaster Castle. John Doherty was a prominent leader of the strike and was subsequently imprisoned for two years. Under these circumstances arson was a possible explanation for the destruction of the mill. A £500 reward was offered for the apprehension of the incendiaries. However, the cotton fluff typical of mills, and their wooden floors, were known fire risks. One newspaper account speculated that the fire was like a spontaneously burning hay rick, with the cotton and dirt mixing to create a combustible substance.[807] But the starting place of the fire, on the second floor of the factory, just above the main entrance, was suspicious. Also, the mill had been inactive for at least 30 hours. Tenuous evidence of ill doing was the *"singular coincidence"* that at the same hour the mill of Swainson and Co of Preston also burned down. [808]

The flames from the Ormerod and Hardcastle fire furnished a midnight spectacle resonating with the destruction of Arkwright's Birkacre Mill in 1779. There were no reported deaths in the mill fire, but a wall did fall on the assembled crowd, injuring many. One eyewitness observed the reprehensible behaviour of some of the onlookers.

"Some of those who disgrace a Christian country, by pilfering and stealing and making a mock at the apparent impending ruin of hundreds."[809]

The destruction of the entire factory being inevitable the water engines turned their attention to the adjacent workers cottages. The homes were saved, though their window frames were scorched from the intense heat. As the eyewitness noted:

"Nothing could be imagined so awful as this scene presented - people (almost naked) in every direction removing furniture etc. with cries of doleful

apprehension, as it regarded the safety of property, friends or relation, rendered more audible by the exceeding calm of the evening.[810]

Nearly one hundred years later the zeppelin indulged in its wayward bombardment of the town. Brownlow Fold Mill, Croft Mill, Gorton Mill, Moor Mill, Egyptian Mill etc. were all passed unscathed. Victoria Mills which had been on their site since 1843, was flown by. The five story, 325,430 spindle Gilnow Mill[811] remained standing and untouched. In the whole town barely, an idle spindle was damaged. The brunt of the attack was borne by the workers in the adjacent terraced cottages. In Kirk Street there were multiple casualties. There had been 5 exploding bombs which destroyed six terraced houses and killed 13 people; 19 families were rendered homeless and 9 people seriously injured. A mother cradling her two year old child was killed. A weaver, *"a bonny girl of 17,"* Miss Gregory also died.[812]

Thousands of people left their homes to see the extent of the destruction and gaze at the retreating zeppelin. The sound of their clogs clattering and sparking on the cobbled streets was seen as an act of defiance, the music of industry ringing *"from the iron shod footwear."*[813] Amid that harsh but reassuring collective sound was the echo of the cries and clatter of the joyously dancing women of the Westhaughton factory burning of 1812, the martial trotting of the Horse Guards at the execution of Bellingham, the menacing cries of the Manchester yeomanry in their charge at Peterloo. Sounds now accompanied by the flash and blasts of bombardment by arial technology. Symbolic of the modernity of this weaponry one of the early casualties, in the vicinity of Kirk Street, was a horse stabled in Back John Street.

In the days which followed the zeppelin attack, the British love of a spectacle manifested itself in the form of thousands of visitors arriving from nearby towns and cities, including Liverpool. It was reported that you could not move freely in the streets for the cars, carts, motorcycles, even donkey carts. A cacophony of the inquisitive and the sound of anxious horns replacing the clatter of clogs and defiance of the solemn days before. It had also been the case in the summer of 1818 as crowds gathered to watch the burning down of the Flash Street factory.

In 1916 what the bombs could not destroy was eventually eroded by foreign competition, with the great textile machines of companies like Dobson and Barlow - especially mules - being exported to overseas competitors. Even in 1859 French noted the worldwide distribution of spinning mules that would underpin competition against British textiles.[814] By 1912, one hundred years after Crompton's disappointing reward for his invention, the

Lancashire cotton industry had reached its peak. The first world war merely the beginning of decline by making exports to some markets impossible. In particular, Japan created a modern textile industry with 24 hours working, easily out competing British manufactures.[815]

§

In the 1860s the terraced streets around the large cotton mills were almost as densely populated as they were in 1916. The cotton industry and the industrial workers were the victims of another war. The American Civil war had led to a shortage of cotton that was leading to widespread unemployment and economic distress. When L21 had circumnavigated the town, it had passed over Fletcher Street which had been the humble abode of John Crompton.[816] The last surviving member of the Crompton family. John was an obscure figure living and working as a cotton warper, a worker who prepared the yarn for weaving. He lived in his terraced property with his wife, 4 daughters, 2 sons and a son in law.[817] John the sailor, the mill owner, had for some thirty years been a worker in the factory system that his father had helped to grow.

All hope of any further recompense for Samuel Crompton's invention had faded, only the challenges of poverty remained. Rising early to the yellowing gas light and the din of early morning factories there was little memory of Samuel. Had the workers cared to read them they would have found some volumes praising his perseverance and practical genius, but the memory of him was in danger of being lost. However, there was to be one further twist in the story of Samuel Crompton and the spinning mule, and it would take the usual form of a grand finale of display, celebration, and unrestrained promise in a dalliance with parsimony. The decorous beast of celebration waltzing with the parsimonious guardian of the purse strings.

Of Poverty and Guilt

In 1859 Gilbert French delivered two lectures to the Mechanics Institute in Bolton. Mechanics Institutes were considered, as in an address by Lord Stanley in 1862, important vehicles for working class education and the *"civilisation"* of the populace.[818]The onus was on French to not only educate a new generation about Crompton's life and genius, but also to provoke their sympathies and convince them of the justice of some substantive form of recognition of Crompton's achievements. The lectures were to form the basis of French's biography of Samuel Crompton, and according to the Bolton Guardian they were *"scintillating and rousing."*[819] Entertained and agitated there were numerous calls from the floor of the lecture hall for the good citizens of the town to make amends for their neglect of this important man. As various speakers thanked Mr. French and seconded the motion for a commemoration there were *"hear hears."* It was reported that the second lecture was even more excitable than the first, with the exchange of smiles and knowing affirmative nods among the members of the audience. A Mr. Barlow proclaimed:

"It was now absolutely necessary for their own credit, and the credit of the town, that something should be done to perpetuate the memory of Crompton. His life had now been so prominently brought before the public, that not only Bolton but the whole of Lancashire was waiting to see what was to be the next move" a statement followed by applause.[820]

However, when it came to practicalities and the organisation of a tribute there was little interest beyond the rhetoric. An early meeting distressed French by its poor attendance. The invitation to subscribe to a commemorative fund, left at the Manchester Exchange, elicited just one guinea. Yet, despite the initial stumbling, and the echoes of earlier disregard, the movement to honour Samuel Crompton gained momentum and plans were made to erect a statue in his honour. Gilbert French finally had his day. On Wednesday September 24ᵗth, 1862, at 10 o clock 'in the forenoon' there was an inaugural ceremony for the statue of Samuel Crompton erected in Nelson Square.

The siting of the Crompton statue was not without controversy. Even the irate ghost of Admiral Nelson wrote a letter of complaint from his residence; the crypt in St Paul's Cathedral, London.[821] The heroic admiral resented sharing the honour of the square celebrating his memory with Samuel Crompton. It was bad enough that he had to bear the grunts of pigs on market day; *"sharing the ground with pigs and bacon."* Now he must associate with an individual, no doubt esteemed, but as he put it only of interest to merchantmen. Demanding an alternative location for himself, and himself alone, he expressed satisfaction with the honours granted to him elsewhere. Another correspondent thought a suggestion that the Crompton statue be placed opposite the Black Horse Inn where the Black Horse Club used to meet was odd, insofar as it celebrated a man's life by gazing on where he took a drink.[822] The writer, declaring himself a mechanic, felt that this was *"the flimsiest idea of all the ideas that have been enunciated"*. Despite these complaints, and Nelson's protestations from the crypt, Nelson Square was the chosen site for the monument.

The grand event, just as its later counterpart celebration in 1927, involved an illustrious procession through the town. After initial objections to the proposed route, it was changed to accommodate some older districts with significant population and property. This included the roads used by Samuel Crompton as he had walked on his sorties between Hall i' th' Wood and the town. [823] The advanced guard in the procession were the yeomanry, followed by brass bands, cavalry and other troops of soldiers. The military feel then softened by the clerks, police, ex mayors of the borough and sundry others, including letter carriers and perhaps a little less popular tax commissioners. The one hundredth psalm sung by the scholars of the various Sunday schools, was followed by a rendition of God Save the Queen. At 4.00 there was the launching of Mr. Coxwell's mammoth balloon, while in the Concert Hall there was a performance of Haydn's Oratorio of the Creation. At 7. o clock yet another musical performance with a Promenade concert by the band of Her Majesties 49th regiment. The culmination of events at 10.0clock was a *"grand display of fireworks"* among which was *"A large, beautiful piece"* involving seven revolving wheels in a variety of colours with sprays of pink stars. The glory of spinning and the Hall i'th' Wood Mule cast in a spectacle of flame.[824]

The seating arrangements for the unveiling of the statue were rigidly organised. There were sections for the shepherds, the ancient order of druids, cloggers, tailors and engineers. The butchers' horses had their place, as did the four rows of spinners and the *Odd Fellows*, a pantheon of occupations agricultural, retail and manufacturing.[825] According to the Bolton Chronicle of 1862 *"every tradesman vied with his fellow"*[826] to produce the most evocative, intricate and colourful decorations. The total effect was one of spectacle, marvel and beauty. The inns of the town were particularly forthcoming and produced a range of decorations from the neat star at the Commercial Hotel (made by Taylor and Galloway) to Mr. Simpsons *"profusion of national flags"* at the Grapes Inn. No one evaded a well-honed motto or philosophical riposte, with banners proclaiming *"unity with all, enmity with none"* at Mr. Hayes fruitier shop. There were the usual proclamations in favour of Crompton, such as *"Honour to Crompton"*[827] at Mr. *Horrocks* wooden cloth mart. At the Victoria Hotel in Hotel Street, Mrs. Grime *"hung out her banner right worthily"*.

Prior to the event there was the inevitable commercial flurry with numerous newspaper advertisements offering banners and mementoes. Flags and banners at Menzies Gallery of Arts. Rosettes and white gloves available at Luke McHales. The Millstone Inn offered *"substantial meat pies and sandwiches.* "Variegated lamps for hire at R.D. Airey's in Bridge Street."[828] In 1859 Selim Rothwell the artist, who had entertainingly depicted the art of trotting, produced a lithograph of Hall i'th' Wood, drawn from nature (5 shillings two tints, 10 shillings and six pence colour), presumably to run alongside French's first edition of Crompton's life story[829]. Rothwell was not slow to capitalise on the 1862 celebrations by reissuing his print of Samuel's portrait.[830]

Rooms, with good view of the procession, were for hire. The Peel Hotel in Bridge Street offered not only a selection of wines and spirits, but also the use of a terrace, that provided *"an extensive panorama of the town and neighbourhood, including Hall i'th' Wood."* Even the words of the song to be sung by 1500 Sunday School scholars were for sale at one penny per copy.[831] The Police reminded the public of the darker side of the celebrations warning them not to leave their houses unprotected, and females not to carry any money or valuables in their outside dress pockets. At the recent festivities of the Preston Guild several houses had been broken into.[832]

The route of the procession was estimated to be about 6 miles, with the pageant approximately three miles in length. The mills, struggling and on short time, were closed for the day. Messrs.' Ormerod and Hardcastle's looms had been stopped for eleven weeks and were currently operating on a three day week.[833] Thousands of people arrived from the surrounding towns and countryside. The railway transported 550 eager souls from Atherton. There was an estimated 15,000 to 16,000 people attending at some time during the day. Seventeen hundred children received a celebratory bun.[834]

The parade did not proceed smoothly, being slower than anticipated. By the time the vanguard had reached the offices of the Bolton Chronicle the Ancient Society of Druids, had not yet moved from Knowsley Street.[835] You cannot rush a Druid. Officials, clergy and dignitaries made good progress with their, light speeding carriages, but the more leaden and burdened carts of the artisans and trades moved at a more ponderous pace. Despite the sense of a planned spectacle not quite playing itself out, the excitement was maintained by the rousing music of the numerous bands. The zealous crowds sought a good view of the proceedings, to the extent that some people were to be seen on the very rooftops of the town. Also, an occasion such as this would not be complete without a vibrant touch of Bolton trotting. The source of much speculation, *"Who is it, what is it?"* was a Victoria Car, in which was situated a creature half horse, a quarter alligator and the remainder *"earthquake"*[836] being *"the best practical trot for many a day."*[837]

One trundling cart displayed a tableau involving Samuel Crompton and the current state of spinning. Described as a *"lorry,"* on which was supported a self-acting mule, a poster of Hall i'th' Wood, and inscriptions relating to Crompton's life. There was a brushwood chair and a bookshelf attached. Seated on the chair was a relative of Samuel Crompton,[838] the unfortunately but affectionately labelled *"relic of five generations of spinners,"*[839] 90 years old John Holt, of Bertenshaw, Turton, late in the employ of Messrs.' Ainsworth at Eagerly Mills. John Holt was a cousin of Crompton's and was famed for having spun alongside him during his time at Hall i'th' Wood. He was the oldest living spinner. The celebratory flag highlighted the spinning mule's evolution with a depiction of Robert's self-acting mule. On the reverse of the flag was the image of a sailing ship transporting cotton goods around the world.

There was one motif that summarised the sentiments of the townspeople, on this auspicious occasion. At Messrs.' Orton and Ward's a banner proclaimed

"The wheel could not keep up with the shuttle; but genius stepped in to remove the difficulty; and gave wings to manufacture that had been creeping on the earth."

This was how Samuel Crompton was perceived, as speeding things up, igniting the chase for scale, boosting the factory system but not responsible for its excesses. But even on this day of celebration there was evidence of poverty with gifts for the poor and the hungry. The cotton famine caused by overproduction and limited supplies of cotton had resulted in widespread poverty and unemployment. So, the celebrations had a painful and dark underside. The extent of impoverishment was reflected in the donations of the wealthy; 2,400 4lb loaves, 1020 lbs. of cheese, 1,130 packages of tea, distributed by the Poor Protection Society on behalf of a committee of gentleman and tradesmen of the town. Other donations in kind were distributed on the Wednesday after the parade, reflecting the inclination of keeping poverty out of sight, though distributing this aid would have been difficult on such a complex and busy day. The London Illustrated News, reporting on the celebrations, also featured a short piece on the charitable donations to the *"distressed operatives of the North,"*[840] with an astonishing

£59,7228 raised by a Mansion House Committee and a significant amount contributed by a Ladies Committee in Birmingham. Donations flooded in from all parts of the country.

The privation of one person in particular was to inform a debate about the celebrations, which though clearly enjoyed by the people of Bolton were seen by some commentators as a matter of hypocrisy. The satirical journal Punch commented caustically - as only Punch could do - on the unveiling of the statue of Crompton in Nelson Square.[841] Rather than a tribute to his inventive genius it was taken as a rebuke to his penury and his ill use. Moreover, the subsequent straightened circumstances of his children, grandchildren and even great grandchildren were noted, with a special emphasis upon his one surviving son John Crompton. John had heard of the ceremony by pure chance. Someone recognising John's hardship had purchased him a suit, *"that he might make a decent appearance."*

The Bolton Chronicle detailed John Crompton's progress on the day of the inauguration. He was a proud man who, like his father, shied away from public attention and blanched at accusations of poverty. John had visited his cousin George Pimbley,[842] a dealer in game who shared a property with his wife Ann and two lodgers, in nearby Foundry Street, where he was treated to lunch. To get a good view of the proceedings he had adjourned to the top story of the Pack Horse Hotel, which abutted Nelson Square. How anguished yet proud he must have been to find that Lancashire was at last celebrating the life and achievements of his father. However, it was clear from the pattern of his movements that he had no formal invitation to the proceedings. Word of his presence must have reached the organisers as he was fetched from the Pack Horse Hotel and escorted by a police officer to join the dignitaries of the town on the main platform.

John was passed a chair to the left of the statue, just outside the iron railings that surround it. He remained seated throughout, except to be encouraged to stand when the schoolchildren sang the national anthem. Mr. Ashworth, cotton manufacturer, singled out John and beseeched the crowd not to forget him. Ashworth announced a subscription for John Crompton *"...to place him above indigence for the remainder of his life."*[843] Subsequently, a special fund was established to support him in his old age. Eventually, after the effusive speeches and the grandstanding of John and his material distress, the statue of Samuel Crompton, designed by W. Calder Marshall, R.A. was unveiled. This was a symbol of technical progress as the figure was made from electro plated Bronze, produced by Elkington's of Birmingham.

The dependence of the Crompton family on appeals and public subscriptions was not lost on the Bolton Chronicle, which reported in full the recent financial circumstances of John and his wife. Three years earlier Gilbert French had raised a subscription from the cotton spinners of the town and added a further 15 shillings a week. However, a nephew of Samuel Crompton, Samuel Crompton of Manchester, claimed that the subscription was demeaning to John and his family. After the inauguration of the statue, he had written to the Manchester Weekly Times to protest.[844] The nephew used the term eleemosynary, deriving from the Elemosiniaria Apolistica, being the office of the Pope responsible for charity. This critical view reflected contemporary Victorian values of independence and self-determination.[845] Samuel Smiles had published his popular book 'Self Help' in 1859.[846] Samuel's nephew thought that *"poverty is seen as a crime."* Members of the family in better circumstances could support John, or any other kin in a similarly straightened state.

John and his wife were outraged by the nephew's intervention. They visited the offices of the Bolton Chronicle, the day after the ceremony, to put the record straight. The money was truly appreciated, and Gilbert French had always acted as a gentleman. The intervention of the Manchester nephew was generally resented. One letter accused him of *"showing want of feeling and good taste."*[847] The nephew generated further anger by objecting to the erection of the statue. If only the people of Bolton had put compensation before ostentation he lamented. In this he shared the view of *Punch* that the commemoration was a hypocritical act. However, despite the furor a committee was formed to devise some means of further supporting John Crompton and his family.[848]

The culpability of the people of Bolton for the treatment of Samuel Crompton, and the poverty of his descendants, was not a view shared by all the members of the appointed committee. Mr. Markland stated that the populace could not be blamed for Samuel's lack of fortune as this was a previous generation. He did, however, feel some responsibility, and proposed a fund to support all members of the Crompton family, regardless of whether they resided in Bolton or London. This proposal was fiercely resisted. Mr. Barlow argued that the committee should focus on that member of the family who was best known to them, the closest relative to Samuel. He found no fault in the people of Bolton, considering the behaviour of Manchester folk equally reprehensible; was it not in the Manchester Exchange that a proposed subscription for Samuel Crompton raised but a single guinea? The rest of Lancashire, and indeed other areas of the country, must accept some of the *blame*. Mr. Barlow was of the firm opinion that any assistance given to John Crompton should not be considered charity but *"in kindly remembrance of his father,"* followed by *"hear hear."* Thus, a fund was established to support John Crompton, with Gilbert French as Treasurer.

There was a feeling amongst the committee members that the day of celebration had been a coming together of the people of Bolton and surrounding districts in recognition of Samuel Crompton's achievements, and through that acclaim offering some comfort to the Crompton family. While the worthy gentlemen debated the extent and nature of any compensation, and the guilt or otherwise of the people of Bolton Le Moors, John Crompton and his wife sat humbly in an adjacent room. They were ready, if required, to be called upon for questioning. When they did appear in front of the committee, they related a sorry tale of misfortune. John was 71 and his wife 69 years of age and he had not worked for two years come Christmas. He thanked Messrs.' Arrowsmith, who had graciously kept him in employment until he could work no more. He was asked if he blamed the people of Bolton for his father's lack of fortune and the decline in his own financial circumstances. He asserted that he did not blame them and that he was grateful for any assistance that he might receive. He believed that he could subsist on the sum of £2 per week. He was perhaps wise to adopt this position and not to inveigh against the populace, particularly the manufacturers.

John Crompton certainly had his humility severely tested when in October 1862 the Prime Minister Lord Palmerston awarded him a meagre gratuity of £50 from the Royal Bounty fund.[849] The last whisper of a goodbye from the parsimonious State. Indeed, the Dundee, Perth and Cupar Advertiser reported this event without seeing fit to identify John by name, merely stating that the gratuity was received by the one surviving son of Samuel Crompton.[850]

The statue of Samuel Crompton still stands and dominates Nelson Square, but perhaps a fitting epithet was a flag displayed during the procession of 1862, on which there was a picture of a rooster and inscribed on the flag the words:

"When this cock crows Crompton will be forgotten."[851]

The cock has crowed, coughed and spluttered through the intervening centuries, perhaps it is time for the flag to flutter and the cock to fall silent again!

Chapter Twenty Four

After Thoughts

"Pain insists on being attended to. God whispers in our pleasures, speaks in our consciences, but shouts in our pains."

CS. Lewis

The period covering Samuel Crompton's life illustrated the more ruthless forms of capitalism, including privateering, slavery and the willful exploitation of the spinning mule at Samuel Crompton's expense. We have seen how Samuel's nature was ill-fitted for a calculating commercial environment. This was also revealed by the struggle that he and his sons had in engaging with and profiting from partnerships. Added to which is the turbulent history of the times, with inventions and inventors treated with awe, but also with suspicion and aggression. It has been a story of how a good and creative man fared as the merciless industrial revolution unfolded.

Though Samuel could manage a business, and had some success, his character did not fulfil the requirements of an exceptionally successful businessman, most amply demonstrated by Sir Richard Arkwright. Success in life, or business, could also depend upon having a patron and being supported by the ruling elite. If you did not have that support and you wished to become a prominent member of the rising manufacturing class, then personality mattered. The brazen Colquitt, or the ultimate trotter and colonial champion Edward Gibbon Wakefield showed the merit of ruthlessness and the primacy of connection. By no means all successful businessmen were villains. You need not be a 'villain', but you did need to have the character to deal with them.

Conversely, judged by the standards of the times, Samuel's *'Manchester Gentlemen'* were fair minded supportive friends, and good employers. The

Swedenborg and other non-conformist religions were also a foundation for both enterprise and philanthropy. Samuel's membership of the Swedenborg church revealed much about his spirituality. We have no extant evidence of his attitude to slavery but given his association with non-conformism and their involvement in the abolitionist movement, it is likely that he would have objected to it profoundly.

Samuel Crompton's discipline, inventiveness and resolve should be acknowledged. There is also the lost memory by some of just how important his invention was as the industrial revolution progressed. His treatment and the later attempts to recompense his family, involve issues that concern us today. For example, how valid is collective responsibility for a past injustice, both philosophically and practically? We are still engulfed by the whispers of the industrial revolution. However, beware of simplistic judgements. This biography illustrated how individual life stories interconnected with broader historical events. The story of Samuel Crompton and the spinning mule demonstrates the complexity of history. It is a tangle of progress, injustice, triumph, tragedy and joy.

Endnotes

1 *Prologue.* Gilbert. J, French, *The Life and Times of Samuel Crompton, Inventor of the Spinning Machine Called the Mule, Being the Substance of Two Papers Read to the Members of the Bolton Mechanics Institution,* 1st edition, Simpkin and Marshall, London, 1859

2. For example, Peter. Mathias, *The First Industrial Nation, An Economic History of Britain 1700-1914*, Methuen, London and New York, 2nd Edition, 1983

3. Phyllis. Deane, *The First Industrial Revolution*, Cambridge University Press, Cambridge, 1965

4. Eric. J, Hobsbawm, *Industry and Empire*, Weidenfeld and Nicolson, London, 4th edition, 1973, 40

5. One significant exception to this neglect of the role of cotton must be: Sven. Beckert, *Empire of Cotton, A New History of Global Capitalism*, Penguin Random House, London, United Kingdom, 2014

6. Works that do note the importance of Samuel Crompton include Michael. M. Edwards, *The Growth of the British Cotton Industry 1780-1815*, Manchester University Press. Manchester, England, 1967. Also, Roger. Osborne, *Iron, Steam and Money, The Making of the Industrial Revolution*, The Bodley Head, London, 2013

7. Christine. MacLeod, *Heroes of Invention: Technology, Liberalism and British Identity, 1750-1914*, Cambridge University Press, Cambridge, 2007

8. See Edward. Baines, *History of the Cotton Manufacture in Great Britain*, H. Fisher, R. Fisher and P. Jackson, London, 1835; also, Roger. Osborne, *Iron, Steam and Money, The Making of the Industrial Revolution*, The Bodley Head, London, 2013

9. *Most Haunted*, Series 11, Universal Living, DVD 827 302.11, Disc 3, Hall i' th" Wood, 2009

10. Sir Robert Peel the politician and industrialist (25 April 1750 – 3 May 1830) not the Prime Minister Sir Robert Peel (5 February 1788 – 2 July 1850) who was his son.

11. Historians have an understandably uneasy relationship with myths and legends and the experience of their use in the concocted Aryan supremacy myths of the Nazi party make this understandable. However, the myths are there to be discussed.

See Simon. Schama, *Landscape and Memory*, Fontana Press, An Imprint of Harper Collins, London, 1996, for a full discussion of this issue.

12. John. Brown, and Samuel. Crompton, *The Basis of Mr. Samuel Crompton's Claims to A Second Remuneration from Parliament for His Discovery of the Mule Spinning Machine*, Charles Simms and Co, Manchester, 1868 (the pamphlet first appeared in 1825)

13. Crompton Papers, ZCR/46, item 1, *Letter Thomas Cropp to George Crompton*, 6th of August 1827.

14. Crompton Papers, ZCR/46, item 2, *Letter from James Crompton Hyde to George Crompton Darwen*, 19th of August 1827.

15. Kennedy subsequently gave a lecture to the Manchester Literary and Philosophical Society: John. Kennedy Esq, *A Brief Memoir of Samuel Crompton, with a Description of his Machine Called the Mule and of the Subsequent improvement of the Machine by Others'*, read February 20th, 1830, *Memoirs and Proceedings of the Manchester Literary and Philosophical Society*

16. There was a tendency to embed Crompton's story in newspaper articles which reported family events; for example, the *Liverpool Mercury*, 18th July 1834, reporting on the marriage of George Crompton to Mary Dewsbury Wood, *Crompton Papers*, ZCR53, item 2. A fuller article is by Alfred. Mallalieu, *The Cotton Manufacture*, Blackwood's Magazine, Edinburgh, vol.39, March 1836, 407-424

17. See Hector. Charles, Cameron, *Samuel Crompton*, The Batchworth Press, London, 1951, 9; who refers to minor errors corrected by George. W, Daniels, *The Early English Cotton Industry*, Manchester University Press, London, New York, Bombay, 1920.

18. Gilbert. J. French, *The Life and Times of Samuel Crompton, Inventor of the Spinning Machine Called the Mule*, Being the Substance of Two Papers Read to the Members of the Bolton Mechanics Institution, 1st edition, Simpkin and Marshall, London, 1859

19. French's book has also provided the only detailed personal reference to the family of Samuel's wife Mary Crompton (nee Pimbley/Pimlot) including a mention of her father William. French, *The Life and Times of Samuel Crompton*, 1859, Chapter VI, 70-72

20. Charles. Simms and Co, Printers, *Publicity Sheet for the Third and Cheap Edition of Gilbert. J, French, FSA, The Life and Times of Samuel Crompton, Opinions of the Press*, price one shilling, 24, September 1862 (Author's private collection)

21. *Gentleman's Magazine, November 1859, 476*

22. *W.A. Townsend and Company, Famous Boys and How they Became Great Men,* New York, 1861

23. J. Hamilton. Fyffe, *The Triumphs of Invention and Discovery*, T. Nelson and Sons, London, Edinburgh and New York, 1863, 74-82

24. E. Littell, Cotton Spinning, *Living Age,* Third Series, Vol. IX, 14, 1861, 2-24

25. Daniels, *The Early English Cotton Industry.*

26. Hector. Charles. Cameron, *Samuel Crompton.*

27. David. Avrom, *The First Total War: Napoleon's Europe and the Birth of Warfare as We Know it,* Bell Houghton Mifflin Harcourt, 2007, 203

Chapter One: A Gathering of Whispers

28. Thomas. Hampson, *Horwich Its History and Legends, and Church,* Wigan Observer Office, Wallgate, Wigan, 1883, 3

29. French, The *Life and Times of Samuel Crompton,* 6-7

30. *Official Souvenir, Samuel Compton Centenary: Bolton June 7th -10th, 1927,* Tillotsons Ltd, Art Printers, Bolton and London,1927, (Authors private collection)

31. *Official Souvenir, Samuel Compton Centenary: Bolton June 7th -10th,*15

32. Thomas. Midgely, *Samuel Crompton 1753-1827: A Life of Tragedy and Service,* Tillotsons, Bolton, England, 1927 (Authors private collection)

33. Cameron, *Samuel Crompton,* 1951, 10

34. Town arms were originally granted to Bolton on the 5th June 1890. The town motto is a Latin pun "Bolton-super-Moras" for "Bolton on the Moors".

35. E. Littell, *Cotton Spinning,* 3

36. Kelly, *Beau Brummell,* Hodder, London, 2005, 147

37. This was certainly Crompton's own view; see French, *The Life and Times of Samuel Crompton,* 188-9

38. John. Harland, FSA, (Editor)' Edward. Baines Esq, *The History of the County Palatine and Duchy of Lancaster, A New Revised and Improved Edition,* Vol 1, George Rutledge and Sons, Manchester, London, 1868, 544.

39. see David Lane, Winter Hill Scrap Book, David Lane, Knutsford, Cheshire, 2007 Also available for download online at www.daveweb.co.uk/whcombined.pdf.

40. Daniels, *The Early English Cotton Industry*, 129

Chapter Two: Of Ships and Enterprise

41. Adam. Nicolson, *The Gentry: Stories of the English*, Harper Collins, London, 2011, 220

42. An anachronism, frequently used in the Crompton Papers to describe a letter.

43. *Lloyds Register*, Liverpool Maritime Museum, Archives, 1764

44. *Letter James Mather to the Admiralty, Navy Board*, 24th October 1768, National Archives, reference: ADM106/1168/261.

45. Admiralty, Navy Board, re *James Mathers Request to Dock His Ship at Portsmouth*, dated 26th of October 1768, National Archives, reference: ADM 106/1168/259.

46. Letter *James Mather to the Admiralty, Navy Board*, dated 24th of October 1768, National Archives, reference: ADM106/1168/261.

47. Unreferenced Letter, Crompton Papers, attached to the back of *James Mather to Cousin William Pimbley*, ZCR1, Item 9, Bolton Museums and Libraries, History Centre.

48. French (710-720) stated that William Pimbley was in partnership with one of the Mather's of Radcliffe Bridge. Further research by the author suggests that a James Mather of Warrington is a more likely associate, A parish register for the Parish of Eccles dated 1766 shows a marriage between a James Mather and Ann (Nancy) Kirkham with a witness John Hope, with the Mather signature matching that on the Mather letters. See Ancestry UK, Manchester England, Marriages and Bans, Parish of Eccles, 9/11/1766, ref:17541930 (1). The reference by French may be to a later generation.

49 Dan. Byrnes, *The Blackheath Connection*, http://www.danbyrnes.com.au/blackheath/thebc34.htm, original posting 2005.

50 National Archives, *Morgan v Mather*, Records created, acquired, and inherited by Chancery, and also of the Wardrobe, Royal Household, Exchequer and various commissions, Division within C - Records of Equity Side : the Six Clerks, C 12 - Court of Chancery : Six Clerks Office : Pleadings 1758 to 1800, reference : C 12/1718/2. Note that James Mather of New Orleans was also a litigant in this case.

51 A Mather of a slightly later period: James Mather (1799-1873). Possibly campaigning in the 1830s. See Tamsin. Lilley, *Remembering Slavery: South Shields' Links to the Trans-Atlantic Slave Trade*, June 2008

52 "Virginia Gleanings in England, 1909", *The Virginia Magazine of History and Biography*, 1909, Volume 17, 72.

53 Crompton Papers, ZCR1, Item 9, *Letter James Mather to His Cousin William Pimbley of New Hey Hall*, Warrington, Posted Liverpool, dated April 14th, 1767.

54. Ian. McIntyre, *Hester: The Remarkable Life of Dr Johnson's 'Dear Mistress'*, Constable, London, 2008, 274

55. James. Wallace, *A General and Descriptive history of the Ancient and Present State, of the Town of Liverpool: comprising, a review of its government, police, antiquities, and modern improvements; the progressive increase of street, square, public buildings, and inhabitants, together with a circumstantial account of the true causes of its extensive African trade*, J. McCreery, Liverpool, 1796, 78

56. Gilbert. French, *The Life and Times of Samuel Crompton*, 70-1.

57. The letter notes that eighteen yards of cloth was left at the Griffen Inn. It was common practice for chapmen to store unsold cloth at inns.

58. The Liverpool Plantation Records state that Brookes was the owner of the General Blakeney.

59. Naval Office Shipping Lists for Kingston, Jamaica, National Archives, reference: CO 142, Kew, London. Also, Richardson, D., Beedham, K., Schofield, M.M, *Liverpool Trade and Shipping, 1744-1786*. [data collection]. Economic and Social Science Research Council, UK Data Service. SN: 2923, http://doi.org/10.5255/UKDA-SN-2923-1;1992; these sources indicate that this was the only Brookes ship to sail around the time of the letter.

60. The Liverpool Plantation records show that a ship named the 'General Blakeney', Brookes owner, John Amery master, sailed from Liverpool on the 15th of April destined for Jamaica, via Cork, *Plantation Records*, Liverpool Maritime Museum.

61. Richardson, D., Beedham, K., Schofield, M.M. *Liverpool Trade and Shipping, 1744-1786*, 1992

62. The National Archives, Kew, Shipping Returns, Jamaica, CO 142/19, 1766-1784

63. French, *The Life and Times of Samuel Crompton*, 71

64. *A List of the Company of Merchants trading to Africa belonging to Liverpool*, 24th of June 1752, reproduced as a book cover for, Gail. Cameron and S. Crooke, *Liverpool the Capital of the Slave Trade*, Picton Press, Liverpool, 1992

65. Michael. Janes, *From Smuggling to Cotton Kings: The Gregg Story*, Memoirs, Cirencester, Gloucestershire, United Kingdom, 2010, 9-10

66 William. Hague, *William Wilberforce, The Life of the Great Anti Slave Trade Campaigner,* Harper Perennial, London, New York, Toronto, Sydney and New Delhi, 2008, 152-3

67. Figures taken from Hugh Thomas, *The Slave Trade. The History of the Atlantic Slave Trade 1440-1870*, Picador, London, United Kingdom, 1997, 249

68. See Eric. Williams *Capitalism and Slavery* , University of North Carolina Press, 1994; also http://www.bbc.co.uk/history/british/abolition/industrialisation_article_01.shtml.

69. See: http://www.liverpoolmuseums.org.uk/ism/resources/slave_trade_ports.aspx

70. A ship at the time is defined as a large sea going vessel having a bowsprit and usually three masts each composed of a lower mast, a topmast, and a top gallant mast.

71. See Gomer. Williams, *History of The Liverpool Privateers and Letters of Marque, with an Account of: The Liverpool Slave Trade*, William Heinemann, London, Liverpool, Edward Howell, Church Street, 1897, 123

72. National Archives, HCA - *Records of the High Court of Admiralty and Colonial Vice-Admiralty Courts,* Division within HCA - Records of the Instance and Prize Courts, HCA/26/5/148

73. National Archives, HCA - Records of the High Court of Admiralty and Colonial Vice-Admiralty courts, Division within HCA - Records of the Instance and Prize Courts, 26/9/81

74. A letter of marquee was a license to an authorised nonmilitary person, that is a privateer to attack and capture enemy vessels.

75. Williams, *History of the Liverpool Privateers* , 57

76. See Williams, *History of the Liverpool Privateers*, 162-70, for a discussion of both adversaries' treatment of prisoners.

77. Newcastle Courant - Saturday 20 January 1759

78. Reported in *Ipswich Journal*, Saturday 21st January 1758. In the same edition of this newspaper is a report that Captain Lockhart arrived at Plymouth with a French

ship on January 14th and a Snow from St Domingo. Both taken by himself and the Magnanim. The 'prizes ' were returned under convoy.

79. *The Scots Magazine,* 7th February 1757

80. see Liza. Picard, *Dr Johnson's London*, Phoenix Press, London, 2000, 107-08.

81. Hague, *William Wilberforce,* 150

82. Williams, *History of The Liverpool Privateers ,,* 284

83. Williams, *History of The Liverpool Privateers,* 284

84. see Daniels, *The Early English Cotton Industry*, 139-142

85. See Arnold. Toynbee, *Lectures on The Industrial Revolution of the Eighteenth Century in England*, Longmans, Green and Co, London, New York and Bombay, 1896, 101

86. Marriage Bonds and Licenses, *Cheshire Archives and Local Studies*

87. The description is adapted from John. Hughes, *Liverpool Banks and Bankers, 1760-1837*, Henry Young and Sons, Liverpool; Simpkin, Marshall, Hamilton, Kent &Co, Ltd, London, 1906, 47. See also a colour plate, frontispiece of the book, a wonderful illustration of this garb.

88. For a full deconstruction of the idea of the 'Gentleman' in English History see Nicolson, 2011. For further reference see Stuart. A. Raymond, *My Ancestor Was a Gentleman*, Society of Genealogists Enterprises Ltd. London, 2012. The subtleties of social class and gentility are excellently discussed in Lawrence. James, *The Middle Class, A History*, Little, Brown, London, 2006, 44-59

89. See Williams, *History of The Liverpool Privateers,* 93. To quote: *"being of the old school,"* wearing *"knee breeches, broad-flapped coat, gold laced waistcoat, broad shoes with gold buckles, and wearing a three-cornered hat".*

90. The Sparling was particularly active during the American War of Independence with two notable engagements: one a six hour battle, escaping the clutches of an American Privateer and then retreating into Kingston. The second the taking of an American Brig, laden with tobacco from Carolina. See, Williams, *History of The Liverpool Privateers,* 210-211

91. Crompton Papers, ZCR1, Item 7, *Receipt Charles Hamilton to the Honourable Thomas Townsend Esquire*, dated 27th of March 1760.

92. No direct relation to Charles Townsend. He was the son of the right hon Thomas Townsend of Frognall Kent and had variously been clerk to the household of the

Prince of Wales 1756-1760, Clerk of the Green Cloth 1760-1762 and a Lord of the Treasury 1765-1767. see Lewis. Namier and John. Brooke, *The House of Commons 1754-1790*, Boydell and Brewer, 1985, 554

93. Hugh Thomas, *The Slave Trade. The History of the Atlantic Slave Trade 1440-1870*, 249

94. There is one extant example of William Pimbley's business networks. A contested will for a William Bird of Warrington notes a bond of £15 (1769) due for payment by William. The will is an example of the extensive lending and extension of credit between merchants etc. which provided the foundation for banking. Lancashire Archives, *WCW, Disputed Probate Papers, Testator William Bird of Blackbrook, Warrington, Yeoman*, 1767

95. Roy. Porter, *English Society in the Eighteenth Century*, Penguin Books, 1982, London, 94

96. James, *The Middle Class, A History*, 77

97. For a fascinating discussion of the contradiction of living with investments in slavery and preaching and practicing benevolence see David. Sekers, *A Lady of Cotton: Hannah Greg, Mistress of Quarry Bank Mill*, The History Press In association with the National Trust, Stroud, Gloucestershire, United Kingdom, 2013

Chapter Three: Preface to a Revolution

98. E.J. Hobsbawm, *Industry and Empire, An Economic History of Britain Since 1750*, 18.

99. The timing of the so called 'Agricultural Revolution' is contentious, as are the nineteenth century claims that it originated with leading innovators such as Townsend and Tull. Overton develops specific criteria for an agricultural revolution and places the major changes from 1750. See Mark. Overton, *Agricultural Revolution in England; The Transformation of the Agrarian Economy, 1500-1850*, Cambridge University Press, Cambridge, 1996

100. Baines, *History of the Cotton Manufacture In Great Britain*, 111

101. Daniels, *The Early English Cotton Industry*, 54

102. See Michael. M. Edwards, *The Growth of the British Cotton Industry 1780-1815*, 27

103. Daniels, The Early English Cotton Industry, 59-60; Here Daniels is citing Aiken, *A Description of the Country from Thirty to Forty Miles Round Manchester*, 182-184

104. Nice story, possibly true, but Hargreave's wife's name was not Jenny. The expression jenny could be a derivative of engine.

105. There is an early reference to the machine, by this name, in the particulars of an auction in 1772; see *Manchester Mercury* - Tuesday 22 of September 1772

106. The business was described as Carding, Slubbing and Spinning of Cotton. *Manchester Mercury* - Tuesday 06 August 1776

107. Edward. Baines, *History of the Cotton Manufacture In Great Britain*, H. Fisher, R. Fisher and P. Jackson, London, 1835, 117

108. Barbara. Hahn, Causes and Effects: The Relationship Between Social and Technological Change, 2016, in Chris. Wrigley (ed), *Industrialisation and Society in Britain*, The Arkwright Society, Cromford Mills, Derbyshire, United Kingdom, 68-86

109. Baines, *History of the Cotton Manufacture In Great Britain*, 113

110 John. Roby, *Traditions of Lancashire*, George Rutledge and Sons, London and Manchester, , 5th Edition, 1872

Chapter Four: Prelude to Fear

111. John. Roby, *Traditions of Lancashire*, 1872, 787-840

112. For a brief bibliographical note see Charles. William. Sutton, *A List of Lancashire Authors, With Brief Biographical and Bibliographical Notes*, Abel. Heywood and Sons, London, 1876, 104; Roby tragically drowned on the wreck of the Orion, near Port Patrick, 18th of June 1850.

113. The Pilkingtons were a prominent local family. For a full and colourful narrative of the history of the Pilkingtons see Thomas. Hampson, *History of Rivington*, Roger and Renwick, Market Street, Wigan and Chronicle Office, Horwich, 1893, 12-19, with other mentions throughout the book.

114. It is possible that the inn at the foot of the Pike was "The Black Boy" later run by Joseph Pimbley, William Pimbley's youngest son.[1] The inn was the meeting place for the school governors of the Grammar School, founded in 1566 by Richard Pilkington under a Charter from Queen Elisabeth Ist. The name 'Black Boy' (later the Blackamoors Head and the New Inn) signified the wealth accruing from slavery.

There is a reference to an auction for timber at the House of Joseph Pimbley at the New Inn, Rivington, in the *Manchester Mercury and Harrop's General Advertiser*, Tuesday, 9th of February 1796.

115. Porter, *English Society In the Eighteenth Century*, 293-4

116. Irving. Babbitt, *Rousseau and Romanticism*, Houghton Mifflin Company, The Riverside Press, Cambridge, USA, 1919, 123

Chapter Five: The Hall i' th' Wood (The Hall in the Wood)

117. *Crompton Papers*, ZCR1, Item 4, *Will of George Crompton of Tong*, 1752

118. French, *The Life and Times of Samuel Crompton*, 15-25

119. French, *The Life and Times of Samuel Crompton*, 22

120. French, *The Life and Times of Samuel Crompton*, Appendix, 248-49

121. See Charles. F. Foster, *Capital and Innovation, How Britain Became the First Industrial Nation*. Arley Hall Archive Press, 2004, which discusses the Pimbleys' (Pimlots') as examples of emerging businesspeople in the Northwest.

122. Arnold. Toynbee, *Lectures on The Industrial Revolution of the Eighteenth Century in England, Longman's, Green and Co, London*, New York and Bombay, 1896, 57-66

123. Toynbee, *Lectures on the Industrial Revolution of the !8th Century in England*, 59, Toynbee also notes that this 'decimation' of the yeoman class became more rapid around 1760; Toynbee, 61.

124. Midgely, *Samuel Crompton 1753-1827, A Life of Tragedy and Service*, 5

125. Midgely, *Samuel Crompton 1753-1827, A Life of Tragedy and Service*, 5

126. French, *The Life and Times of Samuel Compton*, 36

127. The footwear noted here is an obvious matter of speculation, but there is an early reference to the wearing of clogs in John. Whittaker, *The History of Manchester in Four Books, volume 2, Messrs Dodley in Pall Mall, London*, 1775, 257, being described under the heading of Galoche: wooden slipper worn sometimes by men in France and England.

128. For a comprehensive consideration of dress codes, fashion and morality read Aileen. Ribeiro, *Dress and Morality*, Berg Publishers; Revised ed. Edition, Oct. 2003

129. Charles. Hefling and Cynthia. L. Shattuck, *The Oxford Guide to The Book of Common Prayer: A Worldwide Survey*, Oxford University Press, 2006, 97

130. Midgley goes so far as to dismiss the whole story of Uncle Alexander and his supposed influence upon Samuel as a fabrication; and even uses the fact that Alexander was an executor for Samuel's father George's will as evidence that he could not have been lame, as he would never have been given such a responsibility Midgely, *Samuel Crompton 1753-1827, A Life of Tragedy and Service*, 8

131. French, *The Life and Times of Samuel Crompton*, 37

132. Cameron, *Samuel Crompton*, 29

133. Cameron, *Samuel Crompton*, 30

134. French, *The Life and Times of Samuel Crompton*, 38

135. *Caledonian Mercury* - Wednesday 04 December 1765

136. *Chester Chronicle* - Friday 13 September 1776

137. French, *The Life and Times of Samuel Crompton*, 39

138. *Newcastle Chronicle* - Saturday 06 June 1772

139. *Leeds Intelligencer* - Tuesday 24 January 1775

Chapter Six: Ghosts, Riots and Disorder

140. Hubert Walsh, *An History of Coppull*, online PDF, dated 2cnd of June 1978, www.lan-opc.org.uk/Coppull/downloads/CoppullHistory.pdf

141. Arkwright leased the land from landowner, John Chadwick of High Burgh Hall, for 84 years at £150 per year.It had been the site of a forge on the river Yarrow.

142. Anglo-French War (1778–1783). The Anglo-French War was a military conflict fought between France and Great Britain with their respective allies as part of the American Revolutionary War between 1778 and 1783.

143. *The Scots Magazine* - Thursday 01 February 1776

144. *Kentish Gazette* - Wednesday 17 July 1776

145. Reasons for opposition to new technology can be complex. For a full analysis of contemporary issues drawing on historical examples see Calestous. Juma, *Innovation and Its Enemies: Why People Resist New Technologies,* Oxford University Press, 2016

146. French, *Life and Times of Samuel Crompton*, 68; French states 20 spindles, but the point remains.

147. *Oxford Journal*, Saturday, 16 October 1779

148. There are contradictory reports on the actual dating of the riots. Fitton notes two attacks, one on Saturday 2nd October and the second on Monday 4th October, one newspaper puts the first attack on Saturday October 9th while *The Annual Register, October 1779, 229,* also reports events on Saturday 9th October. Given a letter dated by Wedgewood 9th October then the riots are likely to have taken place the week previously making Fitton correct.

149. *The Annual Register* claimed this was on the Sunday and involved a mob of 2000 or more.

150. *Oxford Journal*, Saturday, 16 of October 1779

151. Fitton, notes that those caught and tried for the Birkacre riots were *"a representative group of the industrial population"* and included weavers, spinners, labourers, joiners and even a cotton tradesman. See R.S. Fitton, *The Arkwright's: Spinners of Fortune*, Manchester University Press, Manchester and New York, 1989, 54

152. see Brian. Lewis, *Coalmining in the Eighteenth and Nineteenth Centuries*, Seminal Studies in History, Longman, London, 1971, 28-40

153. *The Annual Register*, October 1779, 229

154. At the time of the disturbances Sir Richard Clayton was soon to be married, a fact that might have heightened his urge to survive. Kentish Gazette, Saturday 11th of December 1779

155. These details noted in James. Folds, *Sayings and Doings of James Folds, Otherwise Parson Folds, Lecturer of Bolton Parish Church, From 1755 to 1820*, George. Winterburn, Deansgate, Bolton,1879, 99

156. Quoted in Fitton, *The Arkwright's: Spinners of Fortune*, 53

157. See *Northampton Mercury* - Monday 18th of October 1779

158. Reported in *Manchester Mercury* - Tuesday 16 of November 1779

159. *Northampton Mercury* - Monday 18th of October 1779

160. Adrian. Randall, *Riotous Assemblies: Popular Protest in Hanoverian England*, OUP, Oxford, 2006, 250

161. R.S. Fitton, P. Alfred and P. Wadsworth, *The Strutts and the Arkwrights, 1758-1830: A Study of the Early Factory System*, Manchester University Press, 1968, 53

162. Michael Andrew Žmolek, *Rethinking the Industrial Revolution: Five Centuries of Transition from Agrarian to Industrial Capitalism in England*, BRILL, 2013, 434

163. *Manchester Mercury* - Tuesday 12 October 1779

164. *Manchester Mercury* - Tuesday 12 October 1779

165. French, *The Life and Times of Samuel Crompton*, 54, footnote 38. (2nd edition, 1970).

166. French, *The Life and Times of Samuel Crompton*, 1970, 55.

167. French, *The Life and Times of Samuel Crompton*, 68

168. Daniels, The Early English Cotton Industry, 54

169. Daniels, *The Early English Cotton Industry*, 82-88

170. Randal, *Riotous Assemblies: Popular Protest in Hanoverian England*, 250

171. The invention was further modified in 1753 so that it only required one person to weave.

172. This argument was made by James. A. Mann, FSS, *The Cotton Trade of Great Britain: Its Rise, Progress and Present Extent*, Simpkin, Marshall & Co, London, Joseph Thomson and Son Manchester, 1860, 16

173. Mann, *The Cotton Trade of Great Britain*, 16 noted the initial deleterious effects on the growth of the textile trade in Blackburn because of the riots concerning Hargreaves spinning jenny.

174. Crompton Papers, ZCR17, Item 11, *Draft Memorandum to Merchant and Manufacturers, Cotton Spinners and Bleachers.*

Chapter Seven: The Reign of the Conjurors

175. Hahn, Causes and Effects: The Relationship Between Social and Technological Change, 70-71

176. Osborne, *Iron, Steam and Money, The Making of the Industrial Revolution*, 36.

177. Charles. F. Foster and Eric. L. Jones, *The Fabric of Society and How it Creates Wealth: Wealth Distribution and Wealth Creation in Europe 1000-1800*, Arley Hall Press, Cheshire, England, 2013, 19. (available online at http://arleyhallarchives.co.uk)

178. Osborne, *Iron, Steam and Money, The Making of the Industrial Revolution,* 44-6

179. Harold. Catling, *The Spinning Mule,* The Lancashire Library, Lancashire County Council Library and Leisure Committees, 1986, (Originally published in 1970 by David and Charles), 32

180. Daniels, *The Early English Cotton Industry,* 116-17

181. Edwards, *The Growth of the British Cotton Industry 1780-1815,* 49; Also, Baines, *History of the Cotton Manufacture of Great Britain,* 323

182. *Crompton Papers,* ZCR15, Item 13, *Petition 20th of April 1811, to Landowners, Merchants etc of Lancashire, Cheshire and Yorkshire,* A similar draft can be found under ref ZCR15, Item 12.

183. For a full technical description see Catling, *The Spinning Mule,* 32-4; while for a short clear exposition see Daniels, T*he Early English Cotton Industry,* 116-7.

184. Arkwright went into partnership with Jedidia Strutt and Samuel Need.

185. French, *The Life and Times of Samuel Crompton,* 172, and fn. 157.

186. E.J. Hobsbawm, *Industry and Empire,* 43

187. French, *The Life and Times of Samuel Crompton,* 201-02

188. Foster, *The Fabric of Society and How It Creates Wealth, Wealth Distribution and Wealth Creation in Europe 1000 to 1800, 31,* offers an argument in terms of the high level of skill required of clock and watch making which though true, the problems of spinning also presented new conceptual challenges.

189. Osborne, *Iron, Steam and Money, The Making of the Industrial Revolution,* 13

190. John. Kennedy Esq, *A Brief Memoir of Samuel Crompton with a Description of his Machine Called the Mule and of the Subsequent Improvements of the Machine by Others* (Read February 20th, 1830.) published in, *Memoirs of the Literary and Philosophical Society of Manchester, Second Series,* Volume V, Baldwin and Cradock, London, 1831

191. Kennedy, *A Brief Memoir of Samuel Crompton with a Description of his Machine Called the Mule and of the Subsequent Improvements of the Machine by Others,* 335-6

192. Kennedy, *A Brief Memoir of Samuel Crompton with a Description of his Machine Called the Mule and of the Subsequent Improvements of the Machine by Others,* 337

193. Manchester Mercury, 8th of December 1789

194. Catling, *The Spinning Mule,* 32

195. Osborne, I*ron, Steam and Money, The Making of the Industrial Revolution, 176*

196. *Derby Mercury* - Friday 27 June 1746

197. *Northampton Mercury* - Saturday 13 May 1786

198. A market stall, possibly in Covent Garden. James Peller Malcolm, *Anecdotes of the Manners and Customs of London, During the Eighteenth Century: With a Review of the State of Society in 1807. To which is Added, a Sketch of the Domestic and Ecclesiastical Architecture, and of the Various Improvements in the Metropolis*, Longman, Hurst, Rees, and Orme, 1810

199. *Kentish Gazette* - Tuesday 16 May 1786

200. The Irish Brigade was a brigade in the French army made up of Irish exiles.

201. Saunders Newsletter and Daily Advertiser, April 1785

202. Fitton, *The Arkwright's: Spinners of Fortune*, 79

203. Mansfield is credited with reforming British Commercial Law, and two major court cases that progressed the abolition of slavery; Somerset v Stewart in 1772 and the case of the Zong in 1783 where slaves were judged not to be chattels for insurance purposes.

204. Figures for the use of the jenny varied widely by area such that Bolton had 882 jenny spindles while Stockport had 83,712. See Crompton Papers, ZCR16B, Item 12, *Account of the Number of Spindles*, 1811

205. Crompton Papers, ZCR2, Item 1, *Newspaper cutting Manchester Mercury-offer of improvement in spinning, in return for £100 subscription, Ainsworth Hall near Bolton (Transcript)*, dated 28th of December 1795.

206. Crompton Papers, ZCR2, Item 2, Memorandum referring to ZCR2, Item 1, 1795

Chapter Eight: Of Heartbreak, Love and Betrayal

207. For a notable exception to this see, Amanda. Vickery, *The Gentleman's Daughter, Women's Lives in Georgian England*, Yale University Press, Newhaven and London, 1998

208. Crompton Papers, , Item 4, *Samuel Crompton, Household Account*, 1790

209. Crompton Papers, ZCR100, Item 8, *Samuel Crompton Account Book*, 1796d

210. Mary's birth date has proved elusive to historians, genealogists and the author. Looking at the dates of birth of her siblings, she is likely to have been younger than Samuel.

211. French, *The Life and Times of Samuel Crompton*, 71

212. Cameron, *Samuel Crompton*, 64

213. Cited in French, *The Life and Times of Samuel Crompton*, 71-2

214. The factory was originally situated in Black Horse Street, Bolton moving to an out of town site, Kay Street, in 1846. See Dobson and Barlow Ltd, *Samuel Crompton: The Inventor of the Spinning Mule, A Brief Survey of His Life and Work with which is incorporated a Short History of Messrs Dobson and Barlow Ltd*, Dobson and Barlow Ltd, Bolton, 1927, 97-98

215. Dobson and Barlow Ltd, *Samuel Crompton: The Inventor of the Spinning Mule, A Brief Survey of His Life and Work with which is incorporated a Short History of Messrs. Dobson and Barlow Ltd, Dobson and Barlow Ltd*, Bolton, 83

216. cited in John. Kennedy Esq, *A Brief Memoir of Samuel Crompton with a Description of his Machine Called the Mule and of the Subsequent Improvements of the Machine by Others*, 321

217. *Famous Boys and How They Became Great Men*, 246

218. French, T*he Life and Times of Samuel Crompton*, 78-80

219. Using a subscription was an anachronism insofar as it would not provide adequate recompense for inventions requiring a significant amount of capital for their development.

220. French, T*he Life and Times of Samuel Crompton*, 83-4

221. see *Manchester Mercury* - Tuesday 28 January 1783

222. J. Brown, and S. Crompton, *The Basis of Mr Samuel Crompton's Claims to A Second Remuneration from Parliament for His Discovery of the Mule Spinning Machine*, Charles Simms and Co, Manchester, 1868, 24.

223. Cited in Robert. Chambers, *The Book of Days: A Miscellany of Popular Antiquities in Connection with the Calendar, Including Anecdote, Biography, & History, Curiosities of Literature and Oddities of Human Life and Character*, Volume 2, 1888, W & R Chambers Ltd.

224. This list can be found in *Crompton Papers*, ZCR1, Item 12 (a), and reproduced in French. *The Life and Times of Samuel Crompton*,271-2

225. Estimates cited in French, Life and Times of Samuel Crompton, 84-5

226. French, relates a wonderful interview with the 83 years old Thomas Brindle, who remembered the Crompton's life at Oldhams; French, *The Life and Times of Samuel Crompton*, 96

227. Chapman speculated that the grandmother mentioned here was most likely to be Alice Pimbley rather than Betty Crompton, see Chapman, *Samuel Crompton*, 72, fn 1

228. There is a dispute about the exact date of his move French having erroneously attributed a move in 1791 to the presence of a Mr William Crompton in the Bolton rate books. Midgley states that William Crompton was no relation. See Midgley, *Samuel Crompton and the Spinning Mule, 16-17*

Chapter Nine: The White Doe of Rylstone

229. Noted by French, *The Life and Times of Samuel Crompton*, 89

230. Lancashire Archives, *Assignment: for 10/- a piece and transfer of land and houses: James Blakeley, Junior, of Rivington, husbandman, to Joseph Pimbley of Rivington, whitster -- land and houses in Horwich -- annual rent 14/- for remainder of term of 300 years begun 1785*, DDX 121, Miscellaneous Documents. In 1797 Joseph acquired the interest of James Blakely Junior in the four properties.

231. Moira Long, *A Study of Occupations in Yorkshire Parish Registers In the Eighteenth and Early Nineteenth Centuries,* www.localpopulationstudies.org.uk/ PDF/LPS71/LPS71-2003-14-39.pdf

232. William. Wordsworth, *The White Doe of Rylstone: Or the Fate of the Nortons,* Longman, Hurst, Rees, Orme and Brown, Paternoster Row, London, 1815

233. The factory later became a corn mill and was demolished in 1827.

234. This story relating to John Heaton is fully related in Edmund. R. Heaton, *The Heaton's of Deane: The Varying Fortunes of a Lancashire Family over 850 years,* Heaton, 2000, 145-146.

235. The distance between spindles.

236. Dobson and Barlow Ltd, *Samuel Crompton: The Inventor of the Spinning Mule, A Brief Survey of His Life and Work with which is incorporated a short history of Messrs Dobson and Barlow Ltd,* Bolton, 1927, 82

237. The Picton Street Mill was taken over by John's son Lambert Heaton, prosperous farmer and manufacturer. The most successful cotton manufacturers of the Heaton family were Thomas and Joseph Heaton who built Delph Mill in 1860, being advantageously located next to the Lancashire and Yorkshire railway line in Lostock.

238. M.S. Anderson, *Europe in the Eighteenth Century ,1713-1789*. Routledge, *London*, 2014, 21-2.

239. John. Lord. Campbell, *Lives of the Lords Chancellors and Keepers of the Great Seal of England*, volume seven, Blanchard and Lea, Philadelphia,1851, 416-18

240. Oliver. Goldsmith, Vicar of Wakefield, in J.F. Dove, *The Novels of Sterne, Goldsmith, Dr Johnson, MacKenzie, Horace Walpole and Clara Reeve*, Hurst Robinson and Co, Pall Mall, London, 1823, 266

241. Elizabeth, Barret-Browning (1806-1861) later used Swedenborgian ideas and imagery to attack social ills, for example slavery in the United States, child labor and political oppression in Italy.

242. See Smoley, in Jonathan S. Rose, Stuart, Shotwell, and Mary Lou Bertucci (editors), *Scribe of Heaven, Swedenborg's Life, Work and Impact*, Swedenborg Foundation, INC, 2005,11. Swedenborg's achievements in science, religious and practical matters were enormous and too extensive to list here, See Smoley, 4-49

243. A lecturer was a junior or assistant curate for a Parish.

244. French, *The Life and Times of Samuel Crompton*, 72

245. James. Folds, *Sayings and Doings of James Folds*, George Winterburn, Deansgate, Bolton, 1879, 110

246. Folds, *Sayings and Doings of James Folds*, 54

247. Bolton Museums and Libraries, History Centre, Rev James Folds, *Book of Sermons and Household Accounts 1750-1788*, ZZ441

248. Folds, *Saying and Doings of James Folds*, 108

249. Folds, *Sayings and Doings of James Folds*, 86

250. Some authors considered that the absence of family, particularly a mother, to assist him in raising his children led to their misguided and at times extravagant behaviour. See Chapman, *Samuel Crompton*, 83-4. However, there was an extended family in the form of the Pimbley and Blakeley families.

251. French, *The Life and Times of Samuel Crompton*, 111

252. It is worth noting that there were local connections with Swedenborg. His major works were translated into English within twenty years of his death in 1772. Translated by Thomas Hartley (1708-1784) a nonresident pastor of Winwick, and by John Cloves (1743-1831) an English Pastor in Manchester.

253. Midgely, *Samuel Crompton*, 17

254. French, *The Life and Times of Samuel Crompton*, 123

255. A theory of 'meaningful coincidences' whereby events may be connected by meaning and not necessarily through causality.

256. The story is recounted by Richard. Smoley, The Inner Journey of Emanuel Swedenborg, in Rose, Shotwell, and Bertucci, *Scribe of Heaven, Swedenborg's Life, Work and Impact*, 34-35

257. See for example *Crompton Papers*, ZCR44 Item 7, Letter from *Betty Dawson to George Crompton,* dated 13th of March 1826.

258. French, *The Life and Times of Samuel Crompton*,125.

259. The Swedenborgians used a purpose built hall in Little Bolton, though lack of funds meant that they had to rent it out as a school during the day. See Cameron, *Samuel Crompton*, 87

Chapter Ten: An Englishman's House is His Factory

260 Simon. Taylor and Julian. Holder, *Manchester's Northern Quarter: The Greatest Meer Village*, Manchester City Council, English Heritage Publication, 2008, 20

261 Taylor and Holder, *Manchester's Northern Quarter: The Greatest Meer Village*, 11

262 French gives examples of engines erected in 1792 at the firm of Peel and Ainsworth and other firms, French, *Life and Times of Samuel Crompton*, 100

263 French notes that the first steam engine to be used for the spinning of cotton in Manchester was erected by a Mr Drinkwater in 1789 and that both Bolton and Glasgow adopted the steam engine for spinning in 1792. See French, *Life and Times of Samuel Crompton*, fn 107, 114.

264 Though factories might not be built in towns urban expansion would mean the town would grow towards the factory. In addition, even with steam driven machinery proximity to a water supply was useful.

265 This is an admittedly contentious interpretation, as some believe it to refer to the orthodox religious output of Oxford and Cambridge while others a burned down and subsequently blackened mill in the city of London (Albion Mill).

266 Erasmus. Darwin, *The Botanic Garden, A Poem in Two Parts; The Economy of Vegetation and the Loves of the Plants, With Philosophical Note*s, 1789, Jones and Company, London 1825

267 *Crompton Papers*, ZCR5, Item 1, *Letter, London, 16th of February 1801*, Letter from Thomas Horrocks to Mr Price re arrangements for collecting rents from Spring Gardens. He sustained a considerable loss on the properties.

268 French notes the arrival of the word factory for the first time in the Bolton rate books for 1792 and that spinning, with the use of mules was still largely operated on a domestic scale. French, *The Life and Times of Samuel Crompton*, 114 (fn 107) and 115

269 *Crompton Papers* ZCR100, Item 3, *Accounts Book, 1790*

270 See Midgley, *Samuel Crompton*, 17

271 Cameron says 1800 as does French. Midgley infers his dates from the Irving documents. The year 1800 is possibly the year in which the idea originated.

272 Noted in Midgely, *Samuel Crompton*, 19

273 Daniels thought the sum was £100, but he was writing before the discovery of the 1927 papers: Daniels, *The Early English Cotton Industry*, 120

274 French, *Life and Times of Samuel Crompton*, 124

275 A list of names survives that indicates the extent of his business activity showing 53 weavers to whom he supplied his rovings between 15/3/1810 and 30/12 1811: *Crompton Papers*, ZCR100 Item 17, *Account Books*

276 See Kelly's own description reproduced in Catling, *The Spinning Mule*, 55-6

277 Noted in French, *The Life and Times of Samuel Crompton*, 125-6. No known sources supply the name of the offending son.

Chapter Eleven: The Curious Case of Ichabod Eccles

278. The etymology of Ichabod is the story of the Israelites loss of the 'Ark of God' in battle with the Philistines, in the aftermath of which Shiloh, the wife of Phinehas, names her newborn child Ichobod, meaning 'no glory' or 'loss of glory'. In fact, she

dies with the utterance that the *"the glory is departed from Israel"*. *Holy Bible*, Samuel 4: verses 19-22

279. *The Annual Register, Or, A View of the History, Politics, and Literature of the Year 1825*, Baldwin, Cradock and Joy, C and J. Rivington, London, 1826, 211

280. Adlington Hall Lancashire not Adlington Hall, Cheshire which is still standing.

281. Unfortunately, this majestic edifice was demolished in the 1960s.

282 http://www.lostheritage.org.ukgraphics/pdf/Lancashire_AdlingtonHall_AdlingtonFocus_history_and_photo.pdf.

283. Edward. Wedlake. Brayley, *The Beauties of England and Wales, Or, Delineations, Topographical*, John Britton, London, 1807, 176

284. Ordinance Survey, 1841, Courtesy of Digi map, https://digimap.edina.ac.uk/

285. Sale Particulars provided courtesy of Chorley Archives, Chorley Heritage Centre, Chorley, Lancashire

286. Brayley, *The Beauties of England and Wales, Or, Delineations, Topographical*, 176

287. Thomas. De. Quincey, *Autobiographic Sketches*, Hurd and Houghton, Cambridge, 1876, 459

288. Richard. Clayton, *A Treatise on Greyhounds: With Observations on the Treatment of Disorders of Them, By a Sportsman*, Lackington, Hughes, Harding, Mayor and Jones, Finsbury Square, London, 1819

289. Supported by the Duke of Portland, he did not attend the house after the recess of 1781, was abroad in 1782 and died in that year. see History of parliament online, http://www.historyofparliamentonline.org/volume/1754-1790/member/bridgeman-henry-simpson-1757-82

290. *Kentish Gazette* - Saturday 02 September 1780

291. *Manchester Mercury* Tuesday 19th September 1780

292. *Manchester Mercury* Tuesday 20th May 1783

293. Brian. Lewis, *Coal Mining in the Eighteenth and Nineteenth Centuries, Seminar Studies in History*, Longman, 1971, 17

294. Philopatris. Varvicensis, *Character of the Late Charles James Fox*, Volume 1, Mawman, London, 1809, 239. The quote is attributed to contemporary reports in the newspapers.

295. Edward. Whitehead, *A Sermon Preached in the Parish Church of Bolton after the Execution of James Holland on Bolton Moor for Croft Breaking*, B. Jackson, Bolton, 1786, 12

296. Anonymously written *Biographical Keepsake*, cited in M. Seymour, *Mary Shelley*, John Murray, London, 2000,191

297. David. Wright, *English Romantic Verse*, Penguin Classics, 1968, 235-9

298. Mary. Shelley, *The Biographical Keepsake*, 1827, 226

299. Crompton Papers, ZCR36, Item 14, *Copy of Statement by John Lancaster for Court of Chancery*, A list on the last of ten pages is dated 1823.

300. Beattie, *A History of Blackburn*, Lancaster, 2007, 23

301. The rights of copyholders are an area in which Lord Chancellor Eldon achieved significant reforms.

302. A notable case is Fisher v Pimbley, 1809, cited in legal textbooks throughout the nineteenth century as an example of arbitration law: for example, John. Simcoe. Saunders, *The Law of Pleading and Evidence in Civil Actions*, S.Sweet et al, Chancery Lane, London, 1828.

303. The National Archives, Kew, *Pimbley v Ratcliffe. Bill and Three Answers. Plaintiffs: Joseph Pimbley.Defendants: John Catlow, Ellis Ratcliffe and Ann Smalley*, 1803, C 13/31/1, [W1803 P18]

304. Lancashire Records Office, Archives and Local Studies, DDX 28/249/61, August 1796, *Affidavits Christopher Schofield, John Roscoe, Ellis Ratcliffe*. Clitheroe Borough Court.

305. Alex. Murray and Son (publishers), *Three Tours of Dr Syntax, In Search of 1. The Picturesque, 2. Of Consolation, 3. Of a Wife*, London, 1871

306. Murray and Son, *Three Tours of Dy Syntax, 1. In Search of the Picturesque*, 6

307. *Manchester Mercury* 14th of March 1792

308. *The London Gazette*, 3 June 1794, Issue 13667, 527; 10 March 1795, Issue 13759, 239; 17 March 1795, Issue 13761, 257; 7 May 1796, Issue 13890, 444; 5 December 1797, Issue 14071, 1170; , 29 August 1797, Issue 14041, 843

309. James. Boswell, *The Life of Samuel Johnson LL.D.*, Wordsworth Classics of World Literature, 1999.

310. Story recounted in Dennis. Rose, *Life, Times and Recorded Works of Robert Dighton (1752-1814), Actor, Artist and Print seller, and Three of His Artist Sons,* Dennis Rose (Publisher), Element Books Ltd (Distributor), 1981, 18

311. Robert Dighton published several caricatures of attorneys including a country attorney and his clients, a sharp between two flats, a bailiff and an attorney: a match for the devil, the devil among lawyers, the lawyers all alive in Westminster Hall. A catalogue of sufficient length to communicate his opinion of the 'profession'.

312. For example, Samuel Crompton used the services of a Mr Edward Partington to arbitrate in a dispute with a William Lord of Pilkington, in 1785. See *Crompton Papers,* ZCR1, Item 15.

313. For example, Samuel Crompton was challenged in the Court of Common Pleas in relation to the nonpayment of wages to Abraham Entwistle and Thomas Thorpe, ZCR38 item 8, 1822.

314. The Chancery documents do mention the financial interest of Mr. John Roscow, a stone cutter, of Haslingdon, who appeared as a new partner.

315. Michael. M. Edwards, *The Growth of the British Cotton Industry 1780-1815,* 194

316. Crompton Papers, ZCR 1 Item 14, *Note from William MacAlpine to Samuel Compton,* dated 15th May 1785

317. *Caledonian Mercury -* Saturday 25 October 1788

318. Crompton Papers, ZCR9 Item 3, *Letter from MacAlpine to Samuel Crompton,* 18th February 1805

319. Crompton Papers, ZCR93 Item 1, *Letter from William MacAlpine London to Samuel Compton,* dated 28th January 1805

320. *Caledonian Mercury -* Thursday 10 November 1808

321. Crompton Papers, ZCR92 Item 1, *Letter from William MacAlpine London to Samuel Compton,* dated 9th February 1805,

322. The offer for sale is recorded in the *Caledonian Mercury -* Monday 15 April 1805, with application to the proprietors; Messrs Hunter, Rainey and Co Glasgow.

323. A lease was offered on the Mill later in the year 1806 with Hunters name absent. The *Caledonian Mercury -* Monday 24 November 1806; the Mill went up for sale in November 1808; *Caledonian Mercury -* Thursday 10 November 1808

324. Crompton Papers, ZCR9 Item 3, *Letter from William MacAlpine to Samuel Crompton,* dated 18th February 1805

325. Water twist was the use of Arkwright's Water Frame.

326. The actual dates for this partnership are unknown but accounts of dealings with Wylde to be found in the Crompton papers suggest dates between 1813 and 1819. See *Crompton Papers*, ZCR 25 Item 5 and ZCR34 Item 1

Chapter Twelve: Wealth Anticipated

327. French, *Life and Times of Samuel Crompton*, 156

328. French, *Life and Times of Samuel Crompton*, 156

329. Crompton Papers, *Account A.S. Stubbs to Messrs George Crompton, Purchase of Broad Cloths*, 27th of Marcg 1804, ZCR8 Item 1

330. Crompton Papers, ZCR14 Item 1, *Bill, Henry Wilson, Manchester to Mr Crompton, Details of Purchases, 12th March 1810*. Note this item is indexed as a bill to Samuel Crompton but given the contents the Mr Crompton noted on the bill is more likely to be George.

331. Crompton Papers *ZCR14 Item 5, Letter Lt Colonel Fletcher to Lt George Crompton*, 8th of April- 31st of December 1810

332. *Lancaster Gazette* -1ˢᵗ of December 1810

333. *Manchester Mercury* - Tuesday 8th of September 1807

334. *Manchester Mercury* - Tuesday 8th of September 1807

335. *Manchester Mercury* - Tuesday 20th of October 1807

336. French, *Life and Times of Samuel Crompton*, 156

337. *Manchester Mercury* - Tuesday 01 December 1807

338. *Manchester Mercury* - Tuesday 24 November 1807

339. *London Gazette*, 1807, vol?, 950

340. Crompton Papers, ZCR19 Item12, *Letter from George Crompton , Manchester to Samuel Crompton, London*, 28th April 1812

341. French was mistaken in stating that Crompton sojourned with Edward Harwood in 1812 as he died in 1797. His continuing London contact with the family was with Mary Harwood (possibly Edwards daughter) who later moved to Liverpool. See Crompton Papers, ZCR2812, *Brief Letter from Pembroke Gardens Liverpool, 1814;* and ZCR2413, *Letter from Kensington, 21st of September 1813*, signed *M. Harwood*.

342. French, *Life and Times of Samuel Crompton*, 156-7

343. Crompton Papers, ZCR12 Item 9, *Certificate of Discharge: John Colquitt Commander of HMS Princess to John Crompton*, 13th August 1808,

344. For example, see Lancashire Archives, DDCS/9/79, Copy: *Sir William Gerard to Captain Colquitt of H.M.S. Princess requesting discharge of men impressed*, Date 25 of September 1807

345. *Lancaster Gazette* - Saturday 20th of August 1803

346. *Lancaster Gazette*, 31st of December 1803.

347. *Lancaster Gazette,* 31st of December 1803.

348. Williams, *History of The Liverpool Privateers and Letters of Marque, with an Account of: The Liverpool Slave Trade*, 341.

349. Jamie. Bruce. Lockhart, *A Sailor in the Sahara: The Life and Travels in Africa of Hugh Clapperton*, Commander RN, I.B. Tauris, 2008, 14

350. *Lancaster Gazette* - Saturday 15 of December 1804

351. *Lancaster Gazzette*, 17th of September 1803

352. St Domingo Estate History, *Liverpool Echo*, 14th January 1955

353. Jones, *Trial of William Sparling*, Esq, 33

354. *Lancaster Gazette* - Saturday 10 March 1804

355. *Gloucester Journal* - Monday 2cnd of April 1804

356. Scarlett, James. 1769-1849, *Dictionary of National Biography*, vol. 50, 399-402.

357. W. Jones (Printer), *Trial of William Sparling, Esq. Late Lieutenant in the Tenth Regiment of Dragoons, Commanded by His Royal Highness the Prince of Wales; Samuel Martin Colquitt, Esq. Captain of his Majesty's Ship Princess. On an Indictment for the murder of Mr. Edward Grayson, of Liverpool, Shipbuilder. Before Sir Alan Chambre, Knignt, One of the Judges of the Common Pleas, At the Assizes, held at Lancaster, on Wednesday, April 4th, 1804. Taken in Shorthand and Collated with the Notes of other Writers*, seventh edition, 56, Castle-street, Liverpool, 1804, 73

358. Jones, T*rial of William Sparling*, Esq., 67

359. Jones, *Trial of William Sparling*, Esq, 45

360. Jones, *Trial of William Sparling*, Esq, 45

361. Jones, *Trial of William Sparling*, Esq, 41

362. Jones, *Trial of William Sparling*, Esq, 41

363. Jones, *Trial of William Sparling, Esq*, Postscript to the Preface of the fifth edition, iv-v11

364. *Carlisle Journal* - Saturday 7th of April 1804

365. *Chester Courant* - Tuesday 15 of January 1805

366. *Royal Cornwall Gazette* - Saturday 7th of February 1807

367. *Cheltenham Looker-On* - Saturday 17th of July 1847

368. Crompton Papers, ZCR13 Item 9, *Letter from Samuel Crompton to his Children*, 10th of October 1809

369. Advertisement in *Lancaster Gazette* - Saturday 26th of March 1808

370. Crompton Papers, ZCR12 Item 8, *Letter from William MacAlpine, London, to Samuel Crompton*, 21st of July 1808,

371. Ainsworth is a common name though there is a birth of a Peter Ainsworth to a Thomas and Betty Ainsworth on the 29 May 1787 Bolton-le-Moors, St Peter, Lancashire, England. A midshipman was an apprentice officer so likely to be from a 'good' family.

372. Reported in the *Lancaster Gazette* - Saturday 24 March 1804

373. French, *The Life and Times of Samuel Crompton*, 163.

374. *Crompton Papers*, ZCR16A Items 1-16

Chapter Thirteen: The Campaign Begins

375. Crompton Papers, ZCR14 Item 3, *Letter Samuel Crompton to unknown recipient referring to his letter to the Royal Society and other matters*, 18th March 1810

376. French, *Life and Times of Samuel Crompton*, 141-3

377. Crompton Papers, *Letter from Charles Taylor, Society of Arts*, 1st of March 1811, ZCR15 Item 7

378. French, *The Life and Times of Samuel Crompton*, 154

379. Crompton Papers, ZCR14 Item 7, *Letter Samuel Crompton to George Rose*, 10th June 1810 ; ZCR14 Item 8, *Letter George Rose to Samuel Crompton*, 16th June 1810; ZCR14 Item 3*Letter Samuel Crompton to unknown recipient referring to his letter to the Royal Society and other matters*, 18th March 1810

380. Crompton Papers, ZCR15 Item 8, *Letter Sir Robert Peel to Samuel Crompton,* 9th March 1811, being a response to Crompton's initial correspondence.

381. Crompton Papers, ZCR181, Letter to Children, London 21st of February 1812

382. Crompton Papers, ZCR15 Item 27 to ZCR15 Item 30, *Various correspondence between Samuel Crompton and Kirkman Finlay of Glasgow,* during December 1811

383. Crompton Papers, ZCR18 Item 11, *Letter Jonathon Bottomley, Halifax to Mr George Crompton, confirms use of mules in Yorkshire and Lancashire,* 13th of March 1812

384. For example, see *Crompton Papers, Letter to Samuel's Children from Lad Lane,* 10th March 1812, ZCR18 Item 8

385. Crompton Papers, ZCR15 Item 5, *Letter Samuel Crompton to Hon George Rose,* 29th January 1811

386. Crompton Papers, ZCR14 item 3. *Letter from Samuel Crompton re unidentified participant (undated).* Given a reference to assistance to earlier weavers then this could be written to George Rose.

387. http://www.historyofparliamentonline.org/volume/1790-1820/member/rose-george-1744-1818

388. Rev. Vernon. Levison, Harcourt (editor), *The Diaries and Correspondence of the Right Hon. George Rose: Containing Original Letters of the Most Distinguished Statesmen of His Day. In Two Volumes.* Entry for Sunday, October 1st, 1809, volume 2, 398-99

389. Crompton Papers, ZCR14 Item6, *Letter George Rose to Samuel Crompton,* 10th May 1810

390. Vernon, *The Diaries and Correspondence of George Rose,* volume 2, 413

391. Crompton Papers, ZCR15 Item 5, *Letter Samuel Crompton to Hon George Rose,* 29 January 1811

392. In October 1795 he achieved the reversion of the office of Clerk of the Parliaments to his eldest son, a matter that followed a bitter Parliamentary debate in April 1794 led by Sheridan and Fox.

393. *Cobbett's Political Register,* 30th March 1816, 193

394. Crompton Papers, *Number of spindles in use in cotton mills within 60 mile radius of Bolton, also includes spindles in Scotland,* 1811, ZCR16A Item 1

395. Crompton Papers, ZCR16A Item 1

396. Crompton Papers, ZCR16 Item11*Letter Samuel Crompton to the author of the article on 'Cotton Spinning' in Dr Brewster's Encyclopedia*, 1811

397. Crompton Papers, ZCR15 Item 8, *Letter from Sir Robert Peel to Samuel Crompton*, London, 9th March 1811.

398. An history of the Stanley family can be found in Francis Espinasse, *Lancashire Worthies*, Simpkin, Marshall and Co, London, Heywood and Son, Manchester, 1874, 1-49, 115-205

399. In his first letter to George Rose Crompton refers to Horrocks as an example of someone who could testify as to the importance of his invention. Crompton Papers, ZCR14 item 3

400. History of Parliament online, http://www.historyofparliamentonline.org

401. Bridgeman was elevated to the House of Lords in 1800. History of Parliament online, http://www.historyofparliamentonline.org/

402. Crompton Papers, *Letter Samuel Crompton, Bolton, to Thomas Stanley esq, London, to Thomas Stanley Esq*, 23rd May 1811, ZCR15 Item 22

403. Crompton Papers, various items of correspondence with Mr Kirkman Finlay: *Letter to Mr Finlay from Samuel Crompton*, Bolton, 2nd December 1811, ZCR15 Item 27; *letter to Kirkman Finlay*, 10th December 1811 ZCR15 Item 28; *letter from Mr Finlay, Glasgow*, 21st December 1811, ZCR15 Item 29

404. Crompton Papers, ZCR15 Item 27, Bolton, 2nd December 1811

405. Crompton Papers, Letter *Finlay, Glasgow, to Samuel Crompton*, 21st December 1811 ZCR15 Item 29

406. Crompton Papers, ZCR17 Item 16, *Letter from John Kennedy to Samuel Crompton*, 11th February 1812

Chapter Fourteen: Of Luddites and Distraction

407. Charlotte. Bronte, *Shirley*, T. Nelson and Sons, 1849, 728

408. Hansard, *Petition from the Weavers and Other Working Manufacturers of Chorley Against Sinecure Places and Corruption*, vol. 22, 4th May 1812, 1156-8

409. Noted in *The Scots Magazine*, 1811; Sands, Brymer, Murray and Cochran, Proceedings of Parliament, for consideration Parliament, 462, for consideration by Committee, 542.

410. Sands, *Brymer, Murray and Cochran,* Proceedings of Parliament, 542.

411. *Bury and Norwich Post* - Wednesday 1st of April 1812

412. *Hampshire Chronicle* - Monday 30th of March 1812

413. J.R. Dinwiddy. *Radicalism and Reform in Britain, 1750-1850,* A&C Black, 1992. 82-3

414. *Hampshire Chronicle* - Monday 30th of March 1812

415. *Caledonian Mercury* - Thursday 16th of April 1812

416. *The Literary Panorama, Being a Compendium of National and Parliamentary Reports,* Vol. XL, C.Taylor, Hatton Garden, Holborn, 1812, 1186

417. An official of the Court of Exchequer.

418. Crompton Papers, ZCR19 Item 3, *Letter, Samuel Crompton Junior, Bolton, to Samuel Crompton, London,* 9th April 1812

419. A burgess was an inhabitant of a town or borough with full rights of citizenship.

420. *Caledonian Mercury* - Thursday 16th of April 1812

421. *Chester Courant* - Tuesday 14th of April 1812

422. *Chester Courant* - Tuesday 14th of April 1812

423. *Caledonian Mercury* - Thursday 16th of April 1812

424. Assuming it was terracotta, which was likely, it would have been destructible.

425. *Chester Courant* - Tuesday 14th of April 1812

426. *Caledonian Mercury* - Thursday 16th of April 1812

427. *Liverpool Mercury* - Friday 24th of April 1812

428. For a clear concise discussion of Luddite activity and motives see Brian. Bailey, *The Luddite Rebellion,* Sutton Publishing, Stroud, Gloucestershire, 1998

429. E.J. Hobsbawm, *The Age of Revolution: Europe 1789-148,* 4th edition, Weidenfield and Nicholson, London, 1962.

430. National Archives, *Home Office Papers,* HO-40-1_3.pdf

431. This was the case of a petition presented by a Mr John Lever outlining the attempts by Fletcher and his son to get him to provoke disturbances and to label him as General Ludd. The petition was negated. See Hansard, *Parliamentary Debates From 1803 to the Present Time, Official Report:Parliamentary Session of 21st of*

December 1819, Conduct of Colonel Fletcher, A Magistrate, 1819-1820, 1446-1448.

432. Crompton Papers, *Letter Samuel Crompton Junior, Bolton to his father, London*, 8th of March 1812, ZCR18 Item 6

433. Bolton Museums, Libraries and History Centre, Dewhurst Family of Halliwell, 1773-1816, *Captain Roger Dewhurst Sketch Book*, Albinson, Archive References ZZ/387 and ZZ/442/1 (Sketch book).

434. In architecture a corbel is a structural piece of stone, wood or metal jutting from a wall to carry a superincumbent weight.

435. Joseph. Gillow Esq, Lostock Hall (1822-24), in N. G. Philips, *Views of the Old Halls of Lancashire and Cheshire*, Henry Gray, London, 1893, 63-4

436. Lancashire Archives, *Will of Joseph Bromilow (Brimelow), husbandman*, 28th of September 1789, *Cheshire: - Wills and Inventories, 1781-1790*

437. *Manchester Mercury*-Tuesday 16th of July 1793

438. Lancashire Archives, *Letters of Administration John Bromilow (Bromiley)*,farmer,1821 (deceased 1817), Cheshire: - Wills and Inventories, 1811-1820 (A-L)

439. S.E. Winbolt, *England and Napoleon (1801-1815)*, Bells English Source Books, G.Bell and Sons Ltd, Ltd, 1915

440. James. Christopher Scholes, *History of Bolton: With Memorials of the Old Parish Church,* edited and completed by William. Pimblett, The Daily Chronicle Office, Bolton, Lancashire, *290*

441. The riot act stated that anyone who had not dispersed one hour after it was read could be accused of a felony and subject to the death penalty.

442.Scholes, *History of Bolton: With Memorials of the Old Parish Church*, 1892, 290

443. Crompton Papers, ZCR 19 Item 8, *Letter Samuel Crompton, Kensington, to his children*, 18th of April 1812

444. Crompton Papers, ZCR19 Item 12, *Letter, George Crompton, Manchester, to his father*, 28th of April 1812,

445. Westhaughton Local History Group, *The Burning of Westhaughton Mill 1812*, For the Bicentenary 24th of April 2012, 11

446. His status as an informer is corroborated in National Archives, *Home Office Papers*, HO-40-1_3.pdf, 21 May 1812, 105-9, a letter which also describes finding a place of safety for Stones and his family.

447. Le Blanc had supported Joseph Pimbley's dispute over the contractual agreement for the mining and sale of coal in the Court of the Kings Bench,1809.

448. For example, in 1809 a trial took place at the Lancaster assizes where a gentleman of independent means, a Mr Hanson, was accused of assisting the Manchester weavers to combine to raise their wages. The jury found for the Crown against Hanson but Le Blanc as the presiding judge reserved judgement, forwarding the case to the Kings bench. Hanson was found guilty and served 6 months in prison and required to pay a fine of £100.

449. For example, the special commission held at York Castle, January 2cnd 1813, with respect to disturbances in the West Riding of Yorkshire.

450. National Archives, Letter Sir Richard Clayton, *Home Office Papers*, HO-42/128

451. Lord Chief Justice Ellingborough was another key member of the Northern Circuit presiding over Luddite trials. Almost as unpopular as Eldon, he also presided over the case in the Kings Bench concerning Joseph Pimbley's dispute in 1809.

452. Hansard, *Preservation of the Public Peace*, Friday 10th of July 1812, 973-4

Chapter Fifteen: The Campaign of 1812

453. Crompton Papers,ZCR18 Item 13 *Letter from Samuel Crompton to his Children, London, Lad Lane*, 21st of March 1812.

454. Crompton Papers, ZCR19Item 2, *Letter from Samuel Crompton to Rt Hon Spencer Percival*, 8th of April 1812.

455. Crompton Papers, ZCR20 Item 16,*Letter from Samuel to M. Harwood, Kensington*, 22cnd of July 1812. Not a direct reference to Parliament but it no doubt encompassed its members.

456. William. Hone, *The Everyday Book: Or Everlasting Calendar of Popular Amusements, Sports, Pastime, Ceremonies, Customs and Events, Incident to Each of the Three Hundred and Sixty Five Days, in the Past and Present Times*, In Three Volumes, Thomas Tegg, 73 Cheapside, London, volume 2, 1827, 963

457. Hone, *The Everyday Book*, 963

458. Joseph Banks referred to in: J.Robins, Anecdotes of Animals, *The Ladies Museum*,Volume 1, January to June,James. Robins and Co, London, 1829, 243

459. Robins, *The Ladies Museum*, 243

460. *Crosby's Merchants and Tradesman's Pocket Dictionary: By a London Merchant Assisted by Several Experienced Tradesmen*, Crosby and Co, Stationers Court, London, 1808, 305

461. John. Britton FSA, *Beauties of England and Wales*, Volume 10, issue 3, Part 1, Vernor, Hood and Sharpe et al, London, 1815, 298-9

462. References to Colonel Stanley's illness recur throughout his correspondence. See Crompton Papers,ZCR17 Item 6, *Letter Samuel Crompton, London to his Children*. 23rd of January 1812;ZCR17 Item8, *Letter Samuel Crompton, London, to Mr Yates, Bury*, 21st of January 1812; ZCR17 Item 10, *Letter Samuel Crompton, London, to Messrs McConnel and Kennedy, Manchester*, 23rd January,1812

463. There are repeated references to Peel's absence See: Crompton Papers, ZCR17 Item 9, *Letter Samuel Crompton to Rt Hon Spencer Percival*, 22nd of January 1812 ; ZCR17 Item 10, *Letter Samuel Crompton to Messrs McConnel and Kennedy, Manchester*, 23rd of January1812; ZCR19 Item 1, *Letter, Samuel Crompton, London to his Children*, 8th of April 1812; ZCR17 Item 6, *Letter Samuel Crompton to his Children*, 14th of January 1812; ZCR17 Item 7, *Letter Samuel Crompton to his Children*,20th of January 1812, ; ZCR17 Item 8, *Letter Samuel Crompton*, London, to Mr Yates Bury, 21st of January 1812,

464. Crompton Papers,ZCR17 Item 8, *Letter Samuel Crompton, London, to Mr Yates, Bury*, 21st of January 1812. Samuel again complains in this letter about the absence from town of the members of Parliament for Lancaster.

465. Crompton Papers,ZCR17 Item 7, *Letter Samuel Compton, London to his Children, 15th of January 1812*.

466. Crompton Papers,ZCR17 Item 15, *Letter from Samuel Crompton Junior, Bolton, to his Father*, 5th of February 1812.

467. Crompton Papers, ZCR18 Item 4, *Letter, Samuel Crompton, London, to his Children*, 6th of March 1812; ZCR18 Item 6*Letter Samuel Crompton Junior to his father*, Bolton, 8th March 1812.

468. Crompton Papers, ZCR22 Item 5, ZCR22 Item 6, *Lists of contacts,*

469. Crompton Papers,ZCR18 Item 4, *Letter Samuel Crompton, London, to Children, London,6th of March 1812,* with a postscript by George Crompton informing Samuel of Thomas Ainsworth's indisposition.

470. See Crompton Papers,ZCR17 Item 13 *Letter from Samuel Crompton, London, to his Children, 30th of January 1812, i*n which he was happy to hear of Georges recovery.

471. Crompton Papers,ZCR19 Item 17, *Letter Samuel Crompton to his Children, 14th of May 1812.* In fact, he had previously purchased new flannel trousers and shoes but was unsure that they would outlast his stay.

472. Crompton Papers,ZCR17 Item8, *Letter Samuel Crompton, London, to Mr Yates, Bury,* 21st of January 1812.

473. Crompton Papers,ZCR17 Item 7, *Letter, Samuel Crompton, London, to his Children,* 15th of January 1812.

474. Crompton Papers,ZCR17 Item 7, *Samuel Crompton, Letter to Children from London,* 15th of January 1812.

475. Crompton Papers,ZCR18 Item 1, *Samuel Crompton, Letter to Children, London* 21st of February 1812.

476. Crompton Papers,ZCR18 Item 1, *Samuel Crompton, Letter to Children, London* 21st of February 1812.

477. See, I. Kelly, *Beau Brummell*, Hodder, London, 2005, 245-253

478. Crompton Papers,ZCR17 Item 9, Letter, *Samuel Crompton to Rt Hon Spencer Percival,* 22nd of January 1812.

479. Crompton Papers,ZCR18 Item 13, *Letter Samuel Crompton, London, to his Children,* 21st of March 1812.

480. Crompton Papers,ZCR17 Item 6, *Letter Samuel Crompton, to his Children,* 14th of January 1812.

481. June. Z. Fullmer, Young Humphry Davy: The Making of an Experimental Chemist, Volume 237, 73, *American Philosophical Society,* 2000, Volume 237, 73

482. Crompton Papers,ZCR17 Item 7, *Letter, Samuel Crompton, to his Children,* 15th of January 1812.

483. Peels wife was Ellen nee Yates daughter of his partner William Yates, married 8th of July 1783

484. The partnership of Peel and Yates in Bury had been dissolved in 1807.

485. Crompton Papers, ZCR17 Item 7, *Letter Samuel Compton, London to his Children, 15th January 1812; ZCR17 Item 8, Samuel Compton, London to W. Yates, 15th of January 1812.*

486. Crompton Papers, ZCR17 Item 8, *Letter Samuel Crompton, London, to William Yates,* 21st of January 1812.

487. Crompton Papers, ZCR17 Item 8, *Letter, Samuel Crompton, to William Yates,* 21st of January 1812.

488. Crompton Papers, *Letter Samuel Crompton to Messrs McConnel and Kennedy, Manchester,* 23rd of January 1812, ZCR17 Item 10

489. Crompton Papers, ZCR18 Item 8, *Samuel Crompton, London, Letter to his Children,* 10th of March 1812.

490. Crompton Papers, ZCR18 Item 8, *Samuel Crompton, London, Letter to his Children,* 10th of March 1812.

491. Crompton Papers, ZCR17 Item 12, *Letter, Samuel Crompton, London, to Peter Marsland (?), Stockport,* 28th of January 1812.

492. Peel had first reviewed the petition on the 21st of February 1812. See Crompton Papers, ZCR18 Item 1, *Letter Samuel Crompton, London, to Children,* 21st of February 1812.

493. Crompton Papers, ZCR18 Item 5, *Letter Samuel Crompton, London, to his Children,* 7th of March 1812.

494. Crompton Papers, ZCR20 Item 10, *Letter, Samuel Crompton to Mr White,* 24th of June 1812.

495. French, *Life and Times of Samuel Crompton,* 195

496. Crompton Papers, ZCR17 Item 18, *Letter, Samuel Crompton to Mr. John Kennedy,* March 1812. Date is unclear so his meeting could have been either before or after the Parliamentary Committee, but a reading of the text and the documentation it discusses suggests it was before.

497. See Andro. Linklater, *Why Spencer Percival Had to Die,* Bloomsbury Publishing PLC, London, 2012

498. Crompton Papers, ZCR18 Item 4, *Letter, Samuel Crompton, London, to his Children,* Lad Lane 6th of March 1812.

499. French, *Life and Times of Samuel Crompton*, Appendix, Minutes of Evidence, 276-83

500. Daniels,T*he Early English Cotton Industry*, 156

501. In the war years in particular exports fluctuated greatly though in some years when exports of cloth declined, as in 1803, the spinners still increased their export trade. See Edwards, *The Growth of the British Cotton Trade*, 15

502. Crompton Papers,ZCR17 Item 5, *Letter, George Lee to Samuel Crompton,* 5th of February 1812.

503. Crompton Papers,ZCR18 Item 13, *Letter, Samuel Crompton, London, to his Children*, 21st of March 1812.

504. Alexander Houstoun MP for Glasgow Burgh who had some interest in relieving distressed cotton workers in Glasgow. See https://www.historyofparliamentonline.org/volume/1790-1820/member/houstoun-alexander-1770-1822.

505. Crompton Papers,ZCR18 Item 12 *Letter, George Lee, London, to McConnel and Kennedy*, 21st of March 1812.

506. Crompton Papers,ZCR19 Item 2, *Letter Samuel Crompton, London to Spencer Percival, 8th of April 1812.*

507. See Crompton Papers,ZCR18 Item 13, *Letter, Samuel Crompton London, to his Children*, 21st of March 1812.

Chapter 16: The 1812 Overcoat

508. *Hampshire Chronicle* - Monday 18th of May 1812

509. French, *Life and Times of Samuel Crompton,*172-4.

510. Andro. Linklater, *Why Spencer Percival Had to Die*, Bloomsbury Publishing PLC, London, 2012, 54

511. Bellingham refused a plea of insanity, though his behaviour suggests that he was mentally ill and may have been treated differently by a modern court of law.

512. Crompton Papers, *Letter Samuel Compton to his sons*, 14th of May 1812, ZCR19 Item 17

513. Campbell, *The Lives of the Lords Chancellors and Keepers of the Great Seal of England*, 239-240

514. Orders in Council were issued on the 6th of January and 11th November 1807 and restricted trade with France, not only for the UK but also its allies and neutral countries such as the United States of America, whose ships were often boarded.

515. Crompton Papers, *ZCR19 Item 17*

516. Crompton Papers, ZCR19 Item 17

517. Crompton Papers, *ZCR19 Item 17*

518. Crompton Papers, *ZCR19 Item 17*

519. Castlereagh received much abuse in public, being considered an extreme reactionary, though he was as usual a complex character. For a magnificent review of his life and character see John. Bew, Castlereagh: *Enlightenment, War and Tyranny*, Quercus, London, 2011

520. Crompton Papers, *ZCR19 Item 17*

521. Thomas. Moore, *Life of Lord Byron: With his Letters and Journals, Volume 3*, Thomas Moore, 1851, John. Murray, London. An anecdote from the book is reported in: *The Lancaster Gazette*, 30th of January 1830.

522. Charles C. F. Greville, ESQ, *The Greville Memoirs A Journal of The Reigns of King George IV. King William, IV. and Queen Victoria*, Henry. Reeve (editor), C.B., D.C.L, Longmans, Green and Co, London New York, Bombay. and Calcutta, 1931; referenced in *The Morning Post,* Monday 18th of January 1875.

523. *Lancaster Gazette*, Saturday, 23rd May 1812.

524. *Morning Chronicle* - Tuesday 24 February 1807 gives a full and detailed description of events and how the tragedy unfolded.Three other people died at another spot away from the crush bringing the total to 30.

525. Tried and imprisoned for sedition, having argued against the use of German troops to flog local militia men in Ely.

526. *Cobbett's Political Register,* Saturday, 23 May, 1812.

527. The Political Register was Cobbett's own radical paper, first published 1802 and continuing until 1836.

528. Friend addressing Cobbett through *The Political Register*; used as an epistolary vehicle for expressing Cobbett's views.

529. Note that Cobbett's uses the term populace ironically and sees it as a pejorative for a disadvantaged hard working people who are considered inclined to rebellion,

[not unlike the Parisian mob]. See *Cobbett's Political Register*, Saturday, 23rd may, 1812.

530. Crompton Papers, ZCR20 Item 2, *Letter, Samuel Crompton to his Children*, 18th of May 1812,

531. Beth. Darlington, *The Love Letters of William and Mary Wordsworth*, Cornell University Press, 2009, 145

532. *Cobbett's Political Register*, Saturday, 23rd of May 1812.

533. *Lancaster Gazette*, Saturday, 23rd of May 1812. It is worth noting that many actual texts of news stories were simply circulated and reproduced, so that this would be a text likely to be found elsewhere.

534. *Lancaster Gazette*, Saturday, 23rd of May 1812.

535. *Cobbett's Political Register*, Saturday 23rd of May, 1812.

536. Crompton Papers, *ZCR20 Item 2*.

537. Possibly 'The Chilam Castle' though a ship of this name was sailing to the West Indies after these events. However, there was no copyright on ships names and a replacement vessel could have readily adopted the same title.

538. Crompton Papers, *Letter, Samuel Crompton, Bolton, to M. Harwood*, Kensington, 22cnd July 1812, ZCR20 Item 16

539. *Bath Chronicle and Weekly Gazette,* Thursday, 21st of May 1812

540. *London Courier and Evening Gazette*, Saturday, 16th of May 1812

541. *Lloyds List*, Friday, 29th of May 1812

542. Crompton Papers, *Letter, Jane Harwood, Kensington to Samuel Crompton, Bolton*, 27th of September 1812, ZCR21 Item 1

543. Though there is no direct evidence for the story of not seeing John, and Samuel does not say as much in his correspondence on the matter. This may be a family story related to Gilbert French in his interview with George Crompton, though it is plausible as Samuel would have been alerted by the request for money and could easily have been present at the docks but not gained sight of John. See French, *Life and Times of Samuel Crompton*, 171-2

544. Crompton Papers, *, Letter Samuel Crompton to Mr. White, 24th of June 1812, ZCR20 Item 10*

545. cited in Illustrated London News - Saturday 22 January 1955, being a review of *Lord Liverpool and His Times* by Sir Charles Petrie Bart, Barrie, 1954

546. Vernon, *The Diaries and Correspondence of George Rose*, volume 2, 429.

547. John. Bew, *Castlereagh: Enlightenment, War and Tyranny*, Quercus, London, 2011, 276

548. Hansard, Great Britain Parliament, 1812, 371

549. Crompton Papers, *Letter, Samuel Crompton, London, to his Children*, 26th of January 1812, ZCR20 Item 11

550. Crompton Papers, ZCR20 Item 16

551. Crompton Papers, ZCR20 Item 15, *Letter, M.Harwood, Kensington, to Samuel Crompton, Bolton*, 15th of July 1812

552. Crompton Papers, ZCR21 Item 10,*Letter Samuel Crompton, Bolton to George White, Newington House*, 22cnd of October 1812

Chapter Seventeen: The Shrouds Over Which Ariel Whispers Breathe

553. Zephyr, a soft gentle breeze (literary), a fine cotton gingham (noun).

554. W.D. Billington (ed),*Captain Dewhurst and His Diary*, Bolton, 1989, 141

555. The execution is also referred to in the diary of Richard Pilkington of Horwich, with the simple chilling line *"a man was hung on Bolton Moor"*. Richard. Pilkington, *The Diary of Richard Pilkington of Horwich, May 1784-January 1792; May 1788-September 1797, Lancashire County Council, Archives, refs, DDPI6/1;DDPI6/2*

556. James. Orrell, *Original Poems on A Variety of Subjects*, Printed and Sold by J. Gardner for the Author, Bolton, 1793

557. *Chester Courant* - Tuesday 18th of September 1798

558. Crompton Papers, ZCR5 Item 5, *Letter from Calais*, 1801

559. The Swedish chemist Scheele discovered chlorine in 1774. In 1785 the French scientist Claude Berthollet saw the potential for bleaching fabrics.

560. Also known as the Vale Bleach Works.

561. Crompton Papers, ZCR 28 Item 16.*Recipe: W.H.Jones, Chemist to Whitehall Bleach Works*, 1814

562. For examples see, Crompton Papers, ZCR25 Item 2, *Valuation: Mr. Stevenson and Mr. Lackingson for Mr. Crompton*, 6th of October 1813; ZCR28 Item 8 *List of purchases including plumbing,*

563. Crompton Papers, ZCR25 Item 1, *Letter, George Crompton, Darwen to Samuel Crompton*, 6th of October 1813. The letter refers to an uncle which is most likely to be William .

564. Crompton Papers, ZCR25 Item 1, *Letter, George Crompton, Darwen to Samuel Crompton*, 6 October 1813

565. See Amy Harris, *Siblinghood and social relations in Georgian England: Share and share alike,* Manchester University Press; Reprint edition (15 th April 2016)

566. Crompton Papers, ZCR33 Item 1, *Letter, James Crompton, Pernambuco, to Samuel Crompton, Bolton, 20th of March 1813,* Note that this is catalogued with the date 1819, but a closer inspection reveals a possibly smudged 1813, this is a date that is more compatible with American aggression towards English vessels, does not exclude George from his partnership in Darwen, and matches an enquiry within the letter as to Georges Commission which by 1819 was almost certainly an abandoned attempt. Plus, shipping data on the Margaret. suggests a date of 1813.

567. See https://www.britannica.com/place/Pernambuco.

568. Crompton Papers, *ZCR33 Item 1*

569. Lloyds List 1813/1814, No 4772, London, Tuesday 25th of May 1813, 2; Notes that the Margaret, Pilkington, from Liverpool was at Pernambuco on the 3rd of April 1813, list available at https://babel.hathitrust.org/cgi/pt?id=mdp.39015005785830;view=1up;seq=91.

570. For example, in early March the Bowes, captain Dixon, on its return from Pernambuco to Liverpool was captured by an American privateer. *Lloyd's List -* Tuesday 23rd of March 1813,1

571. *Lloyds List* 1813/1814, No 4772, London, Tuesday 27th of July 1813, 2

572. *Lloyd's List -* Friday 6th of August 1813, 2

573. *London Gazette*, 16th of July 1811, Issue 16505, 1324.

574. Crompton Papers, ZCR24 Item 1, *Letter George Crompton, London to his father, 11th of June 1813*

575. French, *The Life and Times of Samuel Crompton*, 197-98.

576. Stella. Margetson, *Regency London, Cassell* & Company Ltd, London.1971, 108

577. A picture in a locket, now in the Hall 'ith' Wood Museum.

578. Crompton Papers, ZCR25 Item 6, *George Crompton, Bill for Anderton's Coffee House, Fleet Street, London*, 17th of April 1813

579. *Leighs's New Picture of London: Or a View of the Political, Religious, Medical, Literary, Municipal, Commercial and Moral State of the British Metropolis: Presenting a Brief and Luminous Guide to the Stranger on All Subjects Connected with General Information, Business or Amusement,* 1818, Printed for Samuel Leigh, No 18 The Strand, 353

580. *Cobbett's Political Register*, vol. xvii. No. 7, London, Saturday, 7th of July 1810, 499

581. Crompton Papers, *Copy of a Letter from R. Deighton, Horseguards, To Thomas Ainsworth Esq.*, 23rd of September 1813, ZCR, 24 Item 14

582. Field Marshall Lord Carver, 1984, *The Seven Ages of the British Army*, Weidenfeld and Nicolson, London, 72-3

583. Crompton Papers, ZCR24 Item 12, *Letter from Thomas Ainsworth London to George Crompton*, 18th of September 1813.

584. Carver, *The Seven Ages of the British Army*, 80

585. The Deighton letter, ZCR 24 Item 14, is a copy dated 23 September 1813 incorporated in a letter dated 25th of September 1813.

586. Crompton Papers, ZCR24 Item 3, *Letter, Samuel Crompton, Junior, Dublin, to Samuel Crompton, Bolton*, 15th of July 1813

587. In as letter to his father George notes James's safe arrival. Crompton Papers, ZCR24 Item 1, *Letter George Crompton, Kensington to Samuel Crompton, Bolton, 11th of June 1813*

588. Crompton Papers, *ZCR25 Item 1*

589. Crompton Papers, ZCR 25 Item 1

590. Crompton Papers, ZCR25 Item 1

591. Crompton Papers, ZCR34 Item 6: *Rough draft of notice for auction of Whitehall Bleach Works and adjoining property*, (the date of the auction is known to be 1819 though this document is undated) also see ZCR 37 item 12; ZCR37 item15.

592. See correspondence with Richard Hilton, Crompton Papers, ZCR37 Item 9, *Letter Samuel Crompton to Hilton, re valuation of the bleach works, 11th of November 1820*

593. Crompton Papers, ZCR37 Item 9; ZCR37 Item 12: *Letter Samuel Crompton to Hilton, re valuation of tools and machinery at bleach works, 16 th of November 1822.* ZCR38 Item 10, Letters Samuel Crompton to Mr Hilton, ZCR38 item 11; Letter Mr Hilton to Samuel Crompton, ZCR38 item 12 *Letter Thos Jardine to Messrs Neville and Eccles solicitors, Blackburn, 16th of November 1822.*

594. French, *The Life and Times of Samuel Crompton*, 196-98

595. London Gazette, February 1819 copy in the Crompton Papers, ZCR33 Item 5, ZCR35 Item 8, ZCR33 item 15

596. There is also evidence that George's bleaching croft had suffered damage. See Crompton Papers, ZCR35 item 9. George was tried at Lancaster in the Court of Insolvent Debtors 8th of March 1822, see London Gazette, 12th of February 1822, Issue 17790, 276

597. Various entries in the *London Gazette*, two examples being, *Issue 16301*, 3rd July 1802, 1567; *Issue 16614*, 16th of June 1812, 1182

598. Crompton Papers, *Letter, George Crompton, London, to Samuel Crompton, 11th of June* 1813, ZCR24 Item 1

Chapter Eighteen: George's Unpleasant Affair

599. Crompton Papers, ZCR27 Item 8, *Letter, Samuel Crompton Junior, Bolton, to Samuel Crompton c/o Thomas Lever, Milk Street, London, 30th of May 1814*

600. Crompton Papers, ZCR23 Item 14, Letter, *Thomas Lever, London, to Samuel Crompton*, 25th of May 1814,

601. *London Gazette*, Issue 1664, 16th of June 1812, page 1182.

602. Crompton Papers, ZCR27 Item 9, *Letter, Samuel Crompton Junior, Bolton, to Samuel Crompton, 6th of June 1814*

603. Crompton Papers, ZCR27 Item 8

604. Crompton Papers, ZCR27 Item 8, *Letter, Samuel Crompton Junior, Bolton, to Samuel Crompton, c/o Thomas Lever, Milk Street, London*, 30th of May 1814,

605. Crompton Papers, ZCR27 Item 15, *Letter, George Crompton, London to James Crompton, to , Crompton, London*, 17th of *August 1814*

606. Statute 53 George III, cap102

607. see Hugh Barty-King, 1997, 2nd edition, *The Worst of Poverty, A History of Debt and Debtors,* Budding Books, Stroud, Gloucestershire, United Kingdom, 119-122

608. Crompton's father in law William Pimbley experienced multiple bankruptcies. In 1763 at the age of 26 he was 'gazeted', his financial failure trumpeted to the world, through the pages of the London Gazette (*London Gazette*, 21st of May, Issue 10315, 1763, 4.). He was to call at the house of Mrs Catherine Marshall, known by the sign of the George Inn at Warrington. Here he would have to meet the claims of his creditors and hope that they would agree to terms and not issue a commission of bankruptcy. French attributed Wiliam's financial problems to a dispute over the ownership of his rented residence New Hey Hall. This must relate to: The National Archives, Kew, *Browne v Brotherton*, Chancery Proceedings, C 12/2378/30, 1768.

609. Ancestry.com. London, England, *King's Bench and Fleet Prison Discharge Books and Prisoner Lists, 1734-1862* [database on-line]. Provo, UT, USA: Ancestry.com Operations, Inc., 2014.Original data: *King's (Queen's) Bench, Fleet, Marshalsea and Queen's Prisons: Miscellanea. Records of the King's Bench, Fleet, and Marshalsea prisons*, Original Source: Series PRIS 10. The National Archives, Kew, England.

610. A.H.Bailey and Co, *Scenes and Stories by A Clergyman in Debt Written During his Confinement in the Debtor's Prisons. in Three volumes*, , Cornhill, London. MDCCCXXXV, January 1853, 149

611. For example, in *Lancashire and Cheshire Historical and Genealogical Notes, 1879-1883, volume 2, 1879-1881*. He is noted in this book as not being mentioned in a list of Lancashire authors compiled by Mr C.W. Sutton chief librarian of Manchester Free Libraries, so the article is entitled an *"Unquoted Author"*.

612. *Lancashire and Cheshire Historical and Genealogical Notes*, 1879

613. In these letters to a lady, he fulminates against *"the influence of bigotry, enthusiasm and superstition"*, Nightingale, 3

614. Joseph. Nightingale, *The Bazaar: Its Origin, Nature, and Objects, Explained and Recommended as an Important Branch of Political Economy, in a Letter to the Rt. Hon. George Rose, M.P. To which is Added a Postscript Containing an Account of Every Establishment, Bearing this Name, in the Metropolis*, By the Author, at his house, 42, Skinner Street, 1st of January 1816

615. Nightingale, *The Bazaar*, 24-25

616. *London Gazette*, Issue:16576,18th of February 1812, 344

617. Crompton Papers, ZCR16 Item 8, *Mule Spindle Survey*, this gives number of mule spindles in this enterprise as 10,824 and 4760 throstles, so it was a significant size.

618. Crompton Papers, ZCR24 Item 5, *Letter to Samuel Crompton from Thomas Lever, London, 31st of July 1813*

619. The system of shorthand finally deciphered was of John Byron, born at Kersall, Manchester, in 1691; he invented and used it in 1720.

620. Crompton Papers, Letter, J. *Nightingale, Kensington, to George Crompton*, 31st of October 1814, ZCR27 Item 18

621. Joseph. Nightingale, *English Topography, A Series of Historical and Statistical Descriptions of the Counties of England and Wales*, London; printed for Baldwin, Cradock and Joy, Paternoster Row, 1816

622. Crompton Papers, *Shorthand translation relating to an incident on 12th June 1814, regarding £5 note from Mr Lever, London*, 6th of September 1814, ZCR94 Item 6

623. Crompton Papers, ZCR944, *Translation of a letter to George Crompton from Thomas Smallwood writing from Milk Street 10th of August 1814.*

624. The tenacious and intelligent decoding of this text was undertaken in 1927 by the editor of the Bolton Evening News, using a similar methodology to how hieroglyphics were first decoded. See Crompton Papers, *Letter, T.Midgley, to the Editor of the Bolton Evening News, 14th of November 1927, Enclosing Article on Early Shorthand Systems*, ZCR94 Item 16

625. Crompton Papers, ZCR94 Item 7, *Letter, Joseph Nightingale to George Crompton, 10th of November 1814*

626. Joseph Nightingale also asks if George is to marry a Miss M. Given that he marries Sarah Lancaster in 1821 then this clearly did not happen.

627. Ancestry.com. London, England, *King's Bench and Fleet Prison Discharge Books and Prisoner Lists, 1734-1862*

628. Details of the case taken from the *Public Ledger and Daily Advertiser 02 June 1815 an relates to a case of Fraud in the Court of Insolvent Debtors* concerning the Reverend Joseph Nightingale

629. Crompton Papers, ZCR29 Item 4, *Letter, Rev J. Nightingale, London, to George Crompton*, Darwen, 24th of June 1815

630. There is a suggestion that Nightingale shared prison time with George but there is no evidence for this. Nightingale refers to Holland not yet having taken any action on November 16th, 1814, after George's release.

631. Noted in, James. Grande, *Nineteenth Century London in William Godwin's Diary*, Journal of Victorian Culture, 2010, 15:2, 201-211

632. http://www.georgianindex.net/London/l_merchants.html

633. There is ongoing research into the intellectual networks of Georgian London and "urban romanticism". The availability of Godwin's meticulous diary is adding to knowledge of this period. See http://godwindiary.bodleian.ox.ac.uk/diary/.

634. George was a member of the Bolton Church and King Club See Crompton Papers ZCR29 Item 2, *Invitation to 25th anniversary dinner,17th of February 1815*

635. Crompton Papers, ZCR25 Item 3, *Accounts for Crompton and Wylde, 21st of March 1813*. The earliest date of a transaction with Wylde in these accounts is 25th of October 1812.

636. *London Gazette*, 4th of January 1823, Issue:17884, 11

637. French, *Life and Times of Samuel Crompton*, 200

638. Presented but not elaborated on in French, *Life and Times of Samuel Crompton*, 200-1.

639. French, *Life and Times of Samuel Crompton*, 201.

Chapter Nineteen: Brown: A Cause Resuscitated

640. Many, but not all, of the documents listed by Samuel Crompton as being given to Brown re-appeared in the British Museum; copies of these are now incorporated into the Crompton Papers collection at Bolton Libraries and Museums, History Centre

641. French noted that Samuel Crompton was 72 years of age at the time, which given a birthday of 3rd December 1753 makes the year that he met John Brown, 1824. French, *Life and Times of Samuel Crompton*, 218.

642. J. Brown, *The History of Great and Little Bolton*, Veluti in Speculum", published by Mr Kell, bookseller, Deansgate Bolton and Messrs.' Clark, Marketplace, Manchester, 1824; cited in Lt Colonel Henry. Fishwick FSA,*The Lancashire Library, A Bibliographical Account of Books on Topography, Biography, History, Science and Miscellaneous Literature relating to the County Palatine*, George Routledge and Sons, Warrington:Percival Pearce, 1875, 8

643. This was reported to French by Mr. Bromiley the then resident of Hall i' th' Wood. See French, *Life and Times of Samuel Crompton*, 217.

644.   http://www.historyofparliamentonline.org/volume/1790-1820/member/
blackburne-john-1754-1833#footnote14_lzyhqy7

645. See *The History of Parliament*, http://www.historyofparliamentonline.org/
volume/1790-1820/member/peel-robert-ii-1788-1850

646. Gilbert French, *Life and Times of Samuel Crompton*, 190

647. Crompton Papers, ZCR43 Item 2, *Letter, John Brown to Messrs Hick and
Rothwell*, 7 th of May 1825.

648. Peter Rothwell 1792-1849 was an iron founder and in 1814 was in the
partnership with Dobson and Rothwell making mules in Black Horse Street, Bolton,
though the partnership was dissolved in 1815. He established the Union Foundry
in Blackhorse Street with his son, becoming Rothwell, Hick and Rothwell in 1822-
iron founders, engineers and millwrights (see *Grace's Guide to British Industrial
History*): https://www.gracesguide.co.uk/Grace's_Guide

649. Crompton Papers, ZCR43 Item 2, *Letter, John Brown to Messrs Hick and
Rothwell*, 7th of May 1825.

650. Crompton Papers,*ZCR44 Item 9, Letter John Brown to George Crompton,
dated 22cnd of March 1826*

651. Crompton Papers, ZCR43 Item 8, *Letter, John Brown, London, to Samuel
Crompton, Bolton*, 9th of July 1825

652. Possibly Charles Rossi who was sculptor to the Prince Regent and had also
completed commissioned work for Sir Robert Peel.

653. J. Brown, and S. Crompton, *The Basis of Mr Samuel Crompton's Claims to
A Second Remuneration from Parliament for His Discovery of the Mule Spinning
Machine (1825)*, Charles Simms and Co, Manchester, 1868

654. Brown, *The Basis of Mr Samuel Crompton's Claims to A Second Remuneration
from Parliament for His Discovery of the Mule Spinning Machine*, 15

655. Brown, *The Basis of Mr Samuel Crompton's Claims to A Second Remuneration
from Parliament for His Discovery of the Mule Spinning Machine*, 15

656. French, *The Life and Times of Samuel Crompton*, 210

657. Richard. Guest, *Compendious History of Cotton Manufacture; A Disproval of the
Claim of Sir Richard Arkwright to the Invention of Its Ingenious Machinery*, Printed
by Joseph Pratt, Chapel Walks London, 1823, 32-33.

658. Guest, *Compendious History of Cotton Manufacture*, 32-3

659. Crompton Papers, ZCR44 Item 4, Letter, *J.Brown, Board of Trade Office, to George Crompton (for his father) Sent via Betty. Dawson*, 7th of March 1826

660. Crompton papers, ZCR44 Item 4

661. Crompton Papers, ZCR44 Item 6, *Letter, John Brown to George Compton, Blackburn*, 13th of March 1826

662. Crompton Papers, ZCR44 Item 9, *Letter, John Brown, London, to George Crompton, Darwen*, 22 March, 1826 ; John Brown's suggested arbitrator Mr. Thomas Chapman, lived at the Folds, Bolton. Little is known of him.

663. Crompton Papers, ZCR44 Item 10, *Letter from James Crompton, Hyde, to George Crompton*, Darwen, 5th of April 1826

664. Crompton Papers. Letter John Brown, London to Samuel Crompton, 29th of April 1826, ZCR44 Item 13

665. John Taylor was a Bolton attorney, and family friend and advisor.

666. The guinee may have been a rent payment as much of the letter from Betty is about her difficulties in obtaining rent from a Mr. Greatbatch, and her attempts to meet with John Taylor who may have been agent for the properties.

667. Crompton Papers, ZCR43 Item 5, *Letter, Betty Dawson, Bolton, to her Father, Samuel Crompton, Harrogate*, 9th of June 1825

668. Lord Bexley subsequently accepted Prime Minister Canning's invitation to keep his position in the cabinet of 1828, though when the Duke of Wellington came to office Bexley's cabinet position was not renewed.

669. Crompton Papers, ZCR43 Item 15, *Notes of Brown's interview with Lord Bexley*, 27th of December 1825

670. Crompton Papers, *ZCR43 Item 15*

671. Browns document cites a range of statistics that prove the worth of the mule. See Brown, *The Basis of Mr Samuel Crompton's Claims*, 4-5.

672. Jenner was awarded £10,000 in 1802 and a second amount of £20,000 in 1807. These sums are cited in French, *The Life and Times of Samuel Crompton*, 216.

673. Crompton Papers, *ZCR44 Item 4*

674. Crompton Papers, ZCR44 Item 8, *Letter, J.Brown, London, to George. Crompton, Darwen*, 17th of March 1826

675. Though Brown stated that a petition was presented to Parliament, research by French failed to uncover any such submission. See French, *The Life and Times of Samuel Crompton*, 223

676. Crompton Papers, ZCR44 Item 13, *Letter, John Brown, London, to Samuel Crompton*, 22cnd of April 1826

677. Crompton Papers, *Letter John Brown, London to Samuel Crompton*, 9th of July 1825, ZCR43 Item 8.

678. Eric. J. Evans, *Sir Robert Peel, Statesmanship, Power and Party*, Routledge, Oxford, New York, 1991, 21

679. Crompton Papers, *ZCR 44 Item 6*. There is no explicit evidence of malign intent or obstruction by Peel.

680. Samuel's involvement is unclear and by the 15th of July 1826 Taylor is writing to George Crompton saying that he does not believe that Samuel gave permission for this application to Parliament and calls for a meeting. See Crompton Papers, ZCR44 Item 15, *Letter, J.Taylor, Bolton, to George Crompton*, Darwen, 15th of July 1826

681. Cameron, *Samuel Crompton*, 124, notes that at the time of Brown's campaign, prosperity was returning, but it is evident that the economic environment was not that encouraging.

682. *The Manchester Courier and Lancashire General Advertiser*, Saturday 24 th of December 1825

683. See Emily. Buchnea, The Cotton Triangle Revisited, Global Commodity, Colonial Connections, in Chris. Wrigley (ed), *Industrialisation and Society in Britain: Cromford and Beyond in the Era of the Industrial Revolution*, The Arkwright Society, 2016. 87-98

684. Edward. Baines, *History of the Cotton Manufacture In Great Britain*, H. Fisher, R. Fisher and P. Jackson, London, 1835, 493.

685. Crompton Papers, *ZCR 44 Item 7*

686. Crompton Papers, *ZCR 44 Item 10*

687. Crompton Papers, ZCR 44 Item 11, *Letter, George Crompton, Darwen, to James Crompton, Hyde*, 10th of April 1826

688. Crompton Papers, *ZCR 44 Item 6*

689. *Chester Courant* - Tuesday 02 May 1826 ; and Leeds Intelligencer - Thursday 4th of May 1826

690. A piece of brick used as a missile.

691. A. E. Musson, An Early Engineering Firm: Peel, Williams & Co., of Manchester, *Journal Business History* Volume 3, 1960 - Issue 1, 1960, 8-18

692. All estimates taken from Edward Baines, History and Directory of Lancashire ,1825

693. J. Brown, *A Memoir of Robert Blincoe: An Orphan Boy*, printed for and published by John Doherty, 27, Withy-Grove, Manchester, 1832

694. Doherty was active in both the Amalgamated association of Cotton Spinners, the Manchester Spinners Union and founder of the General Union of Cotton Spinners (1829-1831).

695. For wider implications of the Robert Blincoe story see: John. Waller, *The Real Oliver Twist: Robert Blincoe: A Life that Illuminates an Age*, Icon Books, 2005

696. For a full and lucid treatment of Brown's work on Robert Blencoe see D. Hanson, *Children of the Mill: True Stories from Quarry Bank*, Headline Publishing Group, London, 2014, 102-110.

697. Cobbett was also a critic of the focus of abolitionist; see William. Hague, *William Wilberforce, The Life of the Great Anti Slave Trade Campaigner*, Harper Perennial, London, 2008, 440-441

698. Brown, *A Memoir of Robert Blincoe: An Orphan Boy,* 9

699. Cameron, *Samuel Crompton*, 124, credits Brown's abandoning of his History of Bolton to the time that he spent in pursuing the appeal for Samuel Crompton, an opinion shared by French, *The Life and Times of Samuel Crompton*, 218

700. Brown, *A Memoir of Robert Blincoe: An Orphan Boy*, iii

701. Fishwick FSA, *The Lancashire Library, A Bibliographical Account of Books on Topography, Biography, History, Science and Miscellaneous Literature relating to the County Palatine, 8*

702. This is his last known address. See Crompton Papers

703. Alexander Pope, *Rape of the Lock*

704. Though Harvey Sachs argues that in the post revolutionary period under repressive governments creativity was internalised and romanticism flourished

offering the formulae relief+regret+repression=romanticism? See Harvey. Sachs, *The Ninth: Beethoven and the World in 1824*, Faber and Faber,London, 2011, 61-111

705. Brown, *The Basis of Samuel Crompton's Claims*, 11

Chapter Twenty: Of Boggarts and Dreamers

706. Needless to say, this honour is disputed, with other local sites such as Wilderswood Mill, and another named "The Bobbin Shop" claiming to be the origins of cotton manufacture. See Hampson, *Horwich, Its History, Legends and Church*, 98

707. Crompton Papers, ZCR31 Item 2, *Letter, George Bibby, Chorley, to Mr. Crompton*, 26th of January 1817

708. David. A. Owen, *The Headless Cross Ghost*, Horwich Heritage, undated

709. A version of this story can be read in Phoebe. Hesketh, *Rivington, the Story of a Village*, Peter Davies, Great Britain, 1972, 99-107

710. In the 1960s the legend was changed again A taxi driver reported having seen a sinister figure with a cloak standing by the cross. The apparition was claimed to be an Italian foundling named Guillimo Blanco, driven by a desire to find his lost parents. However, what really brought Blanco back to earth on the eve of each new year, was the fact that the head of the Celtic cross was missing. See Hesketh, Rivington, the Story of a Village, 101-2 Hesketh, *Rivington, the Story of a Village, 101-2*

711. French reflects on her competence. See French, *The Life and Times of Samuel Crompton*, 209

712. Crompton Papers, ZCR43 Item 4, *Letter, Samuel Crompton, Harrogate, to Bette Dawson (his daughter) and family*, 7th of June 1825

713. *Yorkshire Gazette*, 9th of June 1826.

714. Details given in Notice of Auction, *York Herald*, 11th of August 1827

715. In the 1841 census return this lodging house was still in the possession of a Mr John and Mrs Elizabeth Downham of 7, York Place. Findmypast, 1841 census, return for Harrogate.

716. Crompton Papers, ZCR369 Item 8, *Letter, Samuel Crompton, Douglas, Isle of Man, Giving Details of his Health*, 16th of July 1823

717. Crompton Papers, ZCR43 Item 4, *Letter, Samuel Crompton, Harrogate, to Bette Dawson (his daughter) and family,* 7th of June 1825

718. Samuel. Solomon (M.D.), *A Guide to Health: or advice to both sexes, in nervous and consumptive complaints, scurvy, leprosy, and scrofula; also, on a certain disease and sexual debility. To which is added, an address to boys, young men, and guardians of youth, with observations on watering places, hot and cold bathing, Sixty-fifth edition, with additions. With plates, including a portrait,* 1817, 256.

719. French, *The Life and Times of Samuel Crompton*, 122

720. For a wonderfully concise and entertaining outline of Solomon's career, influence and decline read, Ben. Wilson, *Decency and Disorder*, 1789-1837, Faber and Faber, London. 2007, 35-50.

721. Advertised in, *The Birmingham Chronicle and General Advertiser of the Counties*, Thursday, 12th of April 1827. Including claims that 10,500 sold copies were proof of its worth.

722. *Manchester Mercury*, 3rd of July 1827; *Oxford University and City Herald*, 7th of July, 1827; *Manchester Courier and Lancashire General Advertiser*, 7th of July 1827; *Sheffield Independent*, 14th of July, 1827; *London Courier and Evening Gazette* , 10th of July 1827.

723. List referred to and names noted by French, *The Life and Times of Samuel Crompton*, 229

724. French, *The Life and Times of Samuel Crompton*, 229

725. There is an intriguing note by French that in his later years he became *"occasionally less abstemious in his habits,"* French, *The Life and Times of Samuel Crompton*, 225

726. French, *The Life and Times of Samuel Crompton*, 202

727. French, *The Life and Times of Samuel Crompton*, 230

728. Lancashire Archives, *Will, Pimbley, Joseph*, 10th of May 1817, Cheshire: - Wills and Inventories, 1811-1820 (M-Z)

729. Crompton Papers, ZCR45 Item 18, *Probate, Of the Will of Samuel Crompton*, 1st of January 1834

730. Crompton Papers, ZCR39 Item 8, *Letter, Samuel Crompton, Douglas, Isle of Man, Giving Details of his Health,* 16th of July 1823

Chapter Twenty One: Of Trotting and Trotters

731. Taylors, or Victoria Mill, Horwich, Bolton, built 1903-1904 and closed and demolished in 2007.

732. Trotting is only discussed in the 2nd edition of French's biography of Crompton, and not the first edition which is generally referred to in this book. See Gilbert. J. French, *The Life and Times of Samuel Crompton, Inventor of the Spinning Machine Called the Mule, Being the Substance of Two Papers Read to the Members of the Bolton Mechanics Institution*, 2nd edition, Simpkin and Marshall, London, 1860, 103

733. French, *The Life and Times of Samuel Crompton*, 2nd edition, 103

734. *Staffordshire Advertiser*, Saturday 28 September 1805; For an amusing story of the lack of purpose of an Idle club formed in Wolverhampton, searching for a system of balloting requiring no trouble then see *Staffordshire Advertiser*, Saturday 31st of August 1805. An Idle Club was evident in Oxford, 1843. *Oxford University and City Herald*, Saturday 14th of January 1843

735. See French, *The Life and Times of Samuel Crompton*, 205-206

736. See French, *The Life and Times of Samuel Crompton*, 211

737. See French, *The Life and Times of Samuel Crompton*, 228

738. A full description of Samuel Crompton's perceived character and an evaluation of his portrait by the London artist Mr Allingham can be found in French, *The Life and Times of Samuel Crompton*, 126-128; also read George Crompton's observations in French, *The Life and Times of Samuel Crompton*, 127

739. See, Delano, José. *Lopez, Snaring the Fowler: Mark Twain Debunks Phrenology, Skeptical Inquirer*, Volume 26, 1 January / February 2002

740. Joseph Nightingale, died 19th of August 1824

741. The Commercial Travelers Society was possibly a charitable association. A Philanthropic and Commercial Travelers Society, for Manchester, is noted by Joseph Parker, *The Edinburgh Encyclopedia*, (First American Edition), vol. 12, Joseph and Edward Parker,1832, 372

742. For example, see, Crompton Papers, ZCR29 Item 2, *Invitation to Church and King Club for George Crompton*, 17th of February 1815; ZCR45 Item 3*Certificate, The United Grand Lodge of Free Masons to George Crompton, admitting him as a member of the Lodge of Harmony and Industry*, 25th of May 1827; ZCR 32 Item 1, *Receipt, George Crompton, Bolton, Subscription Paid, for 1818, to the Commercial Travelers Society*, 7th of January 1818

743. Crompton Papers, ZCR32 Item 4, *Agreement, Between G.Crompton, J. Neville, J.G. Starkie and H. Dunderdale, Over Darwen, Should Any of These Gentlemen Marry They Will Give a Dinner for the Others*, 16th of April 1818,

744. See Crompton Papers, *ZCR59 Item 2, Letter to George Crompton from his nephew, Manchester*, 29th of January 1840

745. Lancaster Gazette, Saturday 28th of July 1821. Entry: *"Married Thursday last Mr George Crompton Over Darwen to Ms. Sarah Lancaster sister to Mr. Lancaster surgeon of Blackburn"*. Sarah tragically died in June 1822. He married his second wife Mary Wood on the 8th of July 1834.

746. After Sarah Lancaster's death there is a dispute in Chancery involving George and the Lancaster family. See Crompton Papers, ZCR36 Item 14, *Statement of John Lancaster defendant at the Court of Chancery. Plaintiffs being George Crompton and Sarah Nancy Lancaster Crompton his daughter.*

747. *Lancaster Gazette* - Saturday 10th of February 1827

748. The sum of £97 was raised (half of the takings, for the poor of the neighbour hood).

749. *Lancaster Gazette* - Saturday 10th of February 1827

750. A List of attendees and their chosen dress can be found in the *Lancaster Gazette* - Saturday 10th of February 1827

751. Technically she was still married to Wakefield but might not have cared to admit it. The announcement of the dissolution of the marriage can be found in; Worcester Journal - Thursday 31st of May 1827

752. *Caledonian Mercury* - Monday 19th of June 1826

753. *Letters to his Son*, 1746-1747, By the Earl of Chesterfield, on the *Fine Art of becoming a Man of the World and a Gentleman*, letter written 9th of March 1748

754. The story of the first abduction is re-told in the *Caledonian Mercury* - Monday 19th of June 1826 being a copy of an article first appearing in the Liverpool Mercury. The story appears several times in the latter newspaper, see for example, *Liverpool Mercury*- 25th of August 1826

755. *London Courier and Evening Gazette*, 19th of June 1816

756. *Oxford University and City Herald* - Saturday 24th of August 1816

757. *Public Ledger and Daily Advertiser*, 10th of July 1820.

758. Details of the case to be found in various newspaper reports, for example, *Manchester Courier and Lancashire General Advertiser*, 24th of March 1827; Also, a complete transcript of the trial is: Edward. Duncombe (Printer and Publisher), *The Trial at Full Length, of Edw. Gibbon Wakefield, William Wakefield, and Mrs. Frances Wakefield, for a Conspiracy, and the Abduction of Miss Turner with the Whole of the Evidence on Both Sides and the Speeches of Counsel at Full Length; The Judge's Charge to the Jury; Etc. (Second Edition, with Additions and Corrections)*, 188, Fleet Street, London, 1827

759. Mrs Wakefield (nee Davies) had married Edward Gibbon Wakefields father, having met him in Paris where the Wakefield's had their lair.

760. Maria Edgeworth's novel provides an apt metaphor for the travails of the Crompton family, where the Percy family experience a house fire, shipwreck and also suffer from the machinations of an evil relative.

761. Maria. Edgeworth, *Tales and Novels*, London: Printed for Baldwin and Cradock, 1832-1833, 308

762. Duncombe, *The Trial at Full Length, of Edward Gibbon Wakefield*, 13

763. London *Evening Standard*-18th of January 1831

764. Robert. Gouger (Editor), *A Letter from Sydney, The Principal Town of Australasia, Together with the Outline of a System of Colonisation*, Joseph Cross 18 Holborn: Simpkin and Marshall, Stationers Court; and Eppingham Wilson, Royal Exchange, MDCCCXXIX (1829).

765. Neither was Torrens reluctant to capitalise on the idea, being significantly involved in the South Australia Land Company.

766. See *History of Parliament Online*, http:www.historyofparliamentonline.org/volume/1820-1832/member/torrens-robert-1780-1864

767. Another example of Wakefield's work on colonisation is, Edward. Gibbon. Wakefield, *A View of the Art of Colonisation, With Present Reference to the British Empire*, In J.W. Parker, *Letters Between a Statesman and A Colonist*, West Strand, London, 1849. A book that rather laboriously defines colonisation and argues for systematic colonization in the context of contemporary political discussions and issues.

768. Edward. Gibbon. Wakefield, *Facts Relating to The Punishment of Death in The Metropolis, London*: James Ridgeway, 169, PICCADILLY. MDCCCXXXI (1831)

769. See Charles. R. Dodd, 1843, T*he Annual Biography: Being Lives of Eminent or Remarkable Persons who have Died Within the Year MDCCCXLII* (1842), Chapman and Hall, The Strand, London. 1843, 453

770. Herbert L. Sussman, *Victorian Technology: Invention, Innovation, and the Rise of the Machine*, Greenwood Publishing Group. Santa Barbara, California; Denver, Colorado; Oxford, England, 2009

771. Sven. Beckert, *Empire of Cotton, A new History of Global Capitalism,* 164-165

772. Wakefield, *A View of the Art of Colonisation, With Present Reference to the British Empire, In Letters Between a Statesman and A Colonist,* 7

Chapter Twenty Two: The Final Trott

773. Crompton Papers, ZCR39 Item 9, *Letter to George Crompton, from William Turner Blackburn*, 19th of July 1823

774. Bowking is a stage of the bleaching process.

775. Crompton Papers, ZCR39 Item 13, *Letter to George Crompton, from William Turner Blackburn*, dated 30th of September 1823

776. Crompton Papers, ZCR41 Item 13*Letter to George Crompton, from William Turner Blackburn*, dated 3rd of May 1824

777. http://www.cottontown.org/Housing/Parish%20histories/Pages/Mill-Hill-The-Area-where-I-Grow-up.aspx

778. Crompton Papers, ZCR 59 Item 6, *Letter William Turner, Shirley Hall, to George Crompton*, dated 19th of July 1840

779. E. Walford, *The County Families of the United Kingdom, or Royal Manual of the Titled and Untitled Aristocracy of Great Britain & Ireland*, Aristocracy1862, London, Robert Hardwicke, Piccadilly, 649

780. *A Short Account of the Windham Club from its Formation in 1828*, 1923, 34 (B.M. pressmark 10349. W.I). Also see https://www.british-history.ac.uk/survey-london/vols29-30/pt1/pp136-139#fnn14.

781. One newspaper reported that George had applied to be a factory inspector but had been turned down in favour of "the natural son of one of the ex secretaries of state", emphasising the lack of a patron. See *Glasgow Herald* - Friday 28th of October 1859

782. *1841 Census*, Township of Little Hulton, Lancashire, 6, Ancestry.

783. Though most of his efforts to gain compensation were during 1842, there is a letter suggesting that George was in London in penciled in as 1845, visiting friends and meeting with a committee, See Crompton Papers, ZCR66 Item 4. However, there is a reference to Peel dividing the house with a majority of 133 which fits more with 1846.

784. For example, Alfred. Mallalieu, The Cotton Manufacture, *Blackwood's Magazine*, Edinburgh, vol.39, March 1836, 407-424, Also at this point there was Baines, *History of the Cotton Industry*, 1835 and Kennedy, *Brief Life of Samuel Crompton*, 1830

785. Crompton Papers, ZCR63 Item 10, *Names and Testimonies of Supporters of George Crompton on his Petition to Parliament*, 3rd of August 1842

786. Crompton Papers, ZCR63 Item 11, *Petition*, 3rd of August 1842

787. See Crompton Papers, *Letter from Samuel Crompton, cousin of George Crompton, dated 29th of January 1840*, ZCR 59 Item 2. George's cousin notes that he "saw the Queen once or twice but that you would think so little of going to see her than seeing the vicar of Blackburn "and describes her as "anything but popular."

788. Crompton Papers, ZCR 63 Item 7, *Letter George Crompton, London to his wife, Fearnhurst, Blackburn*, dated 2cnd of August 1842.

789. Crompton Papers, ZCR63 Item 8, *Letter, George Crompton, London, to his wife*, 1842

790. John Hornby (19th of August 1810 – 5th of December 1892), British Conservative politician, MP for Blackburn 1841-1852.

791. Crompton Papers, *ZCR63 Item 7*

792. Crompton papers *ZCR63 Item 8*

793. Crompton Papers, ZCR63 Item 9, *Letter, George Crompton to his Wife*, 3 August 1842

794. Crompton Papers, *ZCR63 Item 9*

795. Edward. Bootle, Wilbraham, Hon, Private Secretary to Secretary of State (Stanley), 3rd of September. 1841-23 Dec. 1845 (CO 701/11) in J. C. Sainty (editor), *Office Holders in Modern Britain*: Volume 6, Colonial Office Officials 1794-1870, University of London, London, 1976.

796. See entry for Edward. Bootle Wilbraham, (formerly Wilbraham Bootle, (1771-1853), of Lathom House, Ormskirk, Lancs. and 55 Portland Place, Mdx, in *D.R.*

Fisher (editor), 2009, The History of Parliament: The House of Commons 1820-1832, Cambridge University Press, 2009

797. An obscure fund established by Edmund Burke in 1782. A fund facilitating the patronage of the Prime Minister with no clear accountability, having been used at different times for pensions, grants, gifts and assistance to Huguenot refugees.

798. Crompton Papers, *Letter Colonel Wilbraham to George Crompton*, 10th of October 1842, ZCR63 Item 16

799. *Leicestershire Mercury* - Saturday 22cnd of October 1842, being the copy of a report initially published in the Blackburn Standard.

800. Crompton Papers, ZCR63 Item 15, *Letter, George Crompton*, to Mr. John Taylor, 7 October 1842

Chapter Twenty Three: Of Celebration and Regret

801. Newspaper quote cited in Peter. J. C. Smith, *Zeppelins Over Lancashire; The Story of the Air Raids on the County of Lancashire in 1916 and 1918,* published by Neil Richardson, Manchester, 1991

802. Two months later early morning 28th November 1916, 29 year old Frankenberg and his L21 were shot down in flames off Lowestoft, returning from an extended raid on the Staffordshire potteries. Smith, *Zeppelins Over Lancashire*, 23

803. Peter. J. C. Smith, *Zeppelins Over Lancashire,* 14

804. As calculated by the author using a map of the zeppelins route, *Zeppelins Over Lancashire*, 18

805. Widely reported in the newspapers at the time. See *Manchester Mercury* -21st of July 1818.

806. A description of the fire at the Mill is put in context by an article in the *Stamford Mercury* - Friday 24th of July 1818

807. *Morning Post* - Wednesday 29th of July 1818

808. *Saunders's News-Letter* - Friday 7th of August 1818

809. *Morning Post* - Wednesday 29th of July 1818

810. Eyewitness account reported in *Morning Post* - Wednesday 29th of July 1818

811. *Graces Guide to British Industrial History*, https://www.gracesguide. co.uk/1891_Cotton_Mills_in_Bolton

812. Smith, *Zeppelins Over Lancashire, 17*

813. *Bolton Evening News*, 26 September 1916, cited in Smith, *Zeppelins Over Lancashire*, 22

814. French, *Life and Times of Samuel Crompton*, 243-244

815. Ron. Freethy, *Memories of the Lancashire Cotton Mills*, Countryside Books, 2008 (reprinted 2010), Newbury, Berkshire, United Kingdom, see chapter *The Last Rites: A Sad Cotton Wake*, 129-139. Also, BBC: *Boom to Bust, The Decline of the Cotton Industry*. http://www.bbc.co.uk/nationonfilm/topics/textiles/background_decline.shtml

816. The route of L21 and the sites of bombs and incendiaries dropped can be found in Smith, *Zeppelins Over Lancashire*, 18

817. *1861 Census*, Ancestry UK

818. See address by Lord Stanley, on the opening of a new Mechanics Institute in Stockport on Monday 22 September 1862. Reported in *Manchester Times* - Saturday 27 September 1862. This is most likely Frederick Arthur Stanley, 16th Earl of Derby, (1841 – 1908) second son of Edward Smith Stanley.

819. *The Bolton Guardian*, Crompton Supplement, Wednesday, September 24th, 1862. Material courtesy of (Price One Penny) The Bolton Guardian Saturday, 20th of September 1862.

820. *The Bolton Guardian*, 24 September 1862.

821. *Bolton Chronicle* - Saturday 13th of September 1862

822. *Bolton Chronicle* - Saturday 22cnd March 1862

823. *Bolton Chronicle* - Saturday 13 September 1862, report of the meeting of the organising committee held at the Coroners Court, 8th of September 1862.

824. Programme for the day: Published by authority. *Inauguration of the Crompton Statue*, Printed at the Steam Printing Works of J.Y.Staton, Bridge Street Bolton, Wednesday 24th of September 1862. (Author's private collection).

825. *Inauguration of the Crompton Statue*, Programme, 1862

826. *The Bolton Chronicle*, Saturday, 27th of September 27

827. There was some inevitable sniping in the letter's columns of contemporary newspapers. One letter writer reducing Crompton's contribution to a mere combination of other inventions, was sharply corrected by another correspondent

self-proclaimed as "a Lover of Justice though Tardy". *See Bolton Chronicle*, 9th of August 1862.

828. *Bolton Chronicle*, 20th of September 1862.

829. *Bolton Chronicle*, Saturday 19th of March 1859

830. *Bolton Chronicle*, Saturday 20th of September 1862

831. Sold, along with copies of French's Life of Samuel Crompton, by George Winterburn, Deansgate, Bolton.

832. *Bolton Chronicle* - Saturday 20th of September 1862

833. *Bolton Chronicle*, Saturday, 9th of August 1862.

834. However, according to the *London Illustrated News*, 4th October 1862, there were 2,000 school children involved.

835. Established in London in 1781, The Ancient Society of Druids was not a religious organisation but an association whose members were expected to embrace justice, benevolence and friendship, being those principles thought to be adhered to by the early Druids.

836. The author has failed to determine the precise use of the word 'earthquake' in this context but presumes that there was a jumble of objects, or such like.

837. *Bolton Chronicle*, 27th September 1862

838. *Manchester Times*, Saturday, 27th September 1862.

839. Bolton Chronicle, *20th of September* 1862

840. London Illustrated News, 4th of October 1862

841. *Punch*, 11th of October 1862, 154

842. George Pimbley was son of Joseph Pimbley born in Adlington, Lancashire, 9th of January 1807, Ancestry UK

843. As reported in the *London Illustrated News*, 4th of October 1862

844. *Manchester Weekly Times*, 27 September, 1862. Letter dated 24th of September.

845. It is interesting that the modern phenomenon of 'crowd funding' has parallels with the subscription process.

846. Samuel.Smiles, *Self Help*, John Murray, 1897 edition. Though a true reading of this book suggests that Smiles was not totally averse to charity.

847. *Bolton Chronicle* - Saturday 27th of September 1862. The issue of Crompton's contribution and the towns culpability are widely discussed in this edition of the Chronicle.

848. *The Bolton Chronicle*, Saturday, 18th of October 1862.

849. *The Illustrated London News*, 11th of October 1862

850. *Dundee, Perth, and Cupar Advertiser,* 10th of October 1862

851. *Manchester Times*, 27th of September 1862.

Select Bibliography

Irving. Babbitt, *Rousseau and Romanticism*, Houghton Mifflin Company, The Riverside Press, Cambridge, USA, 1919

A.H. Bailey and Co, *Scenes and Stories by A Clergyman in Debt Written During his Confinement in the Debtor's Prisons, in Three Volumes, Cornhill*, London. MDCCCXXXV, January 1853

Brian. Bailey, *The Luddite Rebellion*, Sutton Publishing, Stroud, Gloucestershire, 1998

Edward. Baines, *History, Directory and Gazetteer, of the County Palatine of Lancaster, with a Variety of Commercial and Statistical Information, in Two Volumes*, WM. Wales & CO, 68 Castle Street, and Longman, Hurst &Co, Paternoster Row, London, 1824

Edward. Baines, *History of the Cotton Manufacture in Great Britain*, H. Fisher, R. Fisher and P. Jackson, London, 1835

Sven. Beckert, *Empire of Cotton, A new History of Global Capitalism*, Penguin Random House, United Kingdom, 2014

W.D. Billington (ed), *Captain Dewhurst and His Diary*, Bolton, 1989

J. Brown, *A Memoir of Robert Blincoe: An Orphan Boy*, printed for and Published by John Doherty, 27, Withy-Grove, Manchester, 1832

J. Brown, and S. Crompton, *The Basis of Mr Samuel Crompton's Claims to A Second Remuneration from Parliament for His Discovery of the Mule Spinning Machine*, Charles Simms and Co, Manchester, 1868

Hector. Charles. Cameron, *Samuel Crompton*, The Batchworth Press, London, 1951

Harold. Catling, *The Spinning Mule,* The Lancashire Library, Lancashire County Council Library and Leisure Committee, originally published by David & Charles (1970), 1986

George. W, Daniels, *The Early English Cotton Industry*, Manchester University Press, London, New York, Bombay, 1920

Dobson and Barlow Ltd, *Samuel Crompton: The Inventor of the Spinning Mule, A Brief Survey of His Life and Work with which is incorporated a Short History of Messrs Dobson and Barlow Ltd*, Dobson and Barlow Ltd, Bolton, 1927

Michael. M. Edwards, *The Growth of the British Cotton Industry 1780-1815*, Manchester University Press. Manchester, England, 1967

Eric. J. Evans, Sir Robert Peel, *Statesmanship, Power and Party, Routledge*, Oxford, New York, 1991

R.S. Fitton, *The Arkwright's: Spinners of Fortune*, Manchester University Press, Manchester and New York, 1989

R.S. Fitton and Alfred. P. Wadsworth, *The Strutt's and the Arkwright's, 1758-1830: A Study of the Early Factory System*, Manchester University Press, 1968

James. Folds, *Sayings and Doings of James Folds*, George Winterburn, Deansgate, Bolton, 1879

Charles. F. Foster, *Capital and Innovation, How Britain Became the First Industrial Nation*. Arley Hall Archive Press, 2004

Charles. F. Foster and Eric. L. Jones, *The Fabric of Society and How it Creates Wealth: Wealth Distribution and Wealth Creation in Europe 1000-1800*, Arley Hall Press, Cheshire, England, 2013

Gilbert. J, French, *The Life and Times of Samuel Crompton, Inventor of the Spinning Machine Called the Mule, Being the Substance of Two Papers Read to the Members of the Bolton Mechanics Institution*, 1st edition, Simpkin and Marshall, London, 1859

Gilbert. J, French, *The Life and Times of Samuel Crompton, with an Introduction by Stanley D. Chapman*, 2nd edition, Augustus M. Kelley publishers, New York, 1970

Thomas. Hampson, *Horwich Its History and Legends, and Church*, Wigan Observer Office, Wallgate, Wigan, Lancashire, 1883

D. Hanson, *Children of the Mill: True Stories from Quarry Bank*, Headline Publishing Group, London, 2014

Reverend. Levenson. Vernon. Harcourt (Editor), *The Diaries and Correspondence of the Honourable George Rose*, in two volumes, Richard Bentley, New Burlington Street, London, 1860

Edmund. R. Heaton, *The Heaton's of Deane: The Varying Fortunes of a Lancashire Family Over 850 years*, Heaton, 2000.

E.J. Hobsbawm, *Industry and Empire, An Economic History of Britain Since 1750*, Weidenfield and Nicholson, 4th edition, London, 1973

E.J. Hobsbawm, *The Age of Revolution: Europe 1789-1848*, Weidenfield and Nicholson, Abacus, 4th edition, London, 1962

John. Hughes, *Liverpool Banks and Bankers, 1760-1837*, Henry Young and Sons, Liverpool; Simpkin, Marshall, Hamilton, Kent &Co, Ltd, London, 1906

Michael. Janes, *From Smuggling to Cotton Kings: The Gregg Story, 2010*, Memoirs, Cirencester, Gloucestershire, United Kingdom

John. Kennedy Esq, A Brief Memoir of Samuel Crompton, with a Description of his Machine Called the Mule and of the Subsequent Improvement of the Machine by Others, read February 20th 1830, in *Memoirs and Proceedings of the Manchester Literary and Philosophical Society*, Second Series, Volume 5, 1831

Brian. Lewis, *Coal Mining in the Eighteenth and Nineteenth Centuries*, Longman, London, 1971

Andro. Linklater, *Why Spencer Percival Had to Die*, Bloomsbury Publishing PLC, London, 2012

MacLeod. Christine, *Heroes of Invention: Technology, Liberalism and British Identity, 1750-1914*, Cambridge University Press, Cambridge, 2007

Thomas. Midgely, *Samuel Crompton 1753-1827: A Life of Tragedy and Service*, Tillotsons (Bolton) Ltd, Bolton, Lancashire, England, 1927

Roger. Osborne, *Iron, Steam and Money, The Making of the Industrial Revolution*, The Bodley Head, London, 2013

Mark. Overton, *Agricultural Revolution in England; The Transformation of the Agrarian Economy, 1500-1850*, Cambridge University Press, Cambridge, 1996

John. Roby, *Traditions of Lancashire*, Volume 2, George Routledge, 1867

Jonathan S. Rose, Stuart. Shotwell, and Mary Lou Bertucci (editors), *Scribe of Heaven, Swedenborg's Life, Work and Impact*, Swedenborg Foundation, Inc, 2005

James. Christopher. Scholes, *History of Bolton: With Memorials of the Old Parish Church*, edited and completed by William. Pimblett, The Daily Chronicle Office, 1892

Peter, J. C. Smith, *Zeppelins Over Lancashire; The Story of the Air Raids on the County of Lancashire in 1916 and 1918*, published by Neil Richardson, Manchester, 1991

Hugh. Thomas, *The Slave Trade. The History of the Atlantic Slave Trade 1440-1870*, Picador, London, United Kingdom, 1997

Arnold. Toynbee, *Lectures on The Industrial Revolution of the Eighteenth Century in England*, Longman's, Green and Co, London, New York and Bombay, 1896

Amanda. Vickery, *The Gentleman's Daughter, Women's Lives in Georgian England*, Yale University Press, Newhaven and London, 1998

Westhoughton Local History Group, *The Burning of Westhoughton Mill 1812*, published for the Bicentenary 24th April 2012

Gomer. Williams, *History of The Liverpool Privateers and Letters of Marque, with an Account of: The Liverpool Slave Trade*, William Heinemann, London, Liverpool, Edward Howell, Church Street, 1897

Chris. Wrigley (ed), *Industrialisation and Society in Britain: Cromford and Beyond in the Era of the Industrial Revolution*, The Arkwright Society, Cromford Mills, Cromford, Derbyshire, 2016

Index

BV - #0010 - 130824 - C18 - 229/152/19 - PB - 9781915972514 - Gloss Lamination